Subverting Justice

How the Former President and His Allies Pressured DOJ to Overturn the 2020 Ellection

Subverting JUSTICE

How the Former President and His Allies Pressured DOJ to Overturn the 2020 Election

Introduction by Thomas Fensch

MAJORITY STAFF REPORT

Copyright 2021 by Thomas Fensch

New Century Books
8821 Rockdale Rd.
N. Chesterfield, Va., 23236

newcentbks@gmail.com

ISBN: 978-1-7379998-8-1 (softcover)
ISBN: 978-1-7379998-9-8 (ebook)

Subverting JUSTICE

How the Former President and His Allies Pressured DOJ to Overturn the 2020 Election

MAJORITY STAFF REPORT

Introduction

It was one of the last attempts by Donald John Trump and his cronies to subvert the 2020 election – and it was perhaps the most egregious.

In 1935, novelist Sinclair Lewis published *It Can't Happen Here*, a scathing attack on our national politics and a warning about a fascist takeover. He wrote it in a white heat of passion – in just a few weeks. It is still as readable today as in 1935, and is still as much a warning today as it was in 1935. (Timeless classics are sometimes written that way: after lengthy false starts, John Steinbeck wrote *The Grapes of Wrath* in 100 days straight and very nearly had a nervous breakdown because of the stress; he apparently could not write a major novel as a long-term project — psychologically for him it had to be a sprint to the end.)

This Department of Justice episode could easily be called *It Almost Happened Here.*

IT. ALMOST. HAPPENED. HERE.

And the *Almost-Happened-Here* aspects of this sordid episode ought to scare the bejesus out of any concerned citizen — concerned with the sometimes fragile nature of our democracy.

* * *

Barbara McQuade received her A.B. degree from the University of Michigan and her J.D. from the University of Michigan Law School. She was Assistant U.S. Attorney in the Eastern District of Michigan from 1998 until becoming U.S. Attorney there in 2010, appointed by President Barack Obama. She was the first woman to serve as U.S. Attorney for the Eastern District of Michigan. She has served as Deputy Chief of the National Security Unit, where she prosecuted cases involving terrorism financing, foreign agents, export violations, and threats. She also prosecuted cases involving violent crime, fraud and racketeering.

Forced out of office by Donald Trump, she now teaches in the University of Michigan Law School and, since 2017, has been a contributor to MSNBC, specializing in commentary about scandals in the Trump Administration.

On October 12, 2021, she published a commentary on the MSNBC website titled "Trump's DOJ officials stopped his January election scheme. But they're not heroes."

She wrote that Trump pressured DOJ department officials on at least nine occasions to undermine the results of the presidential election. Finally culminating in a three-hour meeting in the Oval Office, in which several top DOJ officials, including Acting Attorney General Jeffrey Rosen, Acting Attorney General Richard Donoghue and Assistant Attorney General Steven Engel, all threatened to resign if Trump went through with his scheme to insert his own lackeys at the top of the DOJ.

Such resignations would have far surpassed the infamous "Saturday Night Massacre" during the Nixon administration.

White House counsel Pat Cipollone also threatened to resign, as did his Deputy, Patrick Philbin.

Faced with such possible resignations en masse, with horrific national publicity, Trump was forced to back down.

But, McQuade states, they fell short because they remained silent earlier, when their voices should have been heard. And, she writes,

> "These DOJ officials are no heroes. They may have stopped Trump from overthrowing the results of the 2020 presidential election, but they fell short of what we should expect from public servants of integrity."

The following is the full Senate report of Donald Trump's subversive plan to force the Department of Justice to overthrow the 2020 election.

Suggested readings:

There has been a myriad, indeed, a flood of recent books about politics, Donald John Trump and the Trump Administration.
These are noteworthy:

Lewis, Sinclair. *It Can't Happen Here*. New York: Doubleday, Doran, 1935.

Schiff, Adam. *Midnight in Washington*. New York: Penguin-Random House, 2021.

Woodard, Bob. *Fear*. New York: Simon and Schuster, 2018.

_____. *Rage*. New York: Simon and Schuster, 2020.

Woodward Bob and Robert Costa. *Peril*. New York: Simon and Schuster, 2021.

Thomas Fensch (Introduction):

Thomas Fensch is the author or editor of 42 previous books, published since 1970.

They include, as author:

At the Dangerous Edge of Social Justice: Race, Violence and Death in America (2013);

The Sordid Hypocrisy of To Protect and To Serve: Police Brutality, Corruption and Oppression in America (2015).

Inside Nixon's Enemies List (2019).

As editor:

The C.I.A. and the U-2 Program (2001);
The Kennedy-Khrushchev Letters (2001);
War Diaries from Inside Hitler's Headquarters (2015);
Legal Aspects of Impeachment (2019);
How They Survived and Why We Lost: C.I.A. Analysis 1966 — The Vietnamese Communists' Will To Resist (2019).

Fensch has a doctorate from Syracuse University and lives outside Richmond, Virginia, with three dogs, his faithful Senior Literary Advisors, always ready to fetch yellow pencils, notepads and the like.

Table of Contents

EXECUTIVE SUMMARY 1
    A. The Senate Judiciary Committee's Investigation 1
    B. Key Findings 2

REPORT 6

I. **Applicable Legal Requirements** 6
    A. DOJ's Limited Role in Election Fraud Investigations 6
    B. Limits on White House-DOJ Communications 7
    C. Applicable Federal Laws Governing Political Interference with Investigations 10

II. **December 1 – December 15: Attorney General Barr Announces His Resignation After Declaring that DOJ Has Found No Evidence of Widespread Election Fraud** 11

III. **December 15 – December 27: Following Barr's Announcement, Trump Repeatedly Contacts DOJ's Incoming Leadership About His Election Fraud Claims** 13
    A. December 15, 2020 Oval Office Meeting 13
    B. December 23 and 24 Trump-Rosen Calls 14
    C. December 27 Trump-Rosen Call 15
    D. December 27 Outreach from Congressman Perry to Donoghue 16
    E. December 28 Trump-Donoghue Call 19

IV. **December 28: Jeffrey Clark Urges DOJ Leadership to Intervene in Georgia's Appointment of Electors and to Replicate this "Proof of Concept" in Other States** 19
    A. Clark's Late December Oval Office Meeting With Trump 19
    B. Clark's "Two Urgent Action Items" 20
    C. Rosen and Donoghue Reject Clark's Proposal 22

V. **December 29 – December 30: Meanwhile, Trump Urges DOJ to File a Supreme Court Action Contesting the Election** 24

VI. **December 29 – January 1: White House Pressure on DOJ Escalates** 27
    A. DOJ Leadership is Summoned to a December 31 Oval Office Meeting 27
    B. Clark Reveals Ongoing Contacts With Trump 28
    C. White House Chief of Staff Mark Meadows Asks DOJ to Initiate Baseless Election Fraud Investigations, Contrary to Longstanding Rules Against White House-DOJ Interference 29

VII. **January 2 – 4: DOJ Leadership Thwarts the Trump-Clark Plot, but U.S. Attorney BJay Pak is Ousted** 33

	A.	January 2: Clark's Plans Crystallize and Trump Calls the Georgia Secretary of State . 33
	B.	January 3: Clark Reveals That Trump Will Install Him That Day 35
	C.	The Justice Department Leadership Assembles 37
	D.	The January 3, 2021 Oval Office Meeting 37
	E.	U.S. Attorney Pak Resigns 39

VIII. Recommendations 43

APPENDIX A: CHRONOLOGY OF KEY EVENTS A-1

APPENDIX B: KEY DOCUMENTS A-9

Meeting with DOJ leadership, December 31, 2020 | Photo courtesy of the White House
SJC-Pre-CertificationEvents-000334

EXECUTIVE SUMMARY

A. The Senate Judiciary Committee's Investigation

On January 22, 2021, the *New York Times* reported that Jeffrey Bossert Clark, the former Acting Assistant Attorney General for the Department of Justice's (DOJ) Civil Division, sought to involve DOJ in efforts to overturn the 2020 presidential election results and plotted with then-President Trump to oust Acting Attorney General Jeffrey Rosen, who reportedly refused Trump's demands.[1] On January 23, 2021, the *Wall Street Journal* reported that Trump had urged DOJ to file a lawsuit in the Supreme Court seeking to invalidate President Biden's victory.[2] These reports followed Trump's months-long effort to undermine the results of the election, which culminated in the violent insurrection at the United States Capitol on January 6, 2021.

The Senate Committee on the Judiciary immediately launched an investigation into Trump's reported efforts to enlist DOJ in his election subversion scheme. On January 23, 2021, the Committee asked DOJ to produce documents related to these efforts. DOJ cooperated with the Committee's request, producing several hundred pages of calendars, emails, and other documents in the ensuing months.

On May 20, 2021, following DOJ's production of emails from former White House Chief of Staff Mark Meadows to Rosen asking DOJ to investigate several debunked election fraud claims, the Committee asked the National Archives and Records Administration (NARA) for additional Trump White House records related to Trump's attempts to secure DOJ's help in overturning the election results. The Committee's request sought White House records between November 3, 2020 and the end of Trump's presidency related to meetings and communications between and among White House and DOJ officials. NARA has not responded to date, and has represented to the Committee that the delay in transitioning electronic Trump records from the White House to NARA may prevent the Committee from obtaining a response for several more months.

In addition to obtaining and reviewing documents, the Committee interviewed key former DOJ personnel, including Rosen, former Principal Associate Deputy Attorney General Richard Donoghue, and former U.S. Attorney for the Northern District of Georgia Byung Jin ("BJay") Pak. DOJ and the White House authorized these witnesses to testify about their internal communications without restriction, citing the Committee's "compelling legislative interests ... in understanding these extraordinary events: namely, the question whether former President Trump sought to cause the Department to use its law enforcement and litigation authorities to

---

[1] Katie Benner, *Trump and Justice Dept. Lawyer Said to Have Plotted to Oust Acting Attorney General*, N.Y. Times (Jan. 22, 2021).
[2] Jess Bravin & Sadie Gurman, *Trump Pressed Justice Department to Go Directly to Supreme Court to Overturn Election Results*, Wall St. J. (Jan. 23, 2021).

advance his personal political interests with respect to the results of the 2020 presidential election."[3]

The Committee also requested to interview Clark, whom DOJ authorized to testify on the same terms as the other former DOJ officials. DOJ authorized Clark's appearance on July 26, 2021. More than two months after DOJ authorized him to testify without restriction, Clark still has not agreed to the Committee's request that he sit for a voluntary interview.

B. Key Findings

The Committee continues to investigate Trump's efforts to involve DOJ in his election subversion scheme, including by pursuing Trump White House records that NARA has thus far been unable to produce and additional witness interviews as appropriate. Given the gravity of the misconduct the Committee has uncovered to date, however—and in the interest of making a public record of Trump's efforts to compromise DOJ's independence—the Committee is releasing this interim staff report. The report makes six primary findings:

FINDING 1: President Trump repeatedly asked DOJ leadership to endorse his false claims that the election was stolen and to assist his efforts to overturn the election results. Beginning on the day former Attorney General William Barr announced his resignation and continuing almost until the January 6 insurrection, Trump directly and repeatedly asked DOJ's acting leadership to initiate investigations, file lawsuits on his behalf, and publicly declare the 2020 election "corrupt." Documents and testimony confirm that Rosen, and in some cases other senior DOJ leaders, participated in several calls and meetings where Trump directly raised discredited claims of election fraud and asked why DOJ was not doing more to address them. These calls and meetings included:

- December 15, 2020 – Oval Office meeting including Rosen and Donoghue
- December 23, 2020 – Trump-Rosen Call
- December 24, 2020 – Trump-Rosen Call
- December 27, 2020 – Trump-Rosen-Donoghue Call
- December 28, 2020 – Trump-Donoghue Call
- December 30, 2020 – Trump-Rosen Call
- December 31, 2020 – Oval Office meeting including Rosen and Donoghue
- January 3, 2021 – Oval Office meeting including Rosen and Donoghue
- January 3, 2021 – Trump-Donoghue Call

In attempting to enlist DOJ for personal, political purposes in an effort to maintain his hold on the White House, Trump grossly abused the power of the presidency. He also arguably

---

[3] Letter from Bradley Weinsheimer, Assoc. Dep. Att'y Gen., to Jeffrey Clark (July 26, 2021) (on file with the Committee); Letter from Bradley Weinsheimer, Assoc. Dep. Att'y Gen., to Richard Donoghue (July 26, 2021) (on file with the Committee); Letter from Bradley Weinsheimer, Assoc. Dep. Att'y Gen., to Byung J. Pak (July 26, 2021) (on file with the Committee); Letter from Bradley Weinsheimer, Assoc. Dep. Att'y Gen., to Jeffrey Rosen (July 26, 2021) (on file with the Committee).

violated the criminal provisions of the Hatch Act, which prevent any person—including the President—from commanding federal government employees to engage in political activity.[4]

FINDING 2: White House Chief of Staff Mark Meadows asked Acting Attorney General Rosen to initiate election fraud investigations on multiple occasions, violating longstanding restrictions on White House-DOJ communications about specific law-enforcement matters. Meadows asked Rosen to have DOJ investigate at least four categories of false election fraud claims that Trump and his allies were pushing. Between December 29 and January 1, Meadows asked Rosen to have DOJ:

- Investigate various discredited claims of election fraud in Georgia that the Trump campaign was simultaneously advancing in a lawsuit that the Georgia Supreme Court had refused to hear on an expedited basis;

- Investigate false claims of "signature match anomalies" in Fulton County, Georgia, even though Republican state elections officials had made clear "there has been no evidence presented of any issues with the signature matching process."[5]

- Investigate a theory known as "Italygate," which was promoted by an ally of the President's personal attorney, Rudy Giuliani, and which held that the Central Intelligence Agency (CIA) and an Italian IT contractor used military satellites to manipulate voting machines and change Trump votes to Biden votes. Meadows also asked DOJ to meet with Giuliani on Italygate and other election fraud claims.

- Investigate a series of claims of election fraud in New Mexico that had been widely refuted and in some cases rejected by the courts, including a claim that Dominion Voting Systems machines caused late-night "vote dumps" for Democratic candidates.

These requests violated longstanding policies limiting communications between White House and DOJ officials on specific law enforcement matters.[6] The White House and DOJ established these policies following Watergate to protect DOJ's investigations and prosecutions from partisan political interference and to prevent White House officials from corrupting DOJ for their own personal gain.

FINDING 3: After personally meeting with Trump, Jeffrey Bossert Clark pushed Rosen and Donoghue to assist Trump's election subversion scheme—and told Rosen he would decline Trump's potential offer to install him as Acting Attorney General if Rosen agreed to aid that scheme. Clark pushed Rosen and Donoghue to publicly announce that DOJ was investigating election fraud and tell key swing state legislatures they should appoint

---

[4] 18 U.S.C. § 610.
[5] GA Secretary of State Brad Raffensperger (@GaSecofState), Twitter (Dec. 8, 2020, 7:55 a.m.), https://twitter.com/GaSecofState/status/1336293440338989060.
[6] Memorandum from White House Counsel Donald F. McGahn II to All White House Staff, at 1 (Jan. 27, 2017); *see also* Memorandum from Attorney General Eric Holder for Heads of Department Components, All United States Attorneys, at 1 (May 11, 2009).

alternate slates of electors following certification of the popular vote. He did so following personal communications with Trump, including at least one meeting that Clark attended in the Oval Office without the knowledge of DOJ leadership.

On December 28, 2020, Clark emailed Rosen and Donoghue a draft letter addressed to the Georgia Governor, General Assembly Speaker, and Senate President Pro Tempore. The letter was titled "Georgia Proof of Concept" and Clark suggested replicating it in "each relevant state." The letter would have informed state officials that DOJ had "taken notice" of election irregularities in their state and recommended calling a special legislative session to evaluate these irregularities, determine who "won the most legal votes," and consider appointing a new slate of Electors. Clark's proposal to wield DOJ's power to override the already-certified popular vote reflected a stunning distortion of DOJ's authority: DOJ protects ballot access and ballot integrity, but has no role in determining which candidate won a particular election.

Documents and testimony confirm that Donoghue and Rosen rejected Clark's recommendation but that Clark—potentially with the assistance of lower-level allies within DOJ—continued to press his "Proof of Concept" for the next several days. Clark eventually informed Rosen and Donoghue that Trump had offered to install him in Rosen's place, and told Rosen he would turn down Trump's offer if Rosen would agree to sign the "Proof of Concept" letter. Clark's efforts culminated in an Oval Office meeting where Rosen, Donoghue, and Steven Engel, the Assistant Attorney General for the Office of Legal Counsel, informed Trump that DOJ's senior leaders would resign if Trump carried out his plans.

FINDING 4: Trump allies with links to the "Stop the Steal" movement and the January 6 insurrection participated in the pressure campaign against DOJ. In addition to Trump White House officials, including the President himself, outside Trump allies with ties to the "Stop the Steal" movement and the January 6 insurrection also pressured DOJ to help overturn the election results. They included:

- U.S. Representative Scott Perry of Pennsylvania's 10th Congressional District, who led the objection to counting Pennsylvania's electoral votes on the House floor in the hours immediately following the January 6 insurrection. Perry has acknowledged introducing Clark to Trump, and documents and testimony confirm that he directly communicated with Donoghue about his false Pennsylvania election fraud claims.

- Doug Mastriano, a Republican State Senator from Pennsylvania who participated in Rudy Giuliani's so-called election fraud "hearings," spent thousands of dollars from his campaign account to bus people to the January 6 "Save America Rally," and was present on the Capitol grounds as the insurrection unfolded. Documents show that, like Perry, Mastriano directly communicated with Donoghue about his false election fraud claims.

- Cleta Mitchell, a Trump campaign legal adviser, early proponent of Trump's false stolen election claims, and participant the January 2, 2021 call where Trump pressured Georgia Secretary of State Brad Raffensperger to "find 11,780 votes." Mitchell emailed Meadows a copy of Trump's lawsuit against Raffensperger and offered to send DOJ 1,800 pages of supporting exhibits; Meadows sent the materials to Rosen, asking DOJ to investigate.

FINDING 5: Trump forced the resignation of U.S. Attorney Byung Jin ("BJay") Pak, whom he believed was not doing enough to address false claims of election fraud in Georgia. Trump then went outside the line of succession when naming an Acting U.S. Attorney, bypassing First Assistant U.S. Attorney Kurt Erskine and instead appointing Bobby Christine because he believed Christine would "do something" about his election fraud claims. U.S. Attorney Pak investigated and did not substantiate various claims of election fraud advanced by Trump and his allies, including false claims that a videotape showed suitcases of illegal ballots being tabulated at Atlanta's State Farm Arena. Trump accused Pak publicly and privately of being a "Never Trumper" and told Rosen and Donoghue on January 3 that he wanted to fire him. Trump relented when Donoghue argued that Pak already planned to resign, agreeing not to fire Pak so long as he resigned the following day. Although First Assistant U.S. Attorney (FAUSA) Erskine was next in the line of succession and Christine was already serving as U.S. Attorney for the Southern District of Georgia, Trump told Donoghue he liked Christine and thought he would "do something" about his election fraud claims.

FINDING 6: By pursuing false claims of election fraud before votes were certified, DOJ deviated from longstanding practice meant to avoid inserting DOJ itself as an issue in the election. Prior to the 2020 general election, DOJ's longstanding policy and practice was to avoid taking overt steps in election fraud investigations until after votes were certified, in order to avoid inserting DOJ itself as an issue in the election. Then-Attorney General Barr weakened this decades-long policy shortly before and after the 2020 election, including in a November 9, 2020 memo that directed prosecutors not to wait until after certification to investigate allegations of voting irregularities that "could potentially impact the outcome of a federal election in an individual State." Consistent with this directive and following additional personal involvement by Barr, DOJ took overt steps to investigate false claims of election fraud before certification in one instance detailed to the Committee—and likely others.

***

The Committee's investigation to date underscores how Trump's efforts to use DOJ as a means to overturn the election results was part of his interrelated efforts to retain the presidency by any means necessary. As has been well-documented by other sources, Trump's efforts to lay the foundation of the "Big Lie" preceded the general election by several months; Attorney General Barr inserted DOJ into that initial effort through various public remarks and actions prior to November 3, 2020 that cast doubt on voting by mail procedures implemented to facilitate exercise of the franchise during the worst public health crisis in a century. Concurrent with Trump's post-election attempts to weaponize DOJ, Trump also reportedly engaged in a separate and equally aggressive pressure campaign on Vice President Mike Pence to set aside the electoral votes of contested states. This "back-up plan," as it were, culminated on January 4— one day after Clark's final attempt to wrest control of DOJ from Rosen, and again in the Oval

Office—when Trump and outside attorney John Eastman attempted to convince Pence that he could circumvent the certification through a procedural loophole in the Electoral Count Act.[7] All of these efforts, in turn, created the disinformation ecosystem necessary for Trump to incite almost 1,000 Americans to breach the Capitol in a violent attempt to subvert democracy by stopping the certification of a free and fair election.

REPORT

I. Applicable Legal Requirements

A. DOJ's Limited Role in Election Fraud Investigations

Although states have primary responsibility for the administration of federal elections, DOJ plays an essential, longstanding role in protecting the right to vote and the integrity of the vote. DOJ itself was founded in 1870 in the aftermath of the Civil War and its immediate imperative was to protect and preserve civil rights, particularly the right to vote for recently emancipated African Americans.[8] Today, the DOJ Civil Rights Division enforces a range of voting rights laws, including the Civil Rights Act, the Voting Rights Act of 1965, the Help America Vote Act, the National Voter Registration Act, and the Uniformed and Overseas Citizens Absentee Voting Act. In doing so, the Civil Rights Division, and DOJ more broadly, help ensure the right of every American citizen to vote and to have their vote count.

In addition to protecting ballot access, DOJ also plays an important role in protecting ballot integrity. The Criminal Division's Public Integrity Section (PIN) investigates and prosecutes election fraud, campaign finance violations, and public corruption that impacts elections. PIN's Election Crimes Branch (ECB) provides guidance to prosecutors on investigating election fraud, and has explained that DOJ's role in such cases is limited:

> The Justice Department's goals in the area of election crime are to prosecute those who violate federal criminal law and, through such prosecutions, to deter corruption of future elections. The Department does not have a role in determining which candidate won a particular election, or whether another election should be held because of the impact of the alleged fraud on the election. In most instances, these issues are for the candidates to litigate in the courts or to advocate before their legislative bodies or election boards. Although civil rights actions under 42 U.S.C. § 1983 may be brought by private citizens to redress election irregularities, the federal prosecutor has no role in such suits.[9]

---

[7] Jamie Gangel & Jeremy Herb, *Memo shows Trump lawyer's six-step plan for Pence to overturn the election*, CNN (Sep. 20, 2021).

[8] The importance of DOJ's mission to protect the right to vote and the integrity of the vote was so great that President Ulysses S. Grant appointed Amos T. Akerman to be the first Attorney General to lead this new Department in large part due to his experience prosecuting voter intimidation cases as a U.S. Attorney in Georgia.

[9] Dep't of Justice, Federal Prosecution of Election Offenses at 84 (8th ed., Dec. 2017), *available at* https://www.justice.gov/criminal/file/1029066/download.

Consistent with its limited role in investigating and prosecuting election fraud, DOJ's longstanding policy is to avoid investigative steps that would impact the election at issue. Central to this policy is DOJ's recognition that publicizing a criminal election fraud investigation before the election has concluded could chill voting and "interject[] the investigation itself as an issue" in the adjudication of any election contest.[10] To that end, it is DOJ's general policy "not to conduct overt investigations, including interviews with individual voters, until after the outcome of the election allegedly affected by the fraud is certified."[11] DOJ also requires prosecutors to consult with PIN before taking any investigative steps beyond a "preliminary inquiry" in election fraud matters, including conducting voter interviews before an election is certified.[12]

As discussed below, Attorney General Barr twice relaxed elements of DOJ's longstanding policy, once shortly before the election and the second time immediately afterward. Barr's second change, reflected in a November 9, 2020 memorandum, authorized DOJ to take overt investigative steps such as witness interviews after polls closed and before the vote was certified. This change prompted the longtime head of PIN's Election Crimes Branch to resign his position in protest and led to disputes between PIN and DOJ leadership over DOJ's role in post-election investigations.

B. Limits on White House-DOJ Communications

1. The History Informing Limitations on Communications Between the White House and the Justice Department

DOJ's legitimacy and effectiveness depends on the public's confidence that its administration and enforcement of federal laws is done impartially, free from actual or perceived partisan or political influence. To prevent such improper influence, longstanding DOJ and White House guidelines limit communications between the White House and DOJ regarding specific law enforcement matters. The guidelines restrict who within DOJ and the White House can communicate with one another about pending and contemplated investigations and litigation; they also limit when such communications can occur in the first place.

These limitations were first implemented in 1978 by Attorney General Griffin Bell in an effort to make DOJ "a neutral zone in the Government, because the law has to be neutral, and in our form of government there are things that are non-partisan, and one is the law."[13] The White House-DOJ communications guidelines were implemented in direct response to Watergate. President Richard Nixon's abuses of his presidential powers severely undermined public confidence in several agencies, but none more so than the Justice Department, as President Gerald Ford's Attorney General Edward Levi described at his swearing-in:

---

[10] *Id.*
[11] *Id.* at 9.
[12] Dep't of Justice, Justice Manual § 9-85.210.
[13] Attorney General Griffin B. Bell, An Address Before Department of Justice Lawyers, 3 (Sept. 6, 1978), *available at* https://www.justice.gov/sites/default/files/ag/legacy/2011/08/23/09-06-1978b.pdf.

We have lived in a time of change and corrosive skepticism and cynicism concerning the administration of justice. Nothing can more weaken the quality of life or more imperil the realization of those goals we all hold dear than our failure to make clear by word and deed that our law is not an instrument of partisan purpose, and it is not an instrument to be used in ways which are careless of the higher values which are within all of us.[14]

However, while Watergate was the impetus for these guidelines, the need to maintain DOJ's legitimacy by protecting it from political influence is a longstanding norm. In an address to the Second Annual Conference of U.S. Attorneys in 1940, Attorney General Robert Jackson highlighted "the most important reason why the prosecutor should have, as nearly as possible, a detached and impartial view," stating:

Therein is the most dangerous power of the prosecutor: that he will pick people that he thinks he should get, rather than pick cases that need to be prosecuted...It is in this realm...that the greatest danger of abuse of prosecuting power lies. It is here that law enforcement becomes personal, and the real crime becomes that of being unpopular with the predominant or governing group, being attached to the wrong political views, or being personally obnoxious to or in the way of the prosecutor himself.[15]

The norm that law enforcement must be free from political interference is so critical and so uniformly acknowledged in our system of government that the U.S. State Department regularly cites the politicization of a government's prosecutorial power as grounds for determining that a foreign power is an "authoritarian state."[16]

---

[14] Attorney General Edward Levi, Remarks at His Swearing-in Ceremony (Feb. 7, 1975), *available at* https://www.fordlibrarymuseum.gov/library/document/0248/whpr19750207-008.pdf.

[15] Attorney General Robert H. Jackson, The Federal Prosecutor, An Address at the Second Annual Conference of U.S. Attorneys, 4-5 (Apr. 1, 1940), *available at* https://www.justice.gov/sites/default/files/ag/legacy/2011/09/16/04-01-1940.pdf.

[16] *See, e.g.*, U.S. Dep't of State, Bureau of Democracy, H.R. and Lab., 2020 Country Reports on Human Rights Practices: Belarus (2020), *available at* https://www.state.gov/reports/2020-country-reports-on-human-rights-practices/belarus/; U.S. Dep't of State, Bureau of Democracy, H.R. and Lab., 2020 Country Reports on Human Rights Practices: Tajikistan (2020), *available at* https://www.state.gov/reports/2020-country-reports-on-human-rights-practices/tajikistan/; U.S. Dep't of State, Bureau of Democracy, H.R. and Lab., 2020 Country Reports on Human Rights Practices: Venezuela (2020), *available at* https://www.state.gov/reports/2020-country-reports-on-human-rights-practices/venezuela/; U.S. Dep't of State, Bureau of Democracy, H.R. and Lab., Country Reports on Human Rights Practices for 2011: Vietnam (2015), *available at* https://2009-2017.state.gov/j/drl/rls/hrrpt/humanrightsreport/index.htm?year=2015&dlid=252813; U.S. Dep't of State, Bureau of Democracy, H.R. and Lab., Country Reports on Human Rights Practices for 2011: Belarus (2011), *available at* https://2009-2017.state.gov/j/drl/rls/hrrpt/humanrightsreport/index.htm?dlid=186331 (archived).

2. Guidelines Restricting Communications Between the White House and the Justice Department

The restrictions on White House-DOJ communications are effectuated through internal policies issued by both entities, typically at the start of new presidential administrations. On January 27, 2017, White House Counsel Don McGahn issued guidelines that governed White House communications with the Justice Department for the entire duration of the Trump Administration. These guidelines, which McGahn emphasized in the memorandum "*must be strictly followed*," established four limitations on communications regarding "ongoing or contemplated cases or investigations":

- Only the President, Vice President, Counsel to the President, and designees of the Counsel to the President may be involved in communications about contemplated or pending investigations or enforcement actions. These individuals may designate subordinates, but ongoing contacts pursuant to such a designation should be handled in conjunction with the White House Counsel's Office.

- Communications regarding litigation where the government is or may be a defendant must first be cleared by the White House Counsel's Office.

- Responses to DOJ requests for White House views on any litigation must be made in consultation with the White House Counsel's Office.

- The President, Vice President, Counsel to the President, and Deputy Counsel to the President are the only White House individuals who may initiate a conversation with DOJ about a specific case or investigation. All communications about individual cases or investigations should be routed through the Attorney General, Deputy Attorney General, Associate Attorney General, or Solicitor General, unless the White House Counsel's Office approves different procedures for the specific case at issue.[17]

Additionally, the White House guidelines restricted requests for the Justice Department's Office of Legal Counsel to issue formal legal opinions to only "specific legal questions impacting particular matters before the Executive Branch."[18]

During the Trump administration, the Justice Department never issued guidelines on communications with the White House and left the 2009 guidelines issued by Attorney General Eric Holder in place. As an overarching principle, these guidelines make clear that "[Assistant Attorneys General, the United States Attorneys, and the heads of the investigative agencies in the Department] must be insulated from influences that should not affect decisions in particular criminal or civil cases."[19] The Justice Department guidelines established two main limitations on

---

[17] Memorandum from White House Counsel Donald F. McGahn II to All White House Staff, at 1 (Jan. 27, 2017).
[18] *Id.* at 2.
[19] Memorandum from Attorney General Eric Holder for Heads of Department Components, All United States Attorneys, at 1 (May 11, 2009).

communications with the White House regarding "pending or contemplated criminal or civil investigations and cases":

- The Justice Department will advise the White House concerning pending or contemplated criminal or civil investigations or cases only if it is important for the performance of the President's duties and appropriate from a law enforcement perspective.

- Initial communications concerning pending or contemplated criminal investigations or cases will involve only the Attorney General or the Deputy Attorney General and the President, Vice President, Counsel to the President, and Principal Deputy Counsel to the President. If the communications concern a pending or contemplated civil investigation or case, the Associate Attorney General may also be involved. Where ongoing communications are required, these officials may designate subordinates, but must monitor subordinate contacts and the subordinates must keep their superiors regularly informed of any such contacts.[20]

Additionally, the Justice Department guidelines restrict White House requests for legal advice to those from the President, the Counsel to the President, or one of the Deputy Counsels to the President, directed to the Attorney General and the Assistant Attorney General for the Office of Legal Counsel.[21] The Assistant Attorney General for the Office of Legal Counsel also has an independent duty to "report to the Attorney General and the Deputy Attorney General any communications that, in his or her view, constitute improper attempts to influence the Office of Legal Counsel's legal judgment."[22]

C. Applicable Federal Laws Governing Political Interference with Investigations

Beyond White House and DOJ guidelines, improper White House interference in specific law enforcement actions may implicate several federal laws, depending on the circumstances of that interference. Most notably, federal obstruction of justice statutes create criminal liability for "corrupt conduct capable of producing an effect that prevents justice from being duly administered, regardless of the means employed."[23] As the First and Seventh Circuits have held, obstruction of justice includes even otherwise lawful conduct or conduct within one's lawful authority when it constitutes an obstructive act done with an improper motive.[24] An improper request by a White House official that DOJ initiate or drop a specific law enforcement matter could implicate the obstruction statutes depending on the circumstances of the request.

---

[20] *Id.* at 1-2.
[21] *Id.* at 3
[22] *Id.*
[23] *United States v. Silverman*, 745 F.2d 1386, 1393 (11th Cir. 1984) (citing 18 U.S.C. § 1503).
[24] *See United States v. Cueto*, 151 F.3d 620, 631 (7th Cir. 1998); *United States v. Cintolo*, 818 F.2d 980, 992 (1st Cir. 1987).

Separately, the Hatch Act of 1939 may also be implicated by White House interference in DOJ investigations, to the extent such interference is designed to affect the results of a federal election. Among other provisions, the Hatch Act prohibits all employees, even political appointees,[25] from using their "official authority or influence for the purpose of interfering with or affecting the result of an election."[26] The Act's criminal provisions proscribe using "official authority for the purpose of interfering with, or affecting, the nomination or the election of any candidate for [federal office]," as well as "command[ing] ... any employee of the Federal Government ... to engage in, or not to engage in, any political activity, including, but not limited to ... working or refusing to work on behalf of a candidate."[27]

II. December 1 – December 15: Attorney General Barr Announces His Resignation After Declaring that DOJ Has Found No Evidence of Widespread Election Fraud

Although federal prosecutors routinely and appropriately investigate election fraud allegations, DOJ has long recognized that it "does not have a role in determining which candidate won a particular election."[28] DOJ also recognizes that publicizing a criminal investigation of election fraud allegations before the election has concluded "runs the obvious risk of chilling legitimate voting" and of "interjecting the investigation itself as an issue" in the adjudication of any election contest.[29] For this reason, prior to the 2020 election cycle, DOJ policy prohibited federal investigators and prosecutors from taking overt investigative steps in election fraud cases "until the election in question [had] been concluded, its results certified, and all recounts and election contests concluded."[30]

Following months of false claims by President Trump and Attorney General Barr that mail voting would lead to rampant fraud in the 2020 election, DOJ weakened this longstanding policy in two respects.[31] First, in early October 2020, DOJ announced "an exception to the general non-interference with elections policy," instructing U.S. Attorneys' Offices that they could publicly announce election fraud investigations prior to Election Day if "the integrity of any component of the federal government is implicated by election offenses."[32] The newly announced exception encompassed the U.S. Postal Service and thus claims of mail voting fraud, which DOJ could now announce while voting was underway.

Second, two days after then-candidate Joe Biden was declared the Electoral College winner, Barr issued a memorandum authorizing and encouraging overt, pre-certification

---

[25] 5 U.S.C. § 7322(1)(A)
[26] 5 U.S.C. § 7323(a)(1).
[27] 18 U.S.C. §§ 595, 610.
[28] Federal Prosecution of Election Offenses, *supra* n.9 at 84.
[29] *Id.*
[30] *Id.*
[31] Jane C. Timm, *Fact Check: Echoing Trump, Barr Misleads on Voter Fraud to Attack Expanded Vote-by-Mail*, NBC News (Sept. 19, 2020).
[32] Robert Faturechi & Justin Elliott, *DOJ Frees Federal Prosecutors to Take Steps That Could Interfere With Elections, Weakening Long-Standing Policy*, ProPublica (Oct. 7, 2020).

"election irregularity inquiries."³³ Barr's November 9, 2020 memorandum directly contradicted DOJ's longstanding policy against overtly investigating election fraud allegations before the election results are certified. Barr called DOJ's traditional policy a "passive and delayed enforcement approach" and asserted that "any concerns that overt actions taken by the Department could inadvertently impact the election are greatly minimized, if they exist at all, once voting has concluded, even if certification has not yet been completed." Accordingly, Barr authorized pre-certification investigations "if there are clear and apparently credible allegations of irregularities that, if true, could potentially impact the outcome of a federal election in an individual State"—and called on prosecutors to "timely and appropriately address allegations of voting irregularities so that all of the American people ... can have full confidence in the results of our elections."

Barr's memo prompted the longtime career heard of DOJ's Election Crimes Branch to resign his position.³⁴ It also caused tensions between PIN and DOJ leadership more broadly. According to Donoghue, PIN—with whom the Justice Manual requires prosecutors to consult on election crimes matters—withheld its concurrence to pre-certification investigative activity "several times."³⁵ Donoghue recalled that in one case, following a dispute between PIN and a local U.S. Attorney's Office, Rosen generally determined that the U.S. Attorney's Office would not be permitted to move forward with investigative activity at the time. In most cases, however, DOJ leadership overrode PIN's concerns and allowed the relevant U.S. Attorney's Office or FBI to take the investigative steps to which PIN had objected.³⁶ This included Barr's direction that the FBI interview witnesses concerning allegations that election workers at Atlanta's State Farm Arena secretly tabulated suitcases full of illegal ballots.³⁷ As discussed further below, these claims were pushed by Giuliani at a Georgia Senate hearing and had already been debunked by the Georgia Secretary of State's Office by the time Barr's requested interviews took place.³⁸ PIN concluded that the claims did not fall within the scope of Barr's November 9 memo, which PIN Chief Corey Amundson noted "created an exception to the DOJ Election Non-Interference Policy for substantial, clear, apparently credible, and non-speculative allegations of voting and vote tabulation irregularities 'that, if true, could potentially impact the outcome of a federal election in an individual State.'"³⁹ Barr nonetheless directed the FBI to interview witnesses about the State Farm claims; like the Georgia Secretary of State's Office, the FBI and U.S. Attorney's Office also concluded they were meritless.⁴⁰

---

[33] Memo from Attorney General Barr to United States Attorneys, Assistant Attorneys General, and the FBI Director on Post-Voting Election Irregularity Inquiries, Nov. 9, 2020.

[34] *Id.*; Dartunno Clark & Ken Dilanian, *Justice Department's Election Crimes Chief Resigns After Barr Allows Prosecutors to Investigate Voter Fraud Claims*, NBC News (Nov. 9, 2020).

[35] Transcript of Richard Donoghue Interview at 73 (Aug. 6, 2021) ("Donoghue Tr.").

[36] Donoghue Tr. at 73-74.

[37] *Id.*; Email from Richard Donoghue to David Bowdich (Dec. 7, 2020, 12:09 p.m.) (SJC-PreCertificationEvents-000751-753).

[38] Stephen Fowler, *Fact Checking Rudy Giuliani's Grandiose Georgia Election Fraud Claim*, Georgia Public Broadcasting (Dec. 4, 2020).

[39] Email from Corey Amundson to Redacted (Dec. 7, 2020, 12:34 a.m.) (SJC-PreCertificationEvents-000753).

[40] *See* Transcript of BJay Pak Interview at 22 (Aug. 11, 2021) ("Pak Tr.").

Notwithstanding his efforts to encourage election fraud investigations, on December 1, 2020, Attorney General Barr conceded that DOJ had found no evidence of widespread election fraud. He stated that DOJ and the Federal Bureau of Investigation (FBI) had been working to follow up on specific information they had received, but that "to date, we have not seen fraud on a scale that could have effected a different outcome in the election."[41] Barr added that DOJ and the Department of Homeland Security had "looked into" the conspiracy theory that Dominion Voting Systems "machines were programmed essentially to skew the election results," and that "we haven't seen anything to substantiate that."[42] Barr announced his resignation two weeks later, informing Trump on December 14 that he would step down effective December 23.

III. December 15 – December 27: Following Barr's Announcement, Trump Repeatedly Contacts DOJ's Incoming Leadership About His Election Fraud Claims

A. December 15, 2020 Oval Office Meeting

Following Barr's announcement, Trump immediately initiated a series of contacts with Deputy Attorney General Jeffrey Rosen that would continue through early January. On December 14, Special Assistant to the President and Oval Office Coordinator Molly Michael emailed Rosen two documents "From POTUS": (1) a set of talking points on claims of voter fraud in Antrim County, Michigan; and (2) a purported "forensic report" by Allied Security Operations Group (ASOG) on Dominion Voting Systems' performance in Antrim County.[43]

The ASOG report was authored by Russell Ramsland, a one-time Republican congressional candidate who served as an "expert witness" for Rudy Giuliani at so-called election-integrity hearings in Michigan and other states; Ramsland also authored affidavits in support of several failed election challenges, including an affidavit that erroneously cited data from Minnesota when claiming that more Michigan votes were recorded than there were Michigan voters.[44] The ASOG report and associated talking points contained a series of demonstrably false claims, ranging from a claim that Dominion voting machines caused an error rate of 68 percent when counting Antrim County ballots to a claim that Dominion's software is intentionally designed with inherent errors that enable systemic fraud. These claims have been extensively discredited, including by former Cybersecurity and Infrastructure Security Agency Director Chris Krebs, who called them "factually inaccurate," and by a former Election Assistance Commission official, who called them "preposterous."[45]

---

[41] Michael Balsamo, *Disputing Trump, Barr Says No Widespread Election Fraud*, Associated Press (Dec. 1, 2020).
[42] Katie Benner and Michael S. Schmidt, *Barr Acknowledges Justice Dept. Has Found No Widespread Voter Fraud*, N.Y. Times (Dec. 1, 2020).
[43] Email from Molly Michael to Jeffrey Rosen (Dec. 14, 2020, 4:57 p.m.) (SJC-Pre-CertificationEvents-000425).
[44] *Id.*; Emma Brown, Aaron C. Davis, Jon Swaine, & Josh Dawsey, *The Making of a Myth*, Wash. Post (May 9, 2021).
[45] Todd Spangler, *Former Election Security Chief for Trump Knocks Down Antrim County Report*, Detroit Free Press (Dec. 16, 2020).

On December 15, the day after Molly Michael sent the Antrim County materials to Rosen "From POTUS," Rosen and Donoghue were summoned to a meeting at the White House.[46] Barr was not invited, even though he was still Attorney General and would remain so for more than another week.[47] Other participants included White House Counsel Pat Cipollone, White House Chief of Staff Mark Meadows, and the Department of Homeland Security's Ken Cuccinelli, whom Barr had asked to review the ASOG report.[48] According to Rosen and Donoghue, Trump spent the meeting walking through a series of election fraud claims. The ASOG report was a topic of discussion; so were Trump's assertions that "bad things" had happened in Pennsylvania and Georgia, such as the claim that videotape showed election workers delivering suitcases of ballots in Georgia.[49] Rosen recalled Trump asking why DOJ wasn't "doing more to look at this" and whether DOJ was "going to do its job."[50] Rosen added that Trump was not "belligerent" or "angry" when he asked whether DOJ was going to "do its job," and that Rosen and Donoghue responded by making clear that DOJ was in fact doing its job.[51]

B. December 23 and 24 Trump-Rosen Calls

Trump called Rosen twice the following week. The first call was on December 23, Barr's final day as Attorney General; Rosen recalled this being a short call and mostly small talk, with Trump indicating that he might want to talk to Rosen again.[52] Trump in fact called Rosen again on December 24. According to Rosen, the call lasted approximately 10-15 minutes and Trump brought up the same sorts of election fraud claims he had raised during the December 15 meeting—asserting that there was fraud in Pennsylvania and Arizona, asking whether DOJ had looked into election fraud that "people are saying" had taken place, and telling Rosen to "make sure the Department is really looking into these things that you may have missed."[53]

At some point during the December 24 call, Trump also asked Rosen whether he knew "a guy named Jeff Clark."[54] Rosen recalled thinking it was "odd" and "curious" that the President would have known an Assistant Attorney General, but the significance of Trump's reference to Clark did not become fully apparent until the coming days. As discussed in greater detail below, Rosen called Clark on December 26 and learned that shortly before the December 24 Trump-Rosen call, Clark had met with Trump in the Oval Office.

---

[46] Donoghue Tr. at 26-27; Transcript of Jeffrey Rosen Interview at 28 (Aug. 7, 2021) ("Rosen Tr.").
[47] Rosen Tr. at 28-29.
[48] Rosen Tr. at 16-18, 29. Donoghue additionally recalled that Deputy White House Counsel Patrick Philbin attended, along with the Department of Homeland Security's Chad Mizelle; Rosen did not recall Mizelle attending this meeting.
[49] Donoghue Tr. at 27; Rosen Tr. at 30.
[50] Rosen Tr. at 34.
[51] Rosen Tr. at 33-38.
[52] Rosen Tr. at 41-42.
[53] Rosen Tr. at 81-84.
[54] Rosen Tr. at 82.

C. December 27 Trump-Rosen Call

At the end of their December 24 call, Rosen suggested to Trump that they defer any further discussions until the following Monday because of the upcoming Christmas holiday.[55] Trump did not wait that long to call again, calling Rosen twice on Sunday, December 27. He first called Rosen sometime Sunday morning; Rosen recalled discussing golf and other sports until Trump indicated that he was running late for a golf game, at which point the call ended.[56]

Trump called Rosen again the same afternoon.[57] After about 30 minutes, Rosen called Donoghue and asked to conference him in.[58] Donoghue described the portion of the call he participated in as a "long call ... over an hour after I joined."[59] According to Donoghue, Trump "was going on at some length" about the same sorts of election fraud claims he had raised during the December 15 Oval Office meeting, maintaining that the "election has been stolen out from under the American people" and asking whether DOJ was taking these allegations seriously.[60] Among other things, Trump:

- Claimed that 205,000 more votes were certified in Pennsylvania than were cast;[61]
- Claimed that the State Farm Arena tape "shows fraud" by election workers in Atlanta who had ballots hidden under a table that they tabulated multiple times;[62]
- Said that Donoghue should go to Fulton County, Georgia and conduct a signature verification, and that he would find "tens of thousands" of illegal votes;[63] and
- Complained, "You guys aren't following the Internet the way I do."[64]

Trump also referenced three Republican elected officials who were amplifying his claims of a stolen election[65]: (1) Pennsylvania Rep. Scott Perry, who led the objection to certifying Pennsylvania's electoral votes, even after the January 6 insurrection[66]; (2) Ohio Rep. Jim Jordan, who attended a December 21, 2020 meeting where Trump and House Freedom Caucus members strategized about their plans for January 6[67]; and (3) Pennsylvania State Senator Doug Mastriano, who spent thousands of dollars from his campaign account to bus people to the January 6 "Save

---

[55] Rosen Tr. at 57.
[56] Rosen Tr. at 57-58.
[57] Rosen Tr. at 58.
[58] Donoghue Tr. at 37.
[59] Donoghue Tr. at 38.
[60] Donoghue Tr. at 39.
[61] Donoghue Tr. at 42; Notes of Dec. 27, 2020 Call (SJC-PreCertificationEvents-000735) ("12/27/20 Donoghue Notes").
[62] Donoghue Tr. at 44-45; 12/27/20 Donoghue Notes.
[63] 12/27/20 Donoghue Notes.
[64] Rosen Tr. at 93; Donoghue Tr. at 86.
[65] Donoghue Tr. at 41; 12/27/20 Donoghue Notes.
[66] Andrew Solender, *Majority of House Republicans Vote to Reject Pennsylvania, Arizona Electors*, Forbes (Jan. 7, 2021).
[67] Melissa Quinn, *Trump meets with GOP allies with eye on challenging count of electoral votes*, CBS News (Dec. 22, 2020).

America Rally" and was present on the Capitol grounds as the insurrection unfolded.[68] Trump complained that the Republican officials were trying to address election fraud claims but had limited capacity and authority to do so, whereas DOJ was not doing enough—in Donoghue's words, Trump was "complaining about what he thought to be the Department's lack of action. His displeasure was clear. He felt that we should be doing things that, in his mind, at least, we weren't doing."[69]

Rosen and Donoghue both recalled telling Trump that DOJ was doing its job, with Rosen at one point saying that DOJ "can't and won't just flip a switch and change the election."[70] In response, according to Donoghue's testimony and contemporaneous notes, Trump asked that DOJ "just say the election was corrupt and leave the rest to me and the [Republican] Congressmen," whom Donoghue understood to be the Republican House Members who would be challenging the Electoral College certification on January 6.[71] Rosen similarly recalled Trump telling them that DOJ "should be out there finding [the election fraud] and saying so," and that DOJ should "just have a press conference."[72]

At some point during the discussion Trump referenced Clark, indicating that people were telling him good things about Clark, that Trump should "put him in" to a leadership position, and that Trump should replace DOJ's leadership.[73] This was the first time Donoghue heard Clark's name mentioned in connection with the election, and the reference surprised him because Clark "didn't have anything to do with the Department's election responsibilities."[74] Rosen and Donoghue told Trump he should have the DOJ leadership he wanted, but that replacing DOJ's leadership would not change its position on the election.[75]

D. December 27 Outreach from Congressman Perry to Donoghue

Toward the end of the Rosen-Donoghue-Trump call, Trump asked Donoghue to provide his cell phone number so Trump could have elected officials with relevant information call him.[76] Congressman Perry called Donoghue later the same day.[77] At the time, Perry had been amplifying—both publicly and behind the scenes—Trump's false claims that the 2020 election was stolen. After media outlets reported that Vice President Biden had won the election, Perry was one of the first Republican federal officials to publicly dissent, arguing on Twitter that

---

[68] Pennsylvania Dep't of State, Campaign Finance Report: Doug Mastriano Year 2020 Cycle 7 (Sep. 20, 2021) at 33-34; Katie Meyer, Miles Bryan, & Ryan Briggs, *Mastriano campaign spent thousands on buses ahead of D.C. insurrection*, WHYY (Jan. 12, 2021).
[69] Donoghue Tr. at 43-44.
[70] Rosen Tr. at 93; Donoghue Tr. at 39; 12/27/20 Donoghue Notes (SJC-PreCertificationEvents-000738-39).
[71] Donoghue Tr. at 87; 12/27/20 Donoghue Notes.
[72] Rosen Tr. at 95-96.
[73] 12/27/20 Donoghue Notes; Donoghue Tr. at 88-89.
[74] Donoghue Tr. at 88-89.
[75] 12/27/20 Donoghue Notes; Rosen Tr. at 90-91.
[76] 12/27/20 Donoghue Notes; Donoghue Tr. at 90.
[77] Donoghue's contemporaneous notes are labeled "12/28/20," but Donoghue clarified that this was a mistake and that the call from Rep. Perry actually took place on the evening of December 27.

"[I]legal votes will determine who is POTUS."[78] He was one of the initial House Republicans who signed onto an amicus brief supporting Texas's failed attempt to have the Supreme Court invalidate the election results in four states that President Biden won.[79] And after reportedly meeting with Trump on December 21 to strategize about objecting to the Electoral College results at the January 6 Joint Session of Congress,[80] Perry led efforts to block the certification of Pennsylvania's Electoral College votes—speaking against certification on the House floor even after the January 6 insurrection.[81]

Perry told Donoghue that Trump had asked him to call and that DOJ hadn't done its job with respect to the elections.[82] Perry added something to the effect of, "I think Jeff Clark is great. I like that guy a lot. He's the kind of guy who could really get in there and do something about this."[83] Perry did not explain how he knew Clark and Donoghue did not ask.[84] At the end of the call, Perry indicated that he had information about "things going on in Pennsylvania," including the claim that there were 205,000 more votes than voters.[85] Donoghue responded that Perry could send him information about Pennsylvania but that DOJ had not seen fraud on a scale that would have changed the outcome there.[86]

Following their call, Perry emailed Donoghue a series of documents summarizing numerous Pennsylvania election fraud claims.[87] They included a variety of complaints about voting by mail that mirrored similar complaints made in other contested states. They also included several refuted allegations of election fraud in Pennsylvania, including that:

- An analysis of the Pennsylvania Department of State's Statewide Uniform Registry of Electors (SURE) system found that 205,000 more votes were reported as being cast than registered voters who voted.[88] On December 28, Perry also publicly promoted this particular claim on Twitter, tweeting that it "call[ed] into question the integrity not only of the PA system, but the competency of those charged with its oversight."[89] In reality, Pennsylvania votes cast equaled the same amount as registered voters who

---

[78] Representative Scott Perry (@RepScottPerry), Twitter (Nov. 7, 2020, 1:18 p.m.), https://twitter.com/RepScottPerry/status/1325140625218441225?s=20.
[79] Brief of Amicus Curiae of U.S. Representative Mike Johnson and 125 Other Members of the U.S. House of Representatives in Support of Plaintiff's Motion for Leave to File a Bill of Complaint and Motion for a Preliminary Injunction, Texas v. Pennsylvania, 141 S. Ct. 1230 (2020) (No. 155).
[80] Billy House & Laura Litvan, *Thune Sees Challenge to Biden Win Going Down Like 'Shot Dog'*, Bloomberg (Dec. 21, 2020).
[81] *Editorial: Scott Perry Must Resign*, York Dispatch (Jan. 7, 2021).
[82] Notes of Dec. 27, 2020 Donoghue-Perry Call (SJC-PreCertificationEvents-000705) ("12/27/20 Donoghue-Perry Notes").
[83] Donoghue Tr. at 91.
[84] Donoghue Tr. at 92.
[85] 12/27/20 Donoghue-Perry Notes; Donoghue Tr. at 93.
[86] *Id.*
[87] Email from Scott Perry to Richard Donoghue (Dec. 27, 2020, 8:37 p.m.) (SJC-Pre-CertificationEvents-000001-0000043).
[88] *Id.*
[89] Representative Scott Perry (@RepScottPerry), Twitter (Dec. 28, 2020, 6:01 p.m.), https://twitter.com/RepScottPerry/status/1343693703664308225?s=20.

voted. The so-called "analysis" of the SURE system was based on incomplete data: four of the state's biggest counties had not yet entered individualized voter histories, which was clear at the time this allegation was made from the vote counts certified by the counties hosted on the Secretary of State's website.[90]

- Over 4,000 Pennsylvanians voted more than once.[91] In reality, only three actual efforts to vote twice have been identified to date in the state of Pennsylvania, and all three were attempts to vote twice for Trump.[92] The false claim of over 4,000 double votes stems from a printing error that caused more than 4,000 voters to mistakenly receive two absentee ballots apiece. But that did not translate into any duplicate votes because, as the Pennsylvania Department of State explained, "all the duplicate ballots are coded for the same voter, so if a voter tried to submit more than one, the system would literally prevent the second ballot from being counted."[93] Additionally, all voters who received two absentee ballots were contacted by state election officials about the printing error prior to the election.[94]

- Pennsylvania's Democratic Governor and Secretary of State attempted to create "confusion, chaos, and instilling fear" under the guise of protecting public health by encouraging voters to vote by mail rather than in person.[95] In reality, state officials promoted voting by mail to ensure that voters had access to the ballot during an unprecedented global pandemic.

Donoghue forwarded Perry's email to Scott Brady, the United States Attorney for the Western District of Pennsylvania, with the note: "JFYI regarding allegations about PA voting irregularities, for whatever it may be worth."[96] According to Donoghue, he forwarded the materials to Brady "because a U.S. Attorney had to be looking at this thing, a U.S. Attorney in Pennsylvania."[97] Donoghue and Brady subsequently discussed the claims contained in the documents, to the extent they related to election fraud as opposed to complaints that state elected officials should not have changed certain voting procedures. Brady informed Donoghue that the claims "were not well founded." For example, Brady explained that there were not actually more

---

[90] Statement, Pennsylvania Dep't of State, Response to December 28, 2020, release of misinformation by group of GOP state House members (Dec. 29, 2020), available at https://www.dos.pa.gov/about-us/Documents/statements/2020-12-29-Response-PA-GOP-Legislators-Misinformation.pdf.
[91] Email from Scott Perry to Richard Donoghue (Dec. 27, 2020, 8:37 p.m.) (SJC-Pre-CertificationEvents-000001-0000043).
[92] Rosalind S. Helderman, Jon Swaine, & Michelle Ye Hee Lee, *Despite Trump's intense hunt for voter fraud, officials in key states have so far identified just a small number of possible cases*, Wash. Post (Dec. 23, 2020).
[93] Miles Bryan, *PA Reaching Out To More than 4,000 Voters After Glitch Sends Them Two Mail Ballots*, 90.5 WESA (Oct. 22, 2020).
[94] *Id.*
[95] Email from Scott Perry to Richard Donoghue (Dec. 27, 2020, 8:37p.m.) (SJC-Pre-CertificationEvents-000001-0000043).
[96] Email from Richard Donoghue to Scott Brady (Dec. 27, 2020, 10:05 p.m.) (SJC-PreCertificationEvents-000336-381).
[97] Donoghue Tr. at 94.

votes certified than voters; in reality, the database analyzed by proponents of this false claim was missing data from four Pennsylvania counties.[98]

E. December 28 Trump-Donoghue Call

Trump called Donoghue the following morning. Donoghue recalled this December 28 call as "a very short call" and "essentially a follow-up" to the lengthy Trump-Rosen-Donoghue call the prior afternoon.[99] According to Donoghue, Trump said something to the effect of, "I don't know if I mentioned this last night"—referencing something that Trump had, in fact, raised during the December 27 call. Donoghue did not recall with certainty what topic Trump raised, but indicated that it may have been the claim that the Pennsylvania Secretary of State certified more ballots than were actually cast. Donoghue replied that Trump had raised the issue the prior evening, and the call ended.[100]

IV. December 28: Jeffrey Clark Urges DOJ Leadership to Intervene in Georgia's Appointment of Electors and to Replicate this "Proof of Concept" in Other States

Efforts to involve DOJ in Trump's election subversion scheme continued on December 28, when Clark approached Rosen and Donoghue with an audacious proposal: DOJ should inform the legislatures of Georgia and several other states that it was investigating voting irregularities, and recommend that each state legislature call a special session to consider appointing an alternate slate of electors.

A. Clark's Late December Oval Office Meeting With Trump

Clark initially served in the Trump administration as the Senate-confirmed Assistant Attorney General for ENRD. In this role, Clark reportedly "developed a reputation for pushing aggressive conservative legal principles and taking a hands-on approach that drew kudos from some colleagues but often frustrated career lawyers on his team."[101] Subsequently, Clark became the Acting Assistant Attorney General for the Civil Division in September 2020 when the division's previous Acting Assistant Attorney General, Ethan P. Davis, left DOJ. Prior to joining the Trump administration, Clark had known Rosen in private practice at the Washington, D.C. office of Kirkland & Ellis LLP, which Rosen joined in 1982 and Clark joined in 1996.

Rosen called Clark on December 26 in order to learn more about why Trump had mentioned Clark on their December 24 call. Rosen recalled asking Clark whether there was "something going on that I don't know about" and being "flabbergasted" when Clark admitted that he had met with the President. According to Rosen, Clark described having talked to Congressman Perry, getting caught up in a meeting that Perry asked him to join, and not initially realizing that it would be a meeting with Trump in the Oval Office. Rosen did not recall Clark

---

[98] Donoghue Tr. at 95-96.
[99] Donoghue Tr. at 51-52.
[100] Donoghue Tr. at 52.
[101] Ellen Gilmer, *Divisive Top Trump Environment Lawyer Reviews 'Challenging Job'*, Bloomberg Law (Jan. 19, 2021).

telling him who else participated in the meeting or how Clark had met Perry, who later acknowledged that he discussed election fraud claims with Clark and that "when President Trump asked if I would make an introduction [to Clark], I obliged."[102] Rosen also did not recall Clark's description, if any, of what transpired during the Oval Office meeting.[103]

Rosen recalled Clark indicating that the Oval Office meeting took place a day or two before Christmas, meaning either December 23 or 24.[104] If accurate, this means the meeting took place two or three days after Trump, Perry, Congressman Jordan, and other House Republicans met at the White House on December 21 to strategize about the January 6 Joint Session.

B. Clark's "Two Urgent Action Items"

At 4:40 p.m. on December 28, Clark emailed Rosen and Donoghue with the subject "Two Urgent Action Items." The first action item requested a briefing from the Office of the Director of National Intelligence (ODNI):

> I would like to have your authorization to get a classified briefing tomorrow from ODNI led by DNI Radcliffe on foreign election interference issues. I can then assess how that relates to activating the IEEPA and 2018 EO powers on such matters (now twice renewed by the President).[105]

IEEPA refers to the International Emergency Economic Powers Act, which authorizes the president to declare a national emergency due to "unusual and extraordinary threats" to the United States and to block any transactions and freeze any assets within the jurisdiction of the United States to deal with the threat."[106] The 2018 EO Clark mentions is Executive Order 13848, which operationalizes IEEPA sanctions in the event of foreign interference in a U.S. election.[107]

As the basis for his "urgent" request, Clark cited evidence, supposedly in the public domain, from "white hat hackers" indicating that a "Dominion machine accessed the Internet through a smart thermostat with a net connecting trail leading back to China."[108] Clark did not produce or quote any of this purported evidence, but he wrote that he believed the ODNI "may" have additional classified intelligence on this matter.[109]

---

[102] Rosen Tr. at 84-88; Katie Benner & Catie Edmondson, *Pennsylvania Lawmaker Played Key Role in Trump's Plot to Oust Acting Attorney General*, N.Y. Times (Jan. 23, 2021); Jonathan Tamari & Chris Brennan, *Pa. Congressman Scott Perry Acknowledges Introducing Trump to Lawyer at the Center of Election Plot*, Phila. Inquirer, Jan. 25, 2021.
[103] Rosen Tr. at 87-88.
[104] Rosen Tr. at 86.
[105] Email from Jeffrey Clark to Jeffrey Rosen and Richard Donoghue (Dec. 28, 2020, 4:40 p.m.) (SJC-PreCertificationEvents-000697-702).
[106] 50 U.S.C. §§ 1701(a) & 1702(a)(1)(B).
[107] Exec. Order No. 13848, 83 Fed. Reg. 46843 (Sept. 14, 2018).
[108] Email from Jeffrey Clark to Jeffrey Rosen and Richard Donoghue (Dec. 28, 2020, 4:40 p.m.) (SJC-PreCertificationEvents-000697-702).
[109] *Id.*

The second "urgent action item" was a proposal that DOJ send letters to the elected leadership of Georgia and other contested states, urging them to convene special legislative sessions in order to appoint a different slate of electors than those popularly chosen in the 2020 election. Clark explained his proposal in the email:

> The concept is to send it to the Governor, Speaker, and President Pro Tempore of each relevant state to indicate that in light of time urgency and sworn evidence of election irregularities presented to courts and to legislative committees, the legislatures thereof should each assemble and make a decision about elector appointment in light of their deliberations.[110]

Clark attached a draft letter to this email titled "Georgia Proof of Concept" and addressed to Georgia Governor Brian Kemp, Speaker of the Georgia House David Ralston, and President Pro Tempore of the Georgia Senate Butch Miller.[111] Although Clark's draft was addressed to elected officials in Georgia, his transmittal email proposed sending a version of the letter to "each contested state"—according to Rosen, Pennsylvania, Michigan, Wisconsin, Arizona and Nevada.[112]

Clark's proposed letter opened by stating that DOJ had "taken notice" of irregularities" and that "[i]n light of these developments, the Department recommends that the Georgia General Assembly should convene in a special session so that its legislators are in a position to take additional testimony, receive new evidence, and deliberate on the matter consistent with duties under the U.S. Constitution."[113]

The letter emphasized that "[t]ime is of the essence" to take action due to the impending Joint Session of Congress "to count Electoral College certificates [internal citation removed], consider objections to any of those certificates, and decide between any competing slate of elector certificates...with the Vice President presiding over the session as President of the Senate."[114] The letter attempted to further underscore this "urgency" by highlighting that the Trump campaign's legal challenge to alleged voting irregularities filed on December 4, 2020, had not yet been given a hearing date, stating:

> Given the urgency of this serious matter, including the Fulton County litigation's sluggish pace, the Department believes that a special session of the Georgia General Assembly is warranted and is in the national interest.[115]

The letter then outlined a path for the Georgia General Assembly to take advantage of the Joint Session of Congress's certification procedure and replace the Georgia Presidential Electors

---

[110] Id.
[111] Id.
[112] Rosen Tr. at 105; see also Donoghue Tr. at 99 (proposal entailed sending the letter to each swing state).
[113] Email from Jeffrey Clark to Jeffrey Rosen and Richard Donoghue (Dec. 28, 2020, 4:40 p.m.) (SJC-PreCertificationEvents-000697-702).
[114] Id.
[115] Id.

lawfully chosen by the popular vote with a slate of Electors appointed after-the-fact by the legislature. The letter explained that the "purpose of the special session the Department recommends" is (1) to evaluate alleged voter irregularities; (2) to determine whether any such irregularities affected who "won the most legal votes"; and (3) to "take whatever action is necessary" if the "election failed to make a proper and valid choice."[116]

Despite the unprecedented, sweeping nature of this proposal and the lack of adherence to standard DOJ procedures, such as Office of Legal Counsel review, in the preparation of the letter, Clark expressed no hesitation that this letter was both appropriate and ready to send as is, stating:

> Personally, I see no valid downsides to sending out the letter. I put it together quickly and would want to do a formal cite check before sending but I don't think we should let unnecessary moss grow on this.[117]

C. Rosen and Donoghue Reject Clark's Proposal

Just over an hour later, at 5:50 p.m., Donoghue pushed back on Clark's unsubstantiated claims, declaring in an email, "there is no chance that I would sign this letter or anything remotely like this."[118] Donoghue made clear that no widespread election fraud affected the 2020 election, stating:

> While it may be true that the Department 'is investigating various irregularities in the 2020 election for President (something we typically would not state publicly), the investigations that I am aware of relate to suspicions of misconduct that are of such a small scale that they simply would not impact the outcome of the Presidential Election.[119]

After reiterating that "AG Barr made that clear to the public only last week," Donoghue highlighted specific statements in Clark's "Georgia Proof of Concept" letter that had no support, stating:

> I know of nothing that would support the statement "we have identified significant concerns that may have impacted the outcome of election in multiple states." Despite dramatic claims to the contrary, we have not seen the type of fraud that calls into question the reported (and certified) results of the election.[120]

Donoghue emphasized that it would be "utterly without precedent" for the Justice Department to take such action, stating:

---

[116] *Id.*
[117] *Id.*
[118] Email from Richard Donoghue to Jeffrey Clark (Dec. 28, 2020, 5:50 p.m.) (SJC-PreCertificationEvents-000703).
[119] *Id.*
[120] *Id.*

> I cannot imagine a scenario in which the Department would recommend that a State assemble its legislature to determine whether already-certified election results should somehow be overridden by legislative action. Despite references to the 1960 Hawaii situation (and other historical anomalies, such as the 1876 Election), I believe this would be utterly without precedent. Even if I am incorrect about that, this would be a grave step for the Department to take and it could have tremendous Constitutional, political and social ramifications for the country.[121]

Donoghue ended his response by describing what proper consideration and procedure would look like before the Justice Department could take such action. He stated that research and discussion "that such a momentous step warrants" would be required and "[o]bviously, OLC would have to be involved in such discussions."[122]

At 6:00 p.m., Rosen and Donoghue met with Clark in Rosen's conference room.[123] According to Rosen, Clark reiterated the points from his email and said he wanted Rosen to hold a press conference where he announced that "there was corruption."[124] Clark gave no indication whether he was working with others on the letter, either within DOJ or at the White House.[125] According to Donoghue, however, he did make some reference to his Oval Office meeting with Trump, and to the fact that Trump was considering a leadership change at DOJ.[126]

Donoghue recalled the meeting being "difficult" and "heated," with Donoghue telling Clark he had "no business" involving himself in election fraud matters, asking why the President and Congressman Perry had mentioned his name, accusing him of violating the DOJ-White House contacts policy, and telling him his proof of concept proposal was "wildly inappropriate."[127] Rosen similarly called the meeting "contentious."[128] Rosen and Donoghue recalled making clear that DOJ would not send the letter, and stressing to Clark that it was not DOJ's role to serve as election officials and tell states what to do.[129] Rosen's impression at the time was that Clark accepted his and Donoghue's position.[130]

Following the meeting with Clark, Donoghue emailed Assistant Attorney General for OLC Steven Engel to set up a time to discuss "some antics that could potentially end up on your

---

[121] *Id.*
[122] *Id.*
[123] Jeffrey Rosen Calendar (Dec. 28, 2020); Richard Donoghue Calendar (Dec. 28, 2020); Jeffrey Clark Calendar (Dec. 28, 2020); Rosen Tr. at 102; Donoghue Tr. at 102.
[124] Rosen Tr. at 102. Rosen also recalled Clark asking at the meeting to have his title changed from Acting Assistant Attorney General for the Civil Division to Assistant Attorney General for the Civil Division. Rosen recalled Clark's request—to which Steven Engel, the Assistant Attorney General for the Office of Legal Counsel, was "very opposed"—coming up multiple times.
[125] Rosen Tr. at 103-106.
[126] Donoghue Tr. at 104.
[127] Donoghue Tr. at 103-104.
[128] Rosen Tr. at 103.
[129] Donoghue Tr. at 103; Rosen Tr. at 103.
[130] Rosen Tr. at 104.

radar."[131] Donoghue recalled that he and Rosen wanted to read Engel into the situation because Engel would have been next in line to become Acting Attorney General if Trump fired Rosen. They decided not to share the information beyond Engel at the time, however, for fear it would create panic within DOJ's leadership.[132]

V. December 29 – December 30: Meanwhile, Trump Urges DOJ to File a Supreme Court Action Contesting the Election

While Clark was encouraging Rosen and Donoghue to pursue his "proof of concept" in Georgia and elsewhere, Trump and his allies were simultaneously urging DOJ to take Trump's false claims of a stolen election directly to the Supreme Court. On December 29, 2020, White House Special Assistant and Oval Office Coordinator Molly Michael emailed a draft Supreme Court brief to Rosen, Donoghue, and Acting Solicitor General Jeffrey Wall, telling them: "The President asked me to send the attached draft document for your review. I have also shared with Mark Meadows and Pat Cipollone."[133]

The brief that Trump had directed Michael to share with DOJ was styled as a bill of complaint filed under the Supreme Court's original jurisdiction and against the states of Pennsylvania, Georgia, Michigan, Wisconsin, Arizona, and Nevada.[134] The proposed action asked the Court to declare that the six states administered the 2020 presidential election in violation of the Constitution's Electors Clause and Fourteenth Amendment; declare that the Electoral College votes cast by the electors in the six states were in violation of the Electors Clause and Fourteenth Amendment; enjoin the states from using the 2020 election results to appoint electors; and authorize the states to conduct a special election to appoint new electors. In short, Trump asked DOJ to petition the Supreme Court to overturn the election results.

In support of the relief it sought, the proposed Supreme Court brief made a variety of false factual claims about the election (many of which had already been rejected by courts), as well as claims taking issue with the use of mail ballots in general. Among others, these included claims that:

- In the six states Trump proposed suing, "Democrat voters voted by mail at two to three times the rate of Republicans";
- Georgia used Dominion voting machines, which had "known vulnerabilities to hacking and other irregularities";
- A "forensic audit" conducted by Allied Security Group found that "the Dominion voting system in Antrim County [Michigan] was designed to generate an error rate as high as 81.96%";

---

[131] Email from Richard Donoghue to Steven Engel (Dec. 28, 2020, 11:41 p.m.) (SJC-PreCertificationEvents-000272).
[132] Donoghue Tr. at 105-106.
[133] Email from Molly Michael to Jeffrey Rosen, Richard Donoghue, and Jeffrey Wall (Dec. 29, 2020, 11:17 a.m.) (SJC-Pre-CertificationEvents-000479).
[134] *See generally* SJC-Pre-CertificationEvents-000480-535.

- According to a USPS truck driver, the Wisconsin and Illinois chapter of the USPS dispatched employees to find 100,000 mail ballots, which were delivered to a sorting center in Madison and backdated;
- Nevada processed mail ballots through a sorting system, which "[a]nectdotal evidence suggests ... was prone to false [signature-match] positives";
- A Republican state official in Arizona had claimed that there was unspecified evidence of "tampering" and "fraud" in Maricopa County; and
- Local officials in Philadelphia and Allegheny County, Pennsylvania, excluded Republican poll watchers from the opening, counting, and recording of mail ballots.[135]

At the same time as Molly Michael was emailing the draft brief to Rosen, Donoghue, and Wall, one of its authors attempted to reach Rosen on behalf of President Trump. Kurt B. Olsen, a private lawyer who had served as special counsel to Texas Attorney General Ken Paxton in his failed Supreme Court action against Pennsylvania, emailed Wall: "I represented Texas in the action filed in the SCT against Pennsylvania et al. Last night, the President directed me to meet with AG Rosen today to discuss a similar action to be brought by the United States. I have not been able to reach him despite multiple calls/texts. This is an urgent matter. Please call me ... or ask AG Rosen to contact me asap."[136]

Over the next two days, Olsen contacted DOJ numerous times in an effort to discuss Trump's proposed Supreme Court action with Rosen, sending multiple emails and making multiple phone calls to Rosen's Chief of Staff, John Moran. For example, at 12:45 p.m. on December 29, Olsen emailed Moran to follow up on an apparent call, writing:

> Thank you for calling me on behalf of AG Rosen. Attached is a draft complaint to be brought by the United States modeled after the Texas action. As I said on our call, the President of the United States has seen this complaint, and he directed me last night to brief AG Rosen in person today to discuss bringing this action. I have been instructed to report back to the President this afternoon after this meeting. I can be at Main Justice (or anywhere else in the DC Metropolitan area) within an hour's notice.[137]

Olsen also emailed Moran a letter that Republican Pennsylvania State Senator Doug Mastriano had previously sent Donoghue, asking him to pass the materials along to Rosen and telling him that they "raise[] a litany of serious outcome changing issues re: fraudulent and illegal votes in Pennsylvania, and provides an additional justification for the United States to

---

[135] SJC-Pre-CertificationEvents-000480-535.
[136] Email from Kurt Olsen to Jeffrey Wall (Dec. 29, 2020, 10:57 a.m.) (SJC-Pre-CertificationEvents-000064).
[137] Email from Kurt Olsen to John Moran (Dec. 29, 2020, 12:45 p.m.) (SJC-Pre-CertificationEvents-000071).

bring an action in the Supreme Court."[138] Moran forwarded the email to Rosen without comment.[139]

Mastriano's letter raised a litany of false and debunked claims of widespread election fraud in Pennsylvania, which Mastriano had previously aired at a November 25, 2020 "hearing" at a hotel in Gettysburg featuring Trump campaign lawyers Rudy Giuliani and Jenna Ellis and a phone call from Trump himself.[140] Mastriano would later assume a lead role in the "Stop the Steal" movement, spending thousands of dollars from his campaign account to charter buses to Washington for Trump's January 6, 2021 "Save America Rally."[141] He and his wife took part in the January 6 insurrection, with video footage confirming that they passed through breached barricades and police lines at the U.S. Capitol. To date, no footage has emerged showing Mastriano in the Capitol itself, but his presence on the Capitol grounds and his involvement in funding travel to Washington have prompted calls for his resignation.[142]

Rosen recalled Olsen reaching him on the phone twice during this two-day period. Rosen described having a "general practice" of not meeting with anyone in the Trump campaign, and he recalled his first discussion with Olsen being almost accidental: his DOJ cell phone rang with a number he didn't recognize, and when he picked up, Olsen was on the other line.[143] Rosen recalled being annoyed at himself for answering once he realized it was Olsen, who asked whether Rosen had seen the Pennsylvania brief and stressed the importance of filing it. Rosen asked Olsen what his relationship to Trump was and expressed skepticism that there would be standing to bring the proposed lawsuit, and recalled the phone call ending with a polite brushoff.[144]

Following the call, and recognizing that he would probably need to discuss the Supreme Court proposal with Trump, Rosen asked the Office of Solicitor General (OSG) to prepare a list of points on the proposal.[145] OSG responded on December 30 with a one-page summary of the "numerous significant procedural hurdles" DOJ would face if it filed the proposed action.[146] Among other hurdles, OSG explained that DOJ could not file an original Supreme Court action for the benefit of a political candidate; OSG also explained that there is no general cause of action for DOJ to contest the outcome of an election. At Rosen's request, OLC Assistant Attorney General Engel then prepared a plain-English version of the OSG analysis that would be

---

[138] Email from Kurt Olsen to John Moran (Dec. 30, 2020, 10:17 a.m.) (SJC-Pre-CertificationEvents-000174-179).
[139] Email from John Moran to Jeffrey Rosen (Dec. 30, 2020, 10:49 a.m.) (SJC-Pre-CertificationEvents-000186-193).
[140] Quint Forgey, *Trump Takes His Fraud Claims to a Hotel Ballroom – by Phone*, Politico (Nov. 25, 2020).
[141] Katie Meyer, Miles Bryan & Ryan Briggs, *Mastriano Campaign Spent Thousands on Buses Ahead of D.C. Insurrection*, WHYY (Jan. 12, 2021).
[142] Jeremy Roebuck & Andrew Seidman, *Pa. GOP Lawmaker Doug Mastriano Says He Left the Capitol Area Before the Riot. New Videos Say Otherwise*, Phila. Inquirer (May 25, 2021).
[143] Rosen Tr. at 114-115.
[144] Rosen Tr. at 115.
[145] *Id.*
[146] Email from [Redacted] to Jeffrey Rosen (Dec. 30, 2020, 7:06 p.m.) (SJC-PreCertificationEvents-000710-711).

more easily understood by non-lawyers; Engel's version confirmed that "[t]here is no legal basis to bring this lawsuit."[147]

Olsen reached Rosen again on December 30. Donoghue was present for the entire call and took notes.[148] Rosen recalled Olsen being "aggressive," telling him that Trump wanted DOJ to "file this brief by noon today," and threatening to report Rosen's position back to Trump.[149] Rosen responded that he would discuss the matter with Trump but not Olsen, and recalled this being the last and only time he spoke to an outside Trump ally about challenges to the election results.[150]

Sometime during the afternoon of December 30, following his second call with Olsen, Rosen spoke directly with Trump about the Supreme Court proposal. Rosen did not recall who placed the call—whether Trump called him, or whether he initiated the call after getting a message that Trump wanted to talk.[151] Relying on Engel's points, Rosen told Trump that DOJ couldn't file the Supreme Court action. Although Rosen did not recall with certainty whether the proposal came up at an Oval Office meeting the following day, he recalled it essentially being put to rest during this December 30 call, with Trump accepting that DOJ would not pursue the idea.[152] By contrast, Donoghue recalled Trump revisiting the Supreme Court action the following day, as discussed below.

VI. December 29 – January 1: White House Pressure on DOJ Escalates

White House pressure on DOJ escalated in the waning days of 2020 as Trump continued to complain about DOJ's inaction on his election fraud claims, including during a December 31 Oval Office meeting with Rosen and Donoghue. During the same period of time, White House Chief of Staff Mark Meadows—who had recently shown up unannounced at Georgia's Cobb County Civic Center to question election officials about their mail ballot signature match audit—sent a series of emails to Rosen, directly asking him to have DOJ investigate specific, discredited allegations of election fraud pushed by Trump and his campaign.

A. DOJ Leadership is Summoned to a December 31 Oval Office Meeting

On Thursday, December 31, 2020, Rosen and Donoghue were summoned to the White House for a meeting in the Oval Office with Trump. Meadows, Cipollone, and Deputy White House Counsel Patrick Philbin also attended.[153] Rosen recalled that Trump "seemed unhappy"

---

[147] Rosen Tr. at 115; Email from Steven Engel to Jeffrey Rosen (Dec. 31, 2020, 9:02 a.m.) (SJC-PreCertificationEvents-000708-709).
[148] Donoghue Tr. at 113; Notes of Dec. 30, 2020 Olsen-Rosen-Donoghue Call ("12/30/20 Donoghue Notes") (SJC-PreCertificationEvents-000706).
[149] Rosen Tr. at 116.
[150] *Id.*
[151] Rosen Tr. at 117.
[152] Rosen Tr. at 117-118.
[153] There are conflicting accounts about whether Acting DHS General Counsel Chad Mizelle attended this meeting or the earlier, December 15 Oval Office meeting. Rosen recalled that Acting DHS General Counsel Chad Mizelle attended on December 31; Donoghue recalled that Mizelle had attended the December 15 Oval Office meeting, but

that DOJ still had not "found the fraud," and described their discussion as "more of the same"—but otherwise did not recall granular details from the meeting, which he viewed as less significant than the Oval Office meeting that took place three days later.[154]

Donoghue recalled the meeting in greater detail. He described it as "contentious" and told us that "[Trump's] frustration was increasing," with the President reiterating that Rosen and Donoghue weren't doing their jobs and that people were telling him he should fire both of them and install Clark instead.[155] Donoghue did not recall whether Clark's proposed letter was a specific topic of discussion, but did recall responding that although Trump should have whatever leadership he wanted, DOJ operated based on facts and evidence and that replacing its leadership would not change the outcome.[156]

Donoghue also recalled Trump raising the proposed Supreme Court action that Rosen believed had been put to rest the previous day. According to Donoghue, Trump was "very frustrated" when Rosen and Donoghue repeatedly told him that DOJ lacked standing to file the action, insisting that Olsen and others had told him the case was a slam dunk.[157] Finally, Donoghue told us that Trump raised the prospect of appointing a special counsel to investigate election fraud and told the group "something to the effect of, 'I think Ken Cuccinelli would be a great special counsel.'"[158]

B. Clark Reveals Ongoing Contacts With Trump

Following the December 31 Oval Office meeting, either later that night or sometime on January 1, Rosen spoke to Clark again.[159] Although Clark had previously assured Rosen that he would not speak to Trump again and would notify Rosen or Donoghue of any requests to do so, Clark revealed that he had in fact spoken to Trump again. According to Rosen, Clark disclosed that Trump had asked whether he would be willing to take over as Acting Attorney General if Trump decided to replace Rosen, and requested an answer from Clark by Monday, January 4.[160]

Rosen recalled Clark indicating that he hadn't yet decided whether he would accept Trump's offer, wanted to conduct some "due diligence" on certain election fraud claims, and might turn down the offer if he determined that Rosen and Donoghue were correct that there was no corruption.[161] As part of this "due diligence," Clark renewed the request he initially made in his December 28 email for a classified briefing by the DNI. Rosen told us that because he assumed that Clark would follow up with Trump whether he liked it or not, he decided to

---

that Trump, Meadows, Cipollone, Philbin, Rosen, and Donoghue were the only participants on December 27. Rosen Tr. at 138; Donoghue Tr. at 26-7, 117.
[154] Rosen Tr. at 139-142.
[155] Donoghue Tr. at 118.
[156] Donoghue Tr. at 118-119.
[157] Donoghue Tr. at 119-120.
[158] Donoghue Tr. at 30.
[159] Rosen Tr. at 128 & 137.
[160] Rosen Tr. at 129.
[161] *Id.*

facilitate Clark's request for a DNI briefing in the hopes that the briefing would help Clark understand why his theories were unsound. The briefing took place the following day.[162]

Rosen similarly suggested that Clark call U.S. Attorney Pak, whom he knew would explain that allegations of ballot destruction in Atlanta had been debunked.[163] At 8:24 p.m. on January 1, 2021, Rosen emailed Clark the cell phone number for Byung Jin "BJay" Pak, U.S. Attorney for the Northern District of Georgia.[164] Rosen then checked in with Clark at 8:52 a.m. the next morning, asking: "Were you able to follow up?"[165]

Clark responded at 9:50 a.m. the following morning, reporting: "I spoke to the source and am on with the guy who took the video right now. Working on it. More due diligence to do."[166] Clark did not directly answer Rosen's question about whether he reached out to Pak; as discussed below, Rosen learned the following day that Clark had not.

C. White House Chief of Staff Mark Meadows Asks DOJ to Initiate Baseless Election Fraud Investigations, Contrary to Longstanding Rules Against White House-DOJ Interference

As Trump encouraged DOJ to intervene in his behalf in the Supreme Court and asked Clark to consider replacing Rosen, his Chief of Staff, Mark Meadows, asked DOJ to intervene in the electoral certification by launching baseless election fraud investigations. He did so in a series of direct communications with Rosen between December 29 and January 1. These communications, which are detailed below, violated longstanding restrictions on communications between White House and DOJ officials concerning specific law enforcement matters.

December 29, 2020: At 11:27 a.m., Meadows sent Rosen a copy of a letter dated December 27 and authored by Carlo Goria, an apparent representative of USAerospace Partners, a U.S.-based aviation service group.[167] Meadows emailed Rosen the letter without additional comment. Goria's letter was addressed to Trump and written in Italian, although Meadows later sent an English version to Rosen as well. The letter made several claims related to a conspiracy theory known as "Italygate," which holds that an information technology employee of Italian aerospace company Leonardo S.p.A. coordinated with the CIA to use military satellites to remotely switch Trump votes to Biden votes.

December 30, 2020 (9:31 a.m.): At 9:31 a.m., Meadows forwarded Rosen an email and attachments from Cleta Mitchell, an attorney at Foley & Lardner LLP law firm who had been

---

[162] Rosen Tr. at 129-30.
[163] Rosen Tr. at 130.
[164] Email from Jeffrey Rosen to Jeffrey Clark (Jan. 1, 2021, 8:24 p.m.) (SJC-PreCertificationEvents-000287).
[165] Email from Jeffrey Rosen to Jeffrey Clark (Jan. 2, 2021, 8:52 a.m.) (SJC-PreCertificationEvents-000289).
[166] Email from Jeffrey Clark to Jeffrey Rosen (Jan. 2, 2021, 9:50 a.m.) (SJC-PreCertificationEvents-000290).
[167] Email from Mark Meadows to Jeffrey Rosen (Dec. 29, 2020, 11:27 a.m.) (SJC-Pre-CertificationEvents-000536).

advising the Trump campaign on post-election litigation.[168] Mitchell had written Meadows earlier that morning, attaching a December 4 lawsuit filed by the Trump campaign in Georgia state court and an accompanying press release, which announced that the lawsuit was challenging "literally tens of thousands of illegal votes" in Georgia. She explained to Meadows:

> This is the petition filed in GA state court and the press release issued about it. I presume the DOJ would want all the exhibits – that's 1800 pages total. I need to get someone to forward that to a drop box. Plus I don't know what is happening re investigating the video issues in Fulton County. And the equipment. We didn't include the equipment in our lawsuit but there are certainly many issues and questions that some resources need to be devoted to reviewing.

Meadows forwarded Mitchell's email to Rosen, asking: "Can you have your team look into these allegations of wrongdoing. Only the alleged fraudulent activity. Thanks Mark."

The lawsuit whose allegations Meadows asked DOJ to investigate asserted a variety of false claims of election fraud, and the Georgia Supreme Court had rejected Trump's request to hear it on an expedited basis.[169] Among the false claims it asserted, and that Meadows asked DOJ to investigate, were:

- A claim that 66,247 underage voters had unlawfully cast ballots in Georgia. In reality, Republican elections official Gabriel Sterling made clear that it would be impossible for unregistered and underage voters to cast ballots: "There cannot be a ballot issued to you, there's no way to tie it back to you, there's nowhere for them to have a name to correspond back to unless they're registered voters." Only four Georgians requested absentee ballots before turning 18—and all four turned 18 before Election Day.[170]

- A claim that thousands of votes were unlawfully cast by individuals registered at Post Office boxes; who voted after registering in another state; who voted in Georgia and another state; who moved without re-registering in their new county; and who registered after the voter registration deadline. In reality, these claims originated from Matt Braynard, a Trump campaign data expert whose analysis had been widely discredited and who himself acknowledged that he never verified that any of the thousands of voters was actually illegitimate.[171] Georgia's two recounts and its

---

[168] Email from Mark Meadows to Jeffrey Rosen (Dec. 30, 2020, 9:31 a.m.) (SJC-Pre-CertificationEvents-000598-665); *see also* Michael S. Schmidt & Kenneth P. Vogel, *Trump Lawyer on Call Is a Conservative Firebrand Aiding His Push to Overturn Election*, N.Y. Times (Jan. 15, 2021).
[169] Order, *Trump et al. v. Raffensperger et al.*, No. S21M0561 (Ga. Sup. Ct. Dec. 12, 2020).
[170] Bill McCarthy, *Here's Why Georgia's Republican Officials Are Confident in Their Presidential Election Results*, Politifact (Jan. 5, 2021).
[171] *See* Mark Niesse, *5 Georgia Election Fraud Claims Explained*, Atlanta Journal-Constitution (Dec. 14, 2020).

signature audit confirmed Biden's victory and found no evidence of fraud or vote tampering.[172]

December 30, 2020 (9:43 a.m.): Shortly after asking Rosen to have DOJ investigate allegations of wrongdoing in Georgia, Meadows forwarded him an English version of the Italygate letter from Carlo Goria that he had originally sent the previous day. As before, Meadows sent the letter without additional comment.[173]

January 1, 2021 (2:51-3:39 p.m.): At 2:51 p.m., Rosen emailed Meadows, "Did not receive the video link. Can you re-send?"[174] Rosen told us that Meadows had previously sent a link that didn't work, so he asked him to resend it.[175] Meadows responded at 3:08 p.m., sending Rosen a link to a YouTube video titled "Brad Johnson: Rome, Satellites, Servers: an Update."[176] The thirteen-minute video featured Bradley Johnson, a retired CIA station chief-turned conservative freelance opinion contributor who had been promoting the Italygate conspiracy theory in videos and online posts. As proof of his claim that Leonardo S.p.A and the CIA used military satellites to remotely change Trump votes to Biden votes, Johnson pointed to a sudden increase in Biden votes in several states whose early returns showed Trump leading—in reality, the expected result of Democratic counties reporting their totals, and states reporting Democratic-leaning mail ballot totals, after Republican counties had.[177]

Rosen emailed Meadows to confirm receipt, and then forwarded the exchange and YouTube link to Donoghue. Donoghue responded at 3:39 p.m., "Pure insanity."[178]

January 1, 2021 (4:13 p.m.): Just hours after emailing Rosen a link to Brad Johnson's Italygate video, Meadows asked him to have DOJ investigate disproven allegations of election fraud in Georgia. He wrote: "There have been allegations of signature match anomalies in Fulton County, Ga. Can you get Jeff Clark to engage on this issue immediately to determine if there is any truth to this allegation."[179]

Rosen forwarded Meadows's request to Donoghue, asking, "Can you believe this? I am not going to respond to message below." Donoghue agreed, and—alluding to Meadows's earlier

---

[172] 3rd Strike Against Voter Fraud Claims Means They're out After Signature Audit Finds No Fraud, Georgia Secretary of State, *available at*
https://sos.ga.gov/index.php/elections/3rd_strike_against_voter_fraud_claims_means_theyre_out_after_signature_audit_finds_no_fraud.
[173] Email from Mark Meadows to Jeffrey Rosen (Dec. 30, 2020, 9:43 a.m.) (SJC-Pre-CertificationEvents-000666).
[174] Email from Jeffrey Rosen to Mark Meadows (Jan. 1, 2021, 2:51 p.m.) (SJC-Pre-CertificationEvents-000668).
[175] Rosen Tr. at 147.
[176] Email from Mark Meadows to Jeffrey Rosen (Jan. 1, 2021, 3:08 p.m.) (SJC-Pre-CertificationEvents-000669).
[177] *See* Matt Gertz, Mark Meadows: Searching for 'Italygate,' Media Matters for America, June 7, 2021, *available at* https://www.mediamatters.org/voter-fraud-and-suppression/mark-meadows-searching-italygate.
[178] Email from Jeffrey Rosen to Mark Meadows (Jan. 1, 2021, 3:22 p.m.) (SJC-Pre-CertificationEvents-000671); Email from Richard Donoghue to Jeffrey Rosen (Jan. 1. 2021, 3:39 p.m.) (SJC-Pre-CertificationEvents-000678).
[179] Email from Mark Meadows to Jeffrey Rosen (Jan. 1, 2021, 4:13 p.m.) (SJC-Pre-CertificationEvents-000672).

emails on Italygate—observed, "At least it's better than the last one, but that doesn't say much."[180]

In a response to Donoghue later the same evening, Rosen elaborated on Meadows's efforts to have DOJ investigate Italygate, which included a request that Rosen arrange for Johnson to meet with the FBI. Rosen wrote:

> After this message, I was asked to have FBI meet with Brad Johnson, and I responded that Johnson could call or walk into FBI's Washington Field Office with any evidence he purports to have. On a follow up call, I learned that Johnson is working with Rudy Giuliani, who regarded my comments as "an insult." Asked if I would reconsider, I flatly refused, said I would not be giving any special treatment to Giuliani or any of his "witnesses," and reaffirmed yet again that I will not talk to Giuliani about any of this."[181]

During his interview, Rosen told us that it was Meadows who had called and asked him to follow up on the Italygate allegations. Rosen recalled telling Meadows that the theory was "another one that's debunked," being told "there's more to it," and Meadows asking him to meet with Giuliani. This was not the only time he was asked to talk to Giuliani. Rosen told us that he "had refused to meet with Rudy Giuliani, multiple times over, during the month of December."[182] He could not recall how many times he had been asked to meet with Giuliani, and whether the requests had always come from Meadows as opposed to Trump. Rosen told us he never met with Giuliani, however.[183]

January 1, 2021 (6:56 p.m.): Meadows emailed Rosen again at 6:56 p.m., this time asking DOJ to investigate allegations of election fraud in New Mexico being pushed by Steve Pearce, the state's Republican Party chair. Meadows attached a document titled "New Mexico List of Complaints" and asked Rosen, "Can you forward this list to your team to review the allegations contained herein. Steve Pearce is the chairman of the Republican Party for NM."[184] The "complaints" Meadows asked DOJ to investigate consisted of several claims that had been refuted and/or already rejected by courts, including:

- A claim that poll challengers were removed from the mail ballot certification process. In reality, Republican poll challengers and observers were allowed to participate in the mail and provisional ballot certification process, and the New Mexico Supreme Court had unanimously rejected a lawsuit by the Republican Party of New Mexico challenging the process by which poll watchers monitored mail ballot certification.[185]

---

[180] Email from Richard Donoghue to Jeffrey Rosen (Jan. 1, 2021, 4:28 p.m.) (SJC-Pre-CertificationEvents-000673).
[181] Email from Jeffrey Rosen to Richard Donoghue (Jan. 1, 2021, 7:13 p.m.) (SJC-Pre-CertificationEvents-000678).
[182] Rosen Tr. at 148-149.
[183] Rosen Tr. at 149-150.
[184] Email from Mark Meadows to Jeffrey Rosen (Jan. 1, 2021, 6:56 p.m.) (SJC-Pre-CertificationEvents-000675-77).
[185] Michael Gerstein, *New Mexico GOP Claims Election Violations; County Clerks Dispute*, Santa Fe New Mexican (Nov. 6, 2020); Dan Boyd, *NM Supreme Court Denies GOP Election Petition*, Albuquerque Journal (Oct. 27, 2020).

- A claim that Dominion voting machines were the only ones used in New Mexico, and caused late-night "vote dumps" for Democratic candidates. In reality, so-called "vote dumps" were the expected result of Democratic precincts reporting their totals at different times than Republican ones. For example, Pearce previously claimed that 400 votes "just show[ed] up out of thin air" in Soccoro County, but local elections officials confirmed that those ballots simply arrived at the county clerk's office later than others after being driven there from a Navajo reservation an hour away.[186]

- A claim that mail ballots had been fraudulently requested and returned. In reality, there is no evidence of widespread voter fraud in New Mexico, much less any that would overcome Biden's nearly 11-point victory in the state.[187]

VII. January 2 – 4: DOJ Leadership Thwarts the Trump-Clark Plot, but U.S. Attorney BJay Pak is Ousted

A. January 2: Clark's Plans Crystallize and Trump Calls the Georgia Secretary of State

On January 2, President Trump, joined by Cleta Mitchell, spoke with Georgia Secretary of State Brad Raffensperger for approximately an hour by phone to pressure him to change the state's vote totals from the 2020 election. Trump specifically told Raffensperger to find exactly enough votes to win, stating:

> All I want to do is this. I just want to find 11,780 votes, which is one more than [the 11,779 vote deficit] we have, because we won the state.[188]

During the call, President Trump also mentioned Pak, referring to him as "your never-Trumper U.S. attorney there," and alleged that the Trump campaign had a "new tape that we're going to release" purporting to show "devastating" voter fraud at the State Farm Arena.[189]

Clark met with Rosen and Donoghue the same afternoon. Rosen told us that the purpose of the meeting was twofold: first, to reinforce that Clark should stop meeting with Trump, and second, to determine where he stood after conducting the "due diligence" Rosen and Clark had discussed two days earlier.[190] Rosen asked Donoghue to join him because he didn't want to meet with Clark alone; Donoghue joined and took contemporaneous notes.[191] Clark acknowledged that

---

[186] Michael Gerstein, *New Mexico GOP Claims Election Violations; County Clerks Dispute*, Santa Fe New Mexican (Nov. 6, 2020).
[187] Charles Davis, *New Mexico Republicans Peddle 'Dangerous' Myth of Voter Fraud in a State Trump Lost by Double Digits*, Business Insider (Jan. 7, 2021).
[188] Amy Gardner & Paulina Firozi, *Here's the full transcript and audio of the call between Trump and Raffensperger*, Wash. Post (Jan. 5, 2021).
[189] *Id.*
[190] Rosen Tr. at 131.
[191] Donoghue Tr. at 137; Notes of Jan. 2, 2021 Meeting ("1/2/21 Donoghue Notes") (SJC-PreCertificationEvents-000714).

he had been briefed by the DNI, who confirmed that there was no evidence of ballot or data tampering. He continued to press debunked allegations of election fraud in Georgia, however, insisting that DOJ should send his proposed letter.[192] Clark admitted that he had not called U.S. Attorney Pak, despite being asked to do so by Rosen. Instead, he revealed that he had spoken to a witness who testified at a Georgia Senate hearing and claimed that he had seen trucks moving ballots to a location where they would be shredded.[193]

Donoghue recalled that the meeting "became very heated" as he made clear that Clark's conduct was unacceptable. He told us:

> I reminded [Clark] that I was his boss, that he was apparently continuing to violate the White House contact policy, that that letter was never going out while we were in charge of the Department. And I sort of orally reprimanded him on a number of points, including reaching out to witnesses, and [said] "Who told you to conduct investigations and interview witnesses," and things like that. I was getting very heated. And then he turned to Acting AG Rosen, and he said, "Well, the President has offered me the position of Acting Attorney General. I told him I would let him know my decision on Monday. I need to think about that a little bit more."[194]

Rosen told us that at some point during this discussion, Clark indicated that if Rosen would reconsider his refusal to sign Clark's proposed letter—and send it to the Georgia legislature under Rosen's name—Clark might turn down the President's offer to install him in Rosen's place. Rosen again refused to send the letter.[195] According to Rosen:

> Q. So Jeff Clark framed it as a choice he was giving you, to essentially either go along with the letter that you had previously rejected and sign it under your own name, or he will presumably take the President up on his offer to be installed in your place. Is that how you understood it?
>
> A. Close to that. That he was saying that having done some due diligence as he requested, that he wasn't satisfied that Rich Donoghue and I were on this, but that he still wasn't sure what his answer would be on it. And he raised another thing that he might point to, that he might be able to say no [to the President], is if – that letter, if I reversed my position on the letter, which I was unwilling to do.[196]

Later the same day, at 7:13 p.m., Rosen responded to Donoghue's December 28, 2020, email refutation of Clark's initial proposal, stating:

---

[192] Donoghue Tr. at 138-139; 1/2/21 Donoghue Notes.
[193] Donoghue Tr. at 140-141; 1/2/21 Donoghue Notes; Rosen Tr. at 130-132.
[194] Donoghue Tr. at 141-142.
[195] Rosen Tr. at 145-146.
[196] Rosen Tr. at 145-146.

Rich, thanks for responding to this earlier. I confirmed again today that I am not prepared to sign such a letter.[197]

Donoghue then emailed Engel at 8:08 p.m. to ask him to call when he was free so that Donoghue could "update you on today's events."[198] As discussed previously, Rosen and Donoghue had until this point limited the universe of DOJ officials they read into Clark's activities. They kept Engel and, eventually, Rosen's longtime deputy Patrick Hovakimian apprised[199]; they discussed whether to immediately expand the circle following this January 2 meeting, but decided to defer updating other DOJ officials until they saw how Clark's plans developed.[200]

B. January 3: Clark Reveals That Trump Will Install Him That Day

Clark and Trump's plans came to a head the following day. Rosen recalled receiving a phone call from Clark around noon on Sunday, January 3; Clark told Rosen he wanted to talk further and that it was important.[201] Rosen responded that he was unavailable until the afternoon, and they eventually met in Rosen's conference room around 3:00 p.m. At Clark's request, Rosen agreed to take the meeting alone, without Donoghue—who recalled it being "clear to me at this point [that] Jeff Clark did not want me involved in any of these discussions."[202]

According to Rosen, Clark reported that he had spoken earlier with the President, that Trump had in fact offered to install Clark in Rosen's place, and that Clark had accepted. Clark also revealed that the schedule had been accelerated: Rosen would be replaced that day, not on Monday January 4 or sometime thereafter.[203] Clark told Rosen that he wanted him to stay on as his Deputy Attorney General and that Donoghue would be replaced; Rosen responded that "there was no universe I could imagine in which that would ever happen."[204]

Toward the end of their meeting, Rosen told Clark that he would not accept being fired by his subordinate—and would contact the President to discuss the matter directly.[205] Once the meeting concluded, around 4:00 p.m., Rosen called Meadows and said he needed to meet with Trump that day; Meadows said he would arrange it, and called back shortly thereafter to confirm a 6:15 p.m. meeting. Rosen also called Cipollone, who agreed to join the Oval Office meeting

---

[197] Email from Jeffrey Rosen to Richard Donoghue (Jan. 2, 2021, 7:13 p.m.) (SJC-PreCertificationEvents-000200).
[198] Email from Richard Donoghue to Steven Engel (Jan. 2, 2021, 8:08 p.m.) (SJC-PreCertificationEvents-000291).
[199] Hovakimian was Rosen's Chief of Staff until his nomination to be General Counsel of ODNI required him to formally step down from the role, although he remained on Rosen's staff while his nomination was pending in the Senate. *See* PN1918 (116th Cong.); Donoghue Tr. at 56-57.
[200] Donoghue Tr. at 142-143.
[201] Rosen Tr. at 157.
[202] Rosen Tr. at 158. Donoghue Tr. at 145.
[203] Rosen Tr. at 158.
[204] *Id.*
[205] Rosen Tr. at 159.

and suggested that it would be helpful to know that Rosen and Donoghue were not outliers, and that they had the backing of others in DOJ.[206]

Rosen also updated Donoghue on his conversation with Clark. Donoghue recalled responding, "Well, I guess that's it. Are we going to find out [that we're fired] in a tweet?" Donoghue added, "At that point, I went back to my office and I began taking things off the wall and put them in boxes, because I told the Acting AG I would immediately resign. There was no way I was going to serve under Jeff Clark."[207] At Rosen's request, Donoghue and Hovakimian arranged a call with DOJ's senior leadership to determine whether others would also resign.[208]

As Rosen and Donoghue planned to read a broader group of senior DOJ leaders into Clark and Trump's plans, Clark apparently took steps of his own to rally potential allies within DOJ. At some point either shortly before or after his initial conversation with Rosen, Clark sent a series of emails to Doug Smith, his Chief of Staff and the Deputy Assistant Attorney General for the Civil Division's Torts Branch. At 12:31 p.m. on January 3, 2021, Clark emailed Smith and told him to "please get back to DC immediately."[209] Smith responded at 2:38 p.m. that he had "a flight back tonight but will try to get back earlier."[210] Minutes later, at 2:42 p.m., Clark told Smith to "[t]ry to get back as soon as you can."[211] Sixteen minutes later, at 2:58 p.m., Smith told Clark that he was on his way to the airport and would probably get to Washington, D.C. around 6:00 p.m.[212] After the meeting with Rosen, Clark emailed Smith again at 4:37 p.m. to direct him to come to the Justice Department with "[l]egal pad in hand."[213]

Smith appears to be one of two DOJ officials whose help Clark enlisted, or attempted to enlist, while pursuing his scheme. The other was Civil Division Senior Counsel Kenneth Klukowski. Klukowski emailed Smith at 6:15 p.m. to inform him that he "[j]ust heard from Jeff[rey Clark] that our new meeting time tonight is 8pm... See you soon, sir!"[214] Emails suggest that Klukowski had played a role in Clark's "Proof of Concept" letter, a copy of which Klukowski emailed Clark at 4:20 p.m. on December 28—just twenty minutes before Clark sent the proposal to Rosen and Donoghue.[215] The extent of Klukowski's and Smith's role in Clark's scheme is unclear from the limited documents produced by DOJ; nor were the witnesses we interviewed able to shed light on their involvement.

---

[206] Rosen Tr. at 160.
[207] Donoghue Tr. at 145-146.
[208] Donoghue Tr. At 147; Rosen Tr. At 160.
[209] Email from Jeffrey Clark to Douglas Smith (Jan. 3, 2021, 12:31 p.m.) (SJC-PreCertificationEvents-000294).
[210] Email from Douglas Smith to Jeffrey Clark (Jan. 3, 2021, 2:38 p.m.) (SJC-PreCertificationEvents-000295).
[211] Email from Jeffrey Clark to Douglas Smith (Jan. 3, 2021, 2:42 p.m.) (SJC-PreCertificationEvents-000296).
[212] Email from Douglas Smith to Jeffrey Clark (Jan. 3, 2021, 2:58 p.m.) (SJC-PreCertificationEvents-000297).
[213] Email from Jeffrey Clark to Douglas Smith (Jan. 3, 2021, 4:37 p.m.) (SJC-PreCertificationEvents-000304).
[214] Email from Kenneth Klukowski to Douglas Smith (Jan. 3, 2021, 6:15 p.m.) (SJC-PreCertificationEvents-000323).
[215] Email from Kenneth Klukowski to Jeffrey Clark (Dec. 28, 2020, 4:20 p.m.) (SJC-Pre-CertificationEvents-000044-49).

C. The Justice Department Leadership Assembles

From there, at 4:21 p.m., Hovakimian requested a conference line "for a call tonight,"[216] which Donoghue provided at 4:23 p.m.[217] At 4:28 p.m., Hovakimian emailed DOJ leadership asking them to "join Rich[ard Donoghue] and me for a call at 4:45 p.m."[218] The invitees included:

- Claire Murray, Principal Deputy Associate Attorney General;
- Jeffrey Wall, Acting Solicitor General;
- Makan Delrahim, Assistant Attorney General for the Antitrust Division;
- Steve Engel, Assistant Attorney General for the Office of Legal Counsel;
- John Demers, Assistant Attorney General for the National Security Division;
- Eric Dreiband, Assistant Attorney General for the Civil Rights Division; and
- David Burns, Principal Deputy Assistant Attorney General for the National Security Division and acting Assistant Attorney General for the Criminal Division.

Donoghue and Hovakimian took the call from Hovakimian's office. Donoghue explained what had taken place over the past week and asked the invitees to inform him and Hovakimian if they would resign. According to Donoghue, "essentially, everyone responded either during the call or immediately thereafter that they would resign."[219]

Hovakimian also drafted a resignation email at some point on January 3. The email, which Hovakimian never sent, was addressed to DOJ Component Heads, the Offices of the Attorney General and Deputy Attorney General, and the Chair and Vice Chair of the Attorney General's Advisory Committee. It read:

> This evening, after Acting Attorney General Jeff Rosen over the course of the last week repeatedly refused the President's direct instructions to utilize the Department of Justice's law enforcement powers for improper ends, the President removed Jeff from the Department. PADAG Rich Donoghue and I resign from the Department, effective immediately.[220]

D. The January 3, 2021 Oval Office Meeting

Rosen, Donoghue, and Engel arrived at the White House around 6:00 p.m. Donoghue initially waited in the hallway but joined the meeting at Trump's request about 25 minutes after it

---

[216] Email from Patrick Hovakimian to Nathan Gamble and Maya Suero (Jan. 3, 2021, 4:21 p.m.) (SJC-PreCertificationEvents-000299).
[217] Email from Richard Donoghue to Patrick Hovakimian (Jan. 3, 2021, 4:23 p.m.) (SJC-PreCertificationEvents-000300).
[218] Emails from Patrick Hovakimian to Claire Murray, Jeffrey Wall, Makan Delrahim, Steven Engel, John Demers, David Burns, and Eric Dreiband (collectively, "DOJ leadership") (Jan. 3, 2021, 4:28 and 4:30 p.m.) (SJC-PreCertificationEvents-000302-03).
[219] Donoghue Tr. at 148.
[220] Draft Resignation Letter (SJC-PreCertificationEvents-000729).

started; in all, the meeting lasted somewhere between two to three hours. The participants were Trump, Rosen, Donoghue, Engel, Cipollone, Philbin, and Clark.[221] Rosen also recalled Eric Herschmann, Senior Adviser to the President, participating in the meeting.[222]

According to Rosen, Trump opened the meeting by saying, "One thing we know is you, Rosen, aren't going to do anything to overturn the election."[223] Over the course of the next three hours, the group had what Donoghue called "a wide-ranging conversation" focused on whether Trump should replace DOJ's leadership, install Clark in Rosen's place, and send Clark's proposed letter—and whether Clark was even qualified to assume the Acting Attorney General position.[224] Rosen and Donoghue told us that by this point, Clark's proposed letter and his potential role as Acting Attorney General were intertwined:

> At that point, it was difficult to separate the issue of the letter and Jeff Clark being in the leadership position, because it was very clear, and he stated it repeatedly, that if the President made him the Acting Attorney General, he would send that letter. So it wasn't as if there was a third option where Jeff Clark would become the Acting Attorney General and the letter would not go. They were sort of one and the same at that point.[225]

At some point during the meeting, Donoghue and Engel made clear that all of the Assistant Attorneys General would resign if Trump replaced Rosen with Clark. Donoghue added that the mass resignations likely would not end there, and that U.S. Attorneys and other DOJ officials might also resign en masse. Donoghue told us that he raised the prospect of mass resignations "earlier rather than later" in the meeting because he thought it was important context for the President's decision.[226] Donoghue and Rosen also recalled Cipollone and Philbin pushing back against the proposal to replace Rosen with Clark, with Cipollone calling Clark's letter as a "murder-suicide pact" and the two White House lawyers indicating that they would also resign.[227] Beyond the letter, Rosen described Herschmann as being "highly critical" of Clark's "qualifications and capabilities."[228]

Despite being informed early on that the Clark course of action would prompt mass resignations—and even though every participant in the meeting except Clark advocated strongly against that course of action—Trump continued for some time to entertain the idea of installing Clark in Rosen's place. Donoghue told us that Trump did not reject the Clark course of action

---

[221] Donoghue Tr. at 149-151; Rosen Tr. at 47.
[222] Rosen Tr. at 47.
[223] Rosen Tr. at 112.
[224] Donoghue Tr. at 152.
[225] Donoghue Tr. at 152; Rosen Tr. at 49.
[226] Donoghue Tr. at 155.
[227] Donoghue Tr. at 157, 159; Rosen Tr. at 50.
[228] Rosen Tr. at 164.

until "very deep into the conversation," within the final 15 minutes of the two- to three-hour meeting.[229]

After almost three hours of radio silence, at 9:00 p.m., Hovakimian emailed the Justice Department leadership, stating:

> I only have limited visibility into this, but it sounds like Rosen and the cause of justice won. We will convene a call when Jeff is back in the building (hopefully shortly). Thanks.[230]

Demers responded, "Amazing."[231] At 9:28 p.m., Engel confirmed Hovakimian's announcement to the group, stating "that is correct."[232]

While Clark's specific gambit was rebuffed, Trump himself continued to push DOJ to investigate further Georgia election fraud allegations that very night. Donoghue told us that, shortly after the Oval Office meeting concluded, Trump contacted him to claim a DHS Special Agent was in custody of a truck full of shredded ballots outside of Atlanta.[233] Donoghue recalled telling Trump that he had not heard that, but also reminding Trump:

> If it's a DHS agent, remember they don't belong to DOJ. But if they have an issue that they need our assistance with, they certainly know how to contact us. I'm sure that will happen, if appropriate.[234]

Trump still asked Donoghue to make sure that Ken Cuccinelli at DHS knew about this claim, prompting Donoghue that same night to call Cuccinelli, who also was not aware of this claim.[235] This ballot shredding claim was ultimately determined by DHS, FBI, and the U.S. Attorney's Office in Atlanta to be false. While there were ballots shredded, they were from past elections, and were being cleared out to make room for the storage of the 2020 ballots according to the County's record retention procedures.[236]

E. U.S. Attorney Pak Resigns

At some point during the Oval Office meeting, Trump began to complain about U.S. Attorney Pak. By then Pak's office had investigated and debunked various allegations of election fraud in Georgia, including the false claim about a videotape from Atlanta's State Farm Arena. That claim came to the fore following a December 3, 2020 Georgia Senate hearing, where Rudy Giuliani showed a video that he said showed poll workers bringing suitcases of ballots out from

---

[229] Donoghue Tr. at 157.
[230] Email from Patrick Hovakimian to DOJ leadership (Jan. 3, 2021, 9:07 p.m.) (SJC-PreCertificationEvents-000324).
[231] Email from John Demers to Patrick Hovakimian (Jan. 3, 2021, 9:12 p.m.) (SJC-PreCertificationEvents-000325).
[232] Email from Steven Engel to DOJ leadership (Jan. 3, 2021, 9:28 p.m.) (SJC-PreCertificationEvents-000326).
[233] Donoghue Tr. at 52.
[234] *Id.* at 53.
[235] *Id.*
[236] *Id.* at 54.

under a table to secretly count after Republican poll watchers went home.[237] Pak told us that on December 4, Attorney General Barr asked if he had seen the news about the suitcase allegation; Pak said he had, and Barr asked him to make finding out more about Giuliani's allegations a "top priority" because they might come up at an upcoming meeting Barr would attend at the White House.[238]

By December 4, the Georgia Secretary of State's Office had already investigated and announced that the State Farm Arena allegations were false.[239] In reality, the "suitcase" was a secure ballot container, and the ballots were counted in the presence of poll watchers from both parties.[240] Although the Secretary of State's Office had already refuted the allegations, Pak took steps in response to Barr's request. Pak told us he alerted Donoghue, contacted his office's District Election Officer, and spoke to the FBI following Barr's request that he prioritize looking into Giuliani's allegations.[241] He told us he was "very sensitive" to the need to avoid overt investigative steps that voters in the upcoming January 5 Senate runoff might inadvertently view as lending legitimacy to the claims.[242] On the other hand, Pak did not know what the Secretary of State's investigation consisted of, and because Barr had prioritized the matter, Pak asked the FBI to investigate.[243] Within two or three days of his call with Barr, Pak personally reviewed the tape along with an audio recording of interviews the Secretary of State's Office had conducted, and determined that they were consistent with the Secretary of State's public refutation of Giuliani's allegations.[244] Around the same time, the FBI received authorization to interview a handful of poll workers and other individuals depicted in the State Farm videotape.[245] They received this authorization notwithstanding PIN's objection that witness interviews would be inconsistent with ECB's election non-interference policy and Barr's November 9 memo, discussed more fully above. Following the interviews, the FBI reported to Pak that nothing irregular had happened; Pak then reported to Donoghue and Barr that "there was no substance to the allegations."[246]

Donoghue and Rosen later told Trump that there was no merit to the State Farm Arena allegations, including on their December 27 call. Trump nonetheless continued to insist that there was fraud in Georgia. According to Donoghue, Trump raised Georgia during the January 3 Oval Office meeting; after being told that DOJ had looked into election fraud claims in Atlanta and determined there was no evidence to support them, Trump mentioned Pak. Donoghue told us that Trump looked at a piece of paper on his desk and responded, "Atlanta, Atlanta, no surprise there. They didn't find anything. No surprise because we have a never-Trumper there as U.S.

---

[237] Stephen Fowler, Fact Checking Rudy Giuliani's Grandiose Georgia Election Fraud Claim, Georgia Public Broadcasting (Dec. 4, 2020).
[238] Pak Tr. at 13.
[239] Gabriel Sterling (@GabrielSterling), Twitter (Dec. 4, 2020, 6:41 a.m.), https://twitter.com/GabrielSterling/status/1334825233610633217?s=20org%2Fnews%2F2020%2F12%2F04%2Ffact-checking-rudy-giulianis-grandiose-georgia-election-fraud-claim.
[240] *See* Pak Tr. at 16-17.
[241] Pak Tr. at 14-15.
[242] Pak Tr. at 15.
[243] Pak Tr. at 38-39.
[244] Pak Tr. at 18, 21-22.
[245] Pak Tr. at 22-23.
[246] Pak Tr. at 20.

Attorney." Trump then read a quote, purportedly from Pak, criticizing the impact of Trump's rhetoric on the Republican Party's ability to appeal to minorities.[247]

Donoghue told us that he pushed back against Trump's characterization of Pak as a "never-Trumper" and that Trump disagreed and "was fixated on that for a short period of time." Trump then told Donoghue, "I want you to fire him."[248] Donoghue recalled the ensuring conversation as follows:

> I said, "Mr. President, I'm not going to fire him. There's no reason to fire him." And he said, "Then I'm firing him." And I said, "Well, before you do that, understand that I talked to BJay a couple of days ago, and he is submitting his resignation tomorrow morning," which would have been Monday morning. Pat Cipollone stepped in and said, "We're not firing someone who is resigning in a few hours." And the President said, "That's fine. I'm not going to fire him, then. But when his resignation comes in, it's accepted. Tomorrow is his last day as U.S. Attorney."[249]

In fact, Pak had not previously decided to resign on January 4. He told us that sometime prior to January 3, he had informed his office, the courts, and local law enforcement partners that he intended to remain in his position until Inauguration Day. He also informed Donoghue that he would probably submit his resignation sometime shortly after the January 5 runoff election but that the resignation would be effective as of January 20.[250] Pak told us he considered resigning on January 3 after he learned about Trump's call with Raffensperger, during which the President called Pak a "never Trumper" and continued to press election fraud claims that Pak had told DOJ leadership weren't true. Although Pak was "personally very concerned" that Trump was apparently seeking to overturn the election and represent that there had been irregularities in Georgia, he decided not to submit his resignation on January 3 because he did not want to disrupt the upcoming special election. Instead, Pak decided to "stay with my original plan" to "submit my letter of resignation and give two weeks' notice and leave office on Inauguration Day."[251]

After Trump told Donoghue that January 4 would be Pak's last day as U.S. Attorney, the conversation turned to the question of who would replace him. According to Donoghue, Trump asked, "What do you know about Bobby Christine?"[252] Christine was the U.S. Attorney for the Southern District of Georgia, and Trump added, "I hear great things about him." Trump then told Donoghue he wanted Christine to run the Northern District of Georgia. Donoghue responded that Christine was already running a U.S. Attorney's office, and that Pak had a First Assistant U.S. Attorney who would step in when Pak left. Donoghue was referring to FAUSA Kurt Erskine, who would take over as Acting U.S. Attorney under DOJ's well-established line of succession.

---

[247] Donoghue Tr. at 160.
[248] Donoghue Tr. at 161.
[249] Donoghue Tr. at 161.
[250] Pak Tr. at 93-94.
[251] Pak Tr. at 90-91.
[252] Donoghue Tr. at 161.

Trump insisted on appointing Christine instead, telling Donoghue something to the effect of, "if he's good, he'll find out if there's something there."[253]

> Q. You said the President said something to the effect of "I've heard great things about Bobby Christine, and if I put him in, he'll do something about it." Is that what you said?
>
> A. Something to that effect. Of course it's not a quote, but he said something like, "Well, if this guy is good, maybe something will actually get done."
>
> Q. And by "something getting done," what did you interpret him to mean?
>
> A. That there would be some sort of investigation that hadn't been done. But as I had told him repeatedly, the Department's looked at it. They did their job in the Northern District of Georgia.[254]

Later that night, Donoghue emailed Pak to "[p]lease call ASAP."[255] Pak called him. According to Pak, Donoghue relayed that Trump was "very unhappy" with him, believed he was a never-Trumper, and wanted to fire him. Donoghue also relayed that upon learning that Pak intended to submit his resignation that week, Trump agreed to accept the resignation rather than fire Pak, but that Pak had to resign quickly:

> Mr. Donoghue then asked me ... how long were you planning to stay after you submit your resignation. I told him that, you know, through inauguration. And Mr. Donoghue said no, unfortunately, it can't be that long.[256]

Donoghue indicated that Pak could remain at DOJ in another senior role through the end of the administration, but Pak declined.[257] According to Pak, Donoghue acknowledged that Pak could announce his resignation however he wanted, including by having a press conference or by "mak[ing] a big fuss," but suggested that it would be best for everyone if Pak left quietly. Pak responded that he would think about it.[258] Early the next morning, Pak called Donoghue back and informed him that he would submit a "very bland" resignation, in order to avoid impacting the upcoming special election. Pak also asked Donoghue to clarify why he had been asked to resign early. According to Pak, Donoghue responded that the President believed Pak was "not doing enough" and that the reason he was "not doing enough" was that he was a never-Trumper.[259]

---

[253] Donoghue Tr. at 162.
[254] Donoghue Tr. at 168-169.
[255] Email from Richard Donoghue to BJay Pak (Jan. 3, 2021, 10:09 p.m.) (SJC-PreCertificationEvents-000328).
[256] Pak Tr. at 95-96.
[257] Pak Tr. at 96.
[258] Pak Tr. at 96.
[259] Pak Tr. at 96.

At 7:41 a.m., Pak submitted resignation letters to President Trump and Rosen through the Executive Office of United States Attorneys.[260] At 7:46 a.m., Pak emailed all the U.S. Attorneys (copying Donoghue) a personal announcement of his resignation. After his sentiments, Pak included his "wish and hope that at least some of you will consider continuing to serve our country -- our nation needs patriots like you to uphold the rule of law."[261] Donoghue forwarded this email to Rosen,[262] and replied to Pak: "You are a class act, my friend. Thank you."[263] Engel also separately reached out to Pak to offer "[m]any thanks for all of your service to the Department, and I hope that our paths do cross again."[264]

VIII. Recommendations

To date, the Committee's investigation has uncovered several facets of President Trump's attempts to enlist DOJ and its leadership in his efforts to overturn the results of the 2020 presidential election. These efforts highlight several ways in which bad-faith actors can exploit DOJ policy and norms to provide a platform for election fraud claims even when the claims are not backed by any credible evidence and insert DOJ unnecessarily in political controversies.

Because the Committee's investigation is not yet complete and more documents and interviews are still being pursued, we have not made findings or recommendations concerning possible criminal liability. However, the investigation has uncovered sufficient information to justify providing a set of recommendations on potential legislative and oversight steps to strengthen DOJ's protections against politicization of its investigative and prosecutorial powers and additional measures that should be taken in response to this episode. Additionally, as this interim report makes clear, this entire episode is not merely a policy failure, but also the result of conscious actions by a mix of bad-faith actors seeking to overturn the 2020 general election in favor of their preferred candidate as well as other actors attempting to placate Trump while running out the clock on his administration. As appropriate, federal and state bar associations should consider whether additional accountability measures are warranted to discipline these bad actors and deter future attempts to politicize DOJ.

Finally, some aspects of this episode implicate issues that extend beyond the immediate purview of this investigation, and should be pursued as appropriate by the House Select Committee on the January 6 Attack.

Recommendation #1: Strengthen DOJ-White House Contacts Policy Through Increased Transparency and Enforcement

As this report makes clear, Jeffrey Clark blatantly violated the DOJ-White House contacts policy on multiple occasions by making unauthorized contact with President Trump. As the Senate-confirmed Assistant Attorney General for the Environment and Natural Resources

---

[260] Email from BJay Pak to Karen Winzenburg (Jan. 4, 2021, 7:41 a.m.) (SJC-PreCertificationEvents-000382-384).
[261] Email from BJay Pak to U.S. Attorneys (Jan. 4, 2021. 7:46 a.m.) (SJC-PreCertificationEvents-000385).
[262] Email from Richard Donoghue to Jeffrey Rosen (Jan. 4, 2021, 8:46 a.m.) (SJC-PreCertificationEvents-000387).
[263] Email from Richard Donoghue to BJay Pak (Jan. 4, 2021, 11:12 a.m.) (SJC-PreCertificationEvents-000391).
[264] Email from Steven Engel to BJay Pak (Jan. 4, 2021, 10:53 a.m.) (SJC-PreCertificationEvents-000389).

Division and the acting Assistant Attorney General for the Civil Division, Clark had a responsibility to know that the policy prohibited him from meeting with Trump without authorization. Regardless, prior to his unauthorized meetings with Trump, Clark had constructive knowledge that such contact violated the contacts policy after Donoghue sent that very policy to Clark and other senior DOJ leaders after the 2020 general election on November 11, 2020.[265] Yet even being admonished by Donoghue that his unauthorized meeting in the Oval Office violated the contacts policy, and even though Clark assured Rosen that he would not meet with the President again, Clark brazenly violated the policy at least once more.[266]

Mark Meadows also repeatedly violated the DOJ-White House contacts policy. The White House version of that policy in force at the time made clear that communications with DOJ about pending or contemplated investigations or cases were to involve only the President, Vice President, White House Counsel, and the White House Counsel's designees.[267] The policy, which was enshrined in a memo from former White House Counsel McGahn, stressed, "In order to ensure that DOJ exercises its investigatory and prosecutorial functions free from the fact or appearance of improper political influence, these rules must be strictly followed." Meadows violated the policy each time he contacted Rosen to request that DOJ look into election fraud allegations, whether in Fulton County, New Mexico, or elsewhere.

On July 21, 2021, Attorney General Merrick Garland and White House Counsel Dana Remus updated and reissued DOJ and White House versions of the contacts policies. The updated policies clarify and strengthen the limitations on communications between White House and DOJ officials on specific law enforcement matters. However, the misconduct documented in this report demonstrates why a stricter oversight regime around White House contacts with DOJ is appropriate, particularly given that even the Attorney General does not have the authority to fire a fellow presidentially appointed and Senate-confirmed official—a fact Rosen himself faced when confronted by Clark's repeated violations.[268]

Congress can provide additional teeth to the DOJ-White House contacts policy by requiring greater transparency and enhanced enforcement around covered communications. Current proposals that warrant particular consideration are the Title VI provisions within the Protecting Our Democracy Act (PODA) that would require the Attorney General to maintain a log of designated contacts between the White House and DOJ that is shared with the DOJ OIG, who would then notify the Senate and House Judiciary Committees of any inappropriate or improper contacts.[269] However, PODA only contemplates a semi-annual sharing of the contacts log with DOJ OIG, which would not have alerted OIG or Congress of Clark's violations until well after they occurred.[270] Consequently, it would be advisable for any such legislation to

---

[265] Email from Richard Donoghue to DOJ leadership (Nov. 11, 2020, 6:27 p.m.) (SJC-PreCertificationEvents-000680).
[266] Rosen Tr. at 84-85, 128-129; Donoghue Tr. at 104, 141.
[267] Memorandum from Donald F. McGahn II to All White House Staff (Jan. 27, 2017) (SJC-PreCertificationEvents-000685-686).
[268] Rosen Tr. at 131-132.
[269] Protecting Our Democracy Act, H.R. 5314, 117th Cong. §§ 601-604 (2021).
[270] Id. at §603(c)(1).

require regular IG access to the contacts log, and setting up an immediate "urgent concern" transmission system to the Senate and House Judiciary Committees similar to the one in place for whistleblower complaints in the Intelligence Community and the Intelligence Committees. Relatedly, the bipartisan Inspector General Access Act (IGAA) has a role to play in making any DOJ-White House contacts policy enforceable by expanding the jurisdiction of the DOJ Inspector General to cover matters of attorney misconduct.[271] The Committee has previously reported this legislation out on a bipartisan basis and Congress should enact it this year.

Additionally, while the information in this report demonstrates that various existing criminal provisions regarding the obstruction of justice—such as 18 U.S.C. § 1505's prohibition on obstructing proceedings before departments, agencies, and committees, and 18 U.S.C. § 1512(c)(2)'s prohibition on corruptly obstructing, influencing, or impeding any official proceeding—may apply to aspects of this episode, Congress should consider legislative amendments to related obstruction of justice provisions to ensure they clearly cover similarly corrupt actions. These include, but are not limited to:

- Consider amending 18 U.S.C. § 1505 to clarify that this provision applies to corrupt influence of state proceedings relating to federal elections;

- Consider amending 18 U.S.C. § 1512(c) to clarify that this provision also applies to state proceedings relating to federal elections; and

- Consider amending 18 U.S.C. § 372 to clarify that "corruptly persuading" constitutes a type of "force, intimidation, or threat" prohibited by the statute.

Recommendation #2: Strengthen DOJ's Longstanding Policy of Election Non-Interference

Attorney General Barr twice relaxed elements of DOJ's longstanding policy of election non-interference, shortly before the election and immediately afterwards on November 9, 2020. The result of both actions was to cast public doubt on the integrity of the election where none was warranted and to encourage unwarranted investigative steps into non-credible allegations prior to the certification of the election. Attorney General Garland rescinded Barr's November 9 memo on February 3, 2021 and clarified that until DOJ was able to update the Justice Manual to reflect the newly changed policy, "the Department's forty-year old 'non-interference with elections policy'" contained in the ECB's Federal Prosecution of Election Offenses manual would govern.[272]

---

[271] Inspector General Access Act, S. 426 & H.R. 3064, 117th Cong. (2021).

[272] Memorandum from Attorney General Garland for Heads of Department Components, All United States Attorneys at 1 (Feb. 3, 2021). The February 3 memo also rescinded separate guidance issued by former Attorney General Barr on December 22, 2020, which directed the Civil Rights Division to assume that a state or local government that readopts preexisting voting procedures following the pandemic has done so lawfully, unless the preexisting procedures were previously found to be unlawful. *See* Memorandum from Attorney General Barr to the Assistant Attorney General, Civil Rights Division (Dec. 22, 2020).

As they work to update the Justice Manual to reflect the longstanding policy contained in the ECB manual, DOJ leadership should consider expanding the consultation requirements for election-related cases. There are various forms that such an expansion could take, such as explicitly requiring the approval of career attorneys in PIN before any investigative steps can be taken in election fraud cases (as opposed to merely consulting with PIN), but generally such an expansion should require a written request and approval process that includes a requirement for a written explanation when the initial decision by PIN is overruled by a political appointee, including the Attorney General.

Additionally, DOJ leadership should consider formalizing other existing norms regarding election non-interference, and centralizing all such policies and guidance to better ensure career staff and political appointees all share the same understanding. Specifically, DOJ should reduce the so-called "unwritten 60-day rule" to writing. Under this longstanding principle, in the 60-day period preceding a primary or general election, DOJ should avoid returning indictments against a candidate or taking overt investigative steps related to electoral matters.[273] In 2018, the DOJ Inspector General recommended that DOJ consider providing written guidance to agents and prosecutors concerning their obligations to avoid taking actions that could impact elections. DOJ has not yet implemented that recommendation.[274]

Although this report focuses on conduct during the post-election period, that conduct occurred against the backdrop of Attorney General Barr's pre-election efforts to cast doubt on the election's integrity. These efforts included a September 24, 2020 announcement that the U.S. Attorney's Office for the Middle District of Pennsylvania was investigating claims that mail ballots in Luzerne County had been discarded.[275] They also included Barr's numerous public statements baselessly suggesting that voting by mail would lead to fraud and DOJ's October 2020 directive that prosecutors could take overt, pre-election steps in election fraud investigations involving claims of misconduct by federal officials—including U.S. Postal Service employees.[276] To help ensure that agents and prosecutors adhere to DOJ's longstanding norms against election interference, DOJ should issue written guidance enshrining the 60-day rule.

Recommendation #3: Further Investigation of Clark's Conduct by the District of Columbia Bar

Clark's attempts to enlist DOJ in Trump's effort to overturn the results of the presidential election without evidence or legal authority to do so clearly undermined the rule of law. Clark is

---

[273] *See* Department of Justice Office of the Inspector General, *A Review of Various Actions by the Federal Bureau of Investigation and the Department of Justice in Advance of the 2016 Election* at 17-18 (June 2018).
[274] Department of Justice Office of the Inspector General, *Recommendations Issued by the Office of the Inspector General that were Not Closed as of July 31, 2021* at 114.
[275] Department of Justice, Press Release: Revised Statement of U.S. Attorney Freed on Inquiry into Reports of Potential Issues with Mail-In Ballots (Sept. 24, 2020), *available at* https://www.justice.gov/usao-mdpa/pr/revised-statement-us-attorney-freed-inquiry-reports-potential-issues-mail-ballots.
[276] *See, e.g.,* Jane C. Timm, *Fact Check: Echoing Trump, Barr Misleads on Voter Fraud to Attack Expanded Vote-by-Mail*, NBC News (Sept. 19, 2020); Robert Faturechi & Justin Elliott, *DOJ Frees Federal Prosecutors to Take Steps That Could Interfere With Elections, Weakening Longstanding Policy*, ProPublica (Oct. 7, 2020).

currently barred in the District of Columbia, where DOJ is headquartered and where his offending conduct took place, and as such the District of Columbia Bar's Office of Disciplinary Counsel should evaluate Clark's conduct to determine whether disciplinary action is warranted. To that end, the Committee is concurrently submitting a formal complaint to the District of Columbia Bar based on the findings of our report.

Based on the facts this investigation has uncovered to date, Clark's conduct may implicate multiple Rules of Professional Conduct. This includes Rule 8.4's prohibitions against "conduct involving dishonesty, fraud, deceit, or misrepresentation," "conduct that seriously interferes with the administration of justice" and "stat[ing] or imply[ing] an ability to influence improperly a government agency or official."[277] Clark's conduct may also implicate Rule 1.2(e), which states that a "lawyer shall not counsel a client to engage, or assist a client, in conduct that the lawyer knows is criminal or fraudulent," although a lawyer "may discuss the legal consequences of any proposed course of conduct with a client and may counsel or assist a client to make a good-faith effort to determine the validity, scope, meaning, or application of the law."[278] Clark's continued pursuit of his "Proof of Concept" letter despite being told repeatedly by DOJ leadership that his election fraud claims were baseless may implicate each of these rules.

A determination of whether Clark violated applicable rules of professional conduct would require an assessment of his state of mind, particularly to the extent those rules—like Rule 1.2(e)—include a knowledge element. Testimony by Clark himself would shed additional light on his state of mind, but to date he has not agreed to the Committee's request for a voluntary interview despite repeated follow-up and after more than two months have passed since DOJ authorized him to testify without restriction. Regardless, Clark should not be able to avoid discipline by asserting he subjectively assessed his claims to be factual or reasonable. Knowledge is ascertained by an objective standard,[279] and the disciplinary authority may prove that Clark "knowingly" pushed DOJ to act on baseless grounds through circumstantial evidence,[280] which, as demonstrated by this report, overwhelmingly shows Clark knew and should have known his claims were baseless. On this note, it should be noted that Rudy Giuliani has been suspended from practicing law in New York and faces disbarment for communicating "demonstrably false and misleading statements to courts, lawmakers and the public at large" regarding similar claims.[281] Additionally, nine other attorneys, including Sidney Powell and L. Lin Wood, have already been sanctioned by the Eastern District of Michigan and referred to the relevant disciplinary authorities for their admitting jurisdictions for their "bad faith" effort "to use the judicial process to frame a 'public narrative'" based on "conjecture and speculation" lacking evidentiary support, precisely like Clark.[282] Although Clark did not press the false claims in his "Proof of Concept" letter before a court in the same way that Giuliani, Powell, and Wood

---

[277] D.C. R. Prof. Conduct 8.4.
[278] D.C. R. Prof. Conduct 1.2(e).
[279] Rebecca Roiphe, *The Ethics of Willful Ignorance*, 24 Geo. J. Legal Ethics 187, 196 (2011).
[280] George Cohen, *The State Of Lawyer Knowledge Under The Model Rules Of Professional Conduct*, 3 Am. U. Bus. L. R. 115, 116 (2018).
[281] *Matter of Giuliani*, 146 N.Y.S. 3d 266 (App. Div. 1st Dep't 2021).
[282] *King v. Whitmer*, No. 20-13134, 2021 WL 3771875 *26, *34, *39 (E.D. Mich. Aug. 25, 2021).

did, the fact that those claims and others like them have been rejected in other disciplinary proceedings is at the very least circumstantial evidence that Clark knew they were baseless.

Recommendation #4: Cooperation with the House Select Committee to Investigate Ties Between This Episode and the January 6 Attack

As discussed throughout this report, President Trump's efforts to enlist DOJ and its leadership in his efforts to overturn the results of the 2020 presidential election were aided by numerous allies with clear ties to the "Stop the Steal" movement and the January 6 insurrection. As Trump himself noted to Rosen and Donoghue on December 27, he and his congressional allies could effectively position themselves to overturn the presidential election results with cover from DOJ, asking DOJ to "just say the election was corrupt and leave the rest to me and the [Republican] Congressmen."[283]

Three of these allies and their connections to January 6 are particularly notable: U.S. Representative Scott Perry, Pennsylvania State Senator Doug Mastriano, and Trump campaign attorney Cleta Mitchell. These ties warrant further investigation to better place Trump's efforts to enlist DOJ in his efforts to overturn the presidential election in context with the January 6 insurrection. Because the events of January 6 are outside the immediate purview of the Committee's investigation, this report is being made available to the House Select Committee on the January 6 Attack, as well as the public, to assist their investigation.

---

[283] 12/27/20 Donoghue Notes (SJC-PreCertificationEvents-000738); Donoghue Tr. at 86-87.

APPENDIX A: CHRONOLOGY OF KEY EVENTS

Date	Event
September 2, 2020	In an interview on CNN's *The Situation Room*, Attorney General William Barr baselessly claims that "elections that have been held with mail have found substantial fraud and coercion." This follows months of similarly unfounded claims by Barr, including his July 28, 2020 House Judiciary Committee testimony that mail voting creates a "high risk" of extensive voter fraud.
September 24, 2020	Contrary to its decades-old policy of avoiding overt investigative steps in election fraud matters before the election is certified, DOJ issues a press release announcing an investigation into nine "discarded" mail ballots in Luzerne County, Pennsylvania and stating that seven of the ballots were cast for President Trump.
October 2, 2020	DOJ issues an internal announcement of "an exception to the general non-interference with elections policy," which—contrary to longstanding DOJ policy and practice—authorizes overt, pre-election investigative steps into election fraud allegations involving federal agencies such as the U.S. Postal Service.
November 3, 2020	The 2020 General Election is held.
November 7, 2020	Media outlets confirm that Joseph R. Biden won the Electoral College.
November 9, 2020	President Trump spends the afternoon and evening tweeting about dozens of false voter fraud claims about contested states and Dominion Voting Systems. Attorney General Barr issues a memorandum weakening DOJ's longstanding election non-interference policy and authorizing overt, pre-certification investigative steps "if there are clear and apparently credible allegations of irregularities that, if true, could potentially impact the outcome of a federal election in an individual State." Richard Pilger resigns his position as Director of the Public Integrity Section's (PIN's) Election Crimes Branch in response to Barr's 11/9 memorandum.
November 14, 2020	The Trump campaign itself prepares and distributes an internal memorandum rebutting various allegations regarding Dominion Voting Systems, reflecting its early knowledge that such allegations are baseless.
November 19, 2020	Rudy Giuliani and Sidney Powell hold a press conference at the Republican National Committee office where they continue to make false claims, with Giuliani telling the crowd: "I know crimes. I can smell them. You don't have to smell this one. I can prove it to you 18 different ways."

Introduction by Thomas Fensch

Date	Event
December 1, 2020	Barr announces that DOJ has "not seen fraud on a scale that could have effected a different outcome in the election."
	Chief Operating Officer for the Georgia Secretary of State Gabriel Sterling holds a news conference asking Trump and his allies to "stop inspiring people to commit potential acts of violence. Someone's going to get hurt. Someone's going to get shot. Someone's going to get killed."
December 3, 2020	Giuliani shows a video at a Georgia Senate hearing that he claims shows poll workers at Atlanta's State Farm Arena bringing suitcases of ballots out from under a table to secretly count after Republican poll watcher went home.
December 4, 2020	The Georgia Secretary of State's Office announces that it investigated Giuliani's claims and determined they were false – the suitcases were secure ballot containers and all ballots were counted in the presence of poll watchers from both parties.
	Barr calls U.S. Attorney for the Northern District of Georgia Byung Jin ("BJay") Pak to request that he make finding out more about Giuliani's allegations a "top priority."
	The Trump campaign and David Shafer, the Chairman of the Georgia Republican Party, files a suit in Fulton County Superior Court seeking to invalidate Georgia's presidential election results.
December 5, 2020	The Fulton County Superior Court rejects the Trump campaign's suit to overturn the presidential election results.
December 7, 2020	PIN Chief Corey Amundson notifies the FBI that PIN does not concur in any overt investigative activity concerning the State Farm Arena allegations, including witness interviews authorized by Barr, because those allegations "do not fall within the scope of [Barr's November 9 memo], which created an exception to the DOJ Election Non-Interference Policy for substantial, clear, apparently credible, and non-speculative allegations" of election fraud.
	Principal Associate Deputy Attorney General Richard Donoghue makes clear to U.S. Attorney Pak and FBI Deputy Director David Bowdich that PIN's concurrence is not required and that the interviews should proceed, as directed by Barr. Within days, the FBI confirms the Georgia Secretary of State's conclusion that the State Farm Arena allegations are meritless.
December 8, 2020	The U.S. Supreme Court rejects Pennsylvania Representative Mike Kelly's suit to block Pennsylvania's certification of the election results.
December 9, 2020	West Virginia becomes the final state to certify its presidential election results.
December 11, 2020	The U.S. Supreme Court rejects Texas's suit to overturn the presidential election results in Georgia, Michigan, Pennsylvania, and Wisconsin.

Date	Event
December 12, 2020	The Georgia Supreme Court rejects the Trump Campaign's suit to overturn the presidential election results in Georgia, holding that "petitioners have not shown that this is one of those extremely rare cases that would invoke our original jurisdiction."
December 14, 2020	The Electoral College meets in all 50 state capitals and the District of Columbia and casts 306 electoral votes for Joseph R. Biden and 232 electoral votes for Donald J. Trump.
	Barr announces his resignation, effective December 23.
	Special Assistant to the President Molly Michael emails Deputy Attorney General Jeffery Rosen two documents "From POTUS": (1) a set of talking points alleging voter fraud in Antrim County, Michigan; and (2) a purported "forensic report" by Allied Operations Group on Dominion Voting Systems' performance in Antrim County.
December 15, 2020	Senate Majority Leader McConnell speaks on the Senate floor to remark on the Electoral College vote: "The Electoral College has spoken, so today I want to congratulate President-elect Joe Biden."
	Trump tweets an article titled "Trump's allies slam Mitch McConnell for congratulating Biden" and says "Too soon to give up. Republican Party must finally learn to fight. People are angry!"
	Trump summons Jeffery Rosen and Principal Associate Deputy Attorney General Richard Donoghue to the Oval Office to ask why DOJ was not "doing more to look at" the Antrim County allegations and the "bad things" he claimed happened in Pennsylvania and Georgia. Attorney General Barr was not invited.
December 19, 2020	Trump tweets about the upcoming January 6, Joint Session of Congress: "Big protests in D.C. on January 6. Be there. Will be wild!"
December 21, 2020	Barr reaffirms his December 1 announcement that there was no widespread election fraud and adds that there is no basis for appointing special counsels to look into election fraud allegations.
	Trump meets with Ohio Representative Jim Jordan, Pennsylvania Representative Scott Perry, and other House Freedom Caucus members to strategize about January 6.
December 23, 2020	Barr's last day as Attorney General.
	Trump calls Rosen and indicates he will want to talk again soon.
	On or about this date, Jeffrey Clark violates the DOJ-White House contacts policy and meets with President Trump in the Oval Office, along with Representative Perry.

Introduction by Thomas Fensch

Date	Event
	Trump tweets: "After seeing massive Voter Fraud in the 2020 Presidential Election, I disagree with anyone that thinks a strong, fast, and fair Special Counsel is not needed, IMMEDIATELY. This was the most corrupt election in the history of our Country and it must be closely examined!"
December 24, 2020	President Trump calls Rosen, who is now acting Attorney General, and repeats election fraud claims similar to those in the December 15 meeting. He tells Rosen to "make sure the Department is really looking into these things that you may have missed," and asks if Rosen knew "a guy named Jeff Clark."
December 26, 2020	Rosen calls Clark to learn why President Trump mentioned him by name on the December 24 call. Clark admits that he met with Trump in the Oval Office.
December 27, 2020	Trump twice calls Rosen. During the second call, Rosen conferences in Donoghue, who takes extensive notes on Trump's claims that the "election has been stolen out from under the American people" and that DOJ is failing to respond. Trump mentions efforts made by Pennsylvania Representative Scott Perry, Ohio Representative Jim Jordan, and Pennsylvania State Senator Doug Mastriano, and asks Rosen and Donoghue to "just say the election was corrupt and leave the rest to me and the Republican Congressmen." Trump also references Jeffrey Clark and potentially replacing DOJ's leadership.
December 27, 2020	Trump asks Donoghue for his cell phone number so he can direct people with information about election fraud claims to call him. Pennsylvania Representative Perry then calls Donoghue at Trump's behest to discuss a false claim that Pennsylvania had 205,000 more votes than voters. Perry also tells Donoghue that Jeffrey Clark is "the kind of guy who could really get in there and do something about this."
December 27, 2020	Pennsylvania Representative Perry emails Donoghue five documents summarizing numerous false Pennsylvania election fraud claims.
December 27, 2020	Donoghue forwards Representative Perry's email to the U.S. Attorney for the Western District of Pennsylvania Scott Brady "for whatever it may be worth." Brady subsequently responds that the claims "were not well founded."
December 28, 2020	Trump calls Donoghue to confirm that he had raised a particular election fraud claim the prior afternoon; Donoghue tells him he did.
December 28, 2020	Clark emails Rosen and Donoghue about "Two Urgent Action Items." He requests a classified briefing regarding a conspiracy theory that foreign agents in China accessed a voting machine through a smart thermostat and also proposes that DOJ send a "Proof of Concept" letter he drafted to the elected leadership of Georgia and other states to urge them to convene special legislative sessions in order to appoint a different slate of electors.

Date	Event
	Donoghue replies to Clark's email to say "there is no chance I would sign this letter or anything remotely like this" and highlights specific statements in Clark's "Proof of Concept" letter that had no support.
	Rosen and Donoghue meet with Clark to discuss the "Proof of Concept Letter." Clark tells them he wants Rosen to hold a press conference announcing that there was corruption and mentions that President Trump was considering a leadership change at DOJ.
	Donoghue contacts Assistant Attorney General for the Office of Legal Counsel Steve Engel to read him into "some antics that could potentially end up on [his] radar" given his position as the next in line to become Acting Attorney General if Trump fired Rosen.
December 29, 2020	At Trump's behest, Molly Michael emails Rosen, Donoghue, and Acting Solicitor General Jeffrey Wall a draft bill of complaint purporting to invoke the Supreme Court's original jurisdiction against the states of Pennsylvania, Georgia, Michigan, Wisconsin, Arizona, and Nevada to overturn their presidential election results.
	Rosen, Donoghue, and Engel meet with White House Chief of Staff Mark Meadows, White House Counsel Pat Cipollone, and Deputy White House Counsel Pat Philbin. Among other things, they discuss the draft bill of complaint, but also discuss Trump's trust in John Eastman as well as a conspiracy theory known as "Italygate."
	Meadows sends Rosen a copy of a letter pushing the "Italygate" theory, which claims an employee of an Italian aerospace company coordinated with the CIA to use military satellites to remotely switch Trump votes to Biden votes.
	Kurt Olsen, a private attorney who served as a special counsel to Texas Attorney General Ken Paxton during Texas's failed Supreme Court action against Pennsylvania, makes multiple efforts via email and phone to brief Rosen, at President Trump's behest, about the draft bill of complaint.
	Rosen requests that the Office of Solicitor General prepare a one-pager on the draft bill of complaint.
December 30, 2020	Meadows forwards Rosen an email and attachment from Trump campaign attorney Cleta Mitchell addressing election fraud claims the campaign is pushing in Georgia. Meadows asks Rosen to have DOJ look into the campaign's allegations.
	The Office of Solicitor General provides Rosen with a summary of the "numerous significant procedural hurdles" DOJ would face if it filed the draft bill of complaint, including that DOJ cannot file an original Supreme Court

Date	Event
	action for the benefit of a political candidate and that there is no general cause of action allowing DOJ to contest the outcome of an election.
	Rosen and Donoghue speak with Olsen, who attempts to press DOJ to file the draft bill of complaint "by noon today" and threatened to report Rosen's position on the matter back to Trump.
	Engel provides Rosen with an Office of Legal Counsel summary of the draft bill of complaint that concludes "[t]here is no legal basis to bring this lawsuit."
	Rosen speaks with Trump to explain that DOJ could not file the draft bill of complaint.
December 31, 2020	Trump summons Rosen and Donoghue to the Oval Office for a "contentious" meeting about why DOJ still had not "found the fraud," where Trump tells them that people say he should fire both of them and install Clark. Trump further raises that the draft bill of complaint should be pursued.
	Rosen speaks with Clark again. Clark reveals that he has spoken to Trump again and tells Rosen that Trump asked him whether he would be willing to take over as Acting Attorney General if Trump replaced Rosen, but that Clark wanted to do some "due diligence" on certain election fraud claims before deciding.
January 1, 2021	Clark receives the classified briefing he first requested on December 28.
	Meadows sends Rosen a YouTube video regarding the Italygate conspiracy theory titled "Brad Johnson: Rome, Satellites, Servers: an Update."
	Meadows emails Rosen about disproven allegations of signature match anomalies in Fulton County, Georgia and asks "[c]an you get Jeff Clark to engage on this issue immediately…"
	Meadows calls Rosen about the Italygate conspiracy, and even after Rosen tells Meadows that it was "another one that's debunked," Meadows tells Rosen "there's more to it" and asks Rosen to meet with Giuliani. Rosen refused this request, as he had refused multiple other requests to meet with Giuliani in December 2020.
	Meadows emails Rosen to ask DOJ to investigate false election fraud claims in New Mexico pushed by Steve Pearce, the Chair of the New Mexico Republican Party.
	Trump tweets: "January 6th. See you in D.C."
	Rosen suggests that Clark reach out to U.S. Attorney for the Northern District of Georgia Pak for an explanation of how the allegations of ballot destruction in Atlanta had been discredited.

Date	Event
January 2, 2021	Trump, joined by Meadows and Mitchell, calls Georgia Secretary of State Brad Raffensperger and attempts to pressure him to change the state's vote totals from the presidential election, specifically asking to find exactly enough votes for Trump to win. During the call, Trump refers to U.S. Attorney Pak as the "Never Trumper U.S. Attorney there."
	Clarks meets with Rosen and Donoghue, confirms that his classified briefing produced no evidence of ballot or data tampering, but continues to press that DOJ should send his "Proof of Concept" letter. Clark attempts to get Rosen to reconsider sending the letter by offering to turn down Trump's offer to install him in Rosen's place. Clark also confirms that he has not reached out to Pak to discuss why the Georgia election fraud claims he continues to press are false, and reveals that he has instead spoken to witnesses about those claims.
January 3, 2021	Clark asks Doug Smith, his Chief of Staff and the Deputy Assistant Attorney General for the Civil Division's Torts Branch, to "please get back to DC immediately."
	Clark meets with Rosen to tell him that he accepted Trump's offer to become acting Attorney General, and that Rosen would be replaced that day.
	After telling Clark he will not be fired by his subordinate, Rosen calls Meadows to say that he needed to speak with Trump that day, which Meadows arranges for that evening.
	At Rosen's request, Donoghue and Rosen's longtime deputy Patrick Hovakimian arranged a call with DOJ's senior leadership to determine whether the others would also resign if Clark were installed.
	Rosen, Donoghue, and Engel meet with Trump, Cipollone, Philbin, and Clark in the Oval Office. Early in the meeting, it is established that there will be mass resignations if Trump installs Clark as acting Attorney General, but the meeting continues for hours before Trump decides to keep Rosen in place. At the end of the meeting, Trump claims Pak is a never-Trumper and that if U.S. Attorney for the Southern District of Georgia Bobby Christine replaced Pak "he'll do something about [election fraud]." Donoghue convinces Trump not to fire Pak because he says Pak is already planning to resign. Trump agrees, but makes clear that Pak must leave the very next day.
	Donoghue asks Pak to "[p]lease call ASAP," and during their call tells Pak that Trump would fire him if he did not resign quickly the next day.
	Late at night and following their Oval Office meeting, Trump calls Donoghue to alert him of claims that a DHS agent was in custody of a truck full of shredded ballots in Atlanta.

Introduction by Thomas Fensch

Date	Event
January 4, 2021	U.S. Attorney Pak submits his resignation, effective immediately.
	Trump tweets: "How can you certify an election when the numbers being certified are verifiably WRONG. You will see the real numbers tonight during my speech, but especially on JANUARY 6th. @SenTomCotton Republicans have pluses & minuses, but one thing is sure, THEY NEVER FORGET!"
	President Trump and outside attorney John Eastman attempt to convince Vice President Pence to set aside the Electoral College votes of seven states when he presides over the January 6 Joint Session of Congress.
	President Trump speaks at a Dalton, Georgia Senate Runoff campaign event where he continues to claim that the general election "was a rigged election" and that he would "fight like hell."
January 5, 2021	Christine is appointed acting U.S. Attorney for the Northern District of Georgia, sidestepping the next in the line of succession First Assistant U.S. Attorney Kurt Erskine.
January 6, 2021	President Trump incites his supporters to breach the Capitol in an attempt to stop the certification of the 2020 Electoral College votes.
January 7, 2021	Vice President Pence officially affirms the Electoral College votes and declares Joseph R. Biden the president-elect.
January 20, 2021	Joseph R. Biden is inaugurated as the 46th President of the United States of America.

APPENDIX B: KEY DOCUMENTS

Document	Description
A	Email from Richard Donoghue to BJay Pak regarding State Farm Arena videotape (Dec. 7, 2020, 12:48 p.m.)
B	Email from Molly Michael to Jeffrey Rosen regarding Antrim County, Michigan allegations (Dec. 14, 2020, 4:57 p.m.)
C	Email from Theresa Watson to Michigan USAs Matthew Schneider & Andrew Birge regarding Antrim County, Michigan allegations (Dec. 14, 2020, 4:59 p.m.)
D	Email from Ken Cuccinelli to Richard Donoghue regarding summary of refutations to Antrim, County, Michigan allegations (Dec. 18, 2020, 2:54 p.m.)
E	Notes of Dec. 27, 2020 Trump-Rosen-Donoghue Call
F	Notes of Dec. 27, 2020 Donoghue-Perry Call
G	Email from Richard Donoghue to USA Scott Brady regarding Pennsylvania allegations (Dec. 27, 2020, 10:05 p.m.)
H	Email from Jeffrey Clark to Jeffrey Rosen & Richard Donoghue regarding "Proof of Concept" proposal (Dec. 28, 2020, 4:40 p.m.)
I	Email from Richard Donoghue to Jeffrey Clark responding to the "Proof of Concept" proposal (Dec. 28, 2020, 5:50 p.m.)
J	Email from Richard Donoghue to Steven Engel regarding "antics" (Dec. 28, 2020, 11:41 p.m.)
K	Email from Kurt Olsen to Jeffrey Wall regarding draft Supreme Court Complaint (Dec. 29, 2020, 10:57 a.m.)
L	Email from Molly Michael to Jeffrey Rosen, Richard Donoghue, & Jeffrey Wall regarding draft Supreme Court Complaint (Dec. 29, 2020, 11:17 a.m.)
M	Email from Mark Meadows to Jeffrey Rosen regarding Italygate allegations (Dec. 29, 2020, 11:27 a.m.)
N	Email from Doug Mastriano to Richard Donoghue regarding Pennsylvania allegations (Dec. 29, 2020, 11:28 a.m.)
O	Email from Kurt Olsen to John Moran regarding draft Supreme Court Complaint (Dec. 29, 2020, 12:45 p.m.)
P	Notes of Dec. 29, 2020 Rosen-Donoghue-Engel Meeting with Meadows-Cipollone-Philbin
Q	Email from Mark Meadows to Jeffrey Rosen regarding Trump campaign Georgia allegations (Dec. 30, 2020, 9:31 a.m.)
R	Email from Mark Meadows to Jeffrey Rosen regarding translated Italygate allegations (Dec. 30, 2020, 9:43 a.m.)
S	Notes of Dec. 30, 2020 Olsen-Rosen-Donoghue Call
T	Email from Steven Engel to Jeffrey Rosen transmitting "one pager" on draft Supreme Court Complaint (Dec. 31, 2020, 9:02 a.m.)
U	Email from Steve Engel to Richard Donoghue requesting an update (Dec. 31, 2020, 4:20 p.m.)
V	Email from Jeffrey Rosen to Patrick Hovakimian requesting assistance (Dec. 31, 2020, 6:14 p.m.)

Introduction by Thomas Fensch

Document	Description
W	Email from Richard Donoghue to Jeffrey Rosen discussing Mark Meadows's request to have Jeffrey Clark investigate signature match allegations in Georgia (Jan. 1, 2021, 4:28 p.m.)
X	Email from Mark Meadows to Jeffrey Rosen regarding New Mexico allegations (Jan. 1, 2021, 6:56 p.m.)
Y	Email from Jeffrey Rosen to Richard Donoghue discussing Rosen's refusal to meet with Rudy Giuliani or ask FBI to meet with Brad Johnson about Italygate (Jan. 1, 2021, 7:13 p.m.)
Z	Email from Jeffrey Clark to Jeffrey Rosen discussing whether Clark was able to speak with BJay Pak (Jan. 2, 2021, 9:50 a.m.)
AA	Notes of Jan. 2, 2021 Rosen-Donoghue-Clark Meeting
BB	Email from Jeffrey Rosen to Richard Donoghue replying to Donoghue's earlier response to Jeffrey Clark's "Proof of Concept" proposal (Jan. 2, 2021, 7:13 p.m.)
CC	Email from Steve Engel to Richard Donoghue planning an update call (Jan. 2, 2021, 8:09 p.m.)
DD	Draft Donoghue-Hovakimian Resignation Letter
EE	Email from Jeffrey Clark to Douglas Smith requesting Smith to "get back to DC immediately" (Jan. 3, 2021, 4:37 p.m.)
FF	Email from Patrick Hovakimian to DOJ leadership announcing that "it sounds like Rosen and the cause of justice won" (Jan. 3, 2021, 9:07 p.m.)
GG	Email from Steven Engel to DOJ leadership confirming Patrick Hovakimian's announcement (Jan. 3, 2021, 9:28 p.m.)
HH	Email from Richard Donoghue to BJay Pak asking Pak to call "ASAP" (Jan. 3, 2021, 10:09 p.m.)
II	Email from BJay Pak to Karen Winzenburg submitting his resignation letters (Jan. 4, 2021, 7:41 a.m.)
JJ	Email from BJay Pak to U.S. Attorneys announcing his resignation to all U.S. Attorneys (Jan. 4, 2021, 7:46 a.m.)
KK	Email from Francis Brook to John Moran transmitting official White House Photographer shots of the Dec. 31, 2020 Oval Office meeting (Jan. 5, 2021, 5:20 p.m.)

Key Document A

Introduction by Thomas Fensch

Document ID: 0.7.2774.160403

From: Donoghue, Richard (ODAG) <ricdonoghue@jmd.usdoj.gov>
To: Pak, BJay (USAGAN) <bpak@usa.doj.gov>
Cc:
Bcc:
Subject: FW: [EXTERNAL EMAIL] - Georgia Video Consult
Date: Mon Dec 07 2020 12:48:45 EST
Attachments:

JFYI. Please do not forward.

From: Donoghue, Richard (ODAG)
Sent: Monday, December 7, 2020 12:09 PM
To: Bowdich, David L. (DO) (FBI)
Subject: RE: [EXTERNAL EMAIL] - Georgia Video Consult

Dave,

Thanks for forwarding. It is antiquated indeed.

Unfortunately, this is a continuation of a policy disagreement between the Election Crimes Branch (ECB) of PIN and the AG. While I understand ECB's concerns and the reasons for their historic practice, the AG simply does not agree with what he termed their "passive and delayed enforcement approach" (11/9/20 AG Memorandum) and has clearly directed that Department components should undertake preliminary inquiries and investigations of election-related allegations in certain circumstances even if election-related litigation is still ongoing. While this may be different from ECB's traditional approach (which was essentially to allow election fraud to take its course and hope to deter such misconduct in future elections through intervening prosecutions), the AG gets to make that call. PIN recognizes that much when they say below that he "has ultimate decision-making authority on this issue." As I relayed last night, the AG told me last night that the FBI should conduct some interviews relating the State Farm Arena allegations so that we are not relying entirely on the work/assessments of non-federal law enforcement authorities. It may well be that the GA SOS is correct in concluding that nothing nefarious happened there, but the fact is that millions of Americans have come to believe (rightly or wrongly) that something untoward took place and it is incumbent on the Department to timely conduct a limited investigation to assure the American people that we have looked at these claims. If we come to the same conclusion as the GA SOS, then that should give the public increased confidence in the election results in GA. If we come to a different conclusion, then we'll deal with that. Either way, the AG made it clear that he wants to be sure that we are actually doing our job and not just standing on the sidelines.

While PIN says below that they do not "concur" in proceeding with interviews, their concurrence is not required by the Justice Manual, nor has it ever been required. That is language they use to imply that they have approval/disapproval authority when, in fact, they do not. The only requirement in the Justice Manual is for consultation with PIN and that clearly has been done here. Moreover, given that the AG has specifically directed that the FBI conduct some interviews here (he leaves the number and depth of the interviews entirely up to the FBI), the decision has been made. We all have a chain of command for a reason.

Sorry that you and your team have been dragged into this again. Unfortunately, this is the reality of working here these days.

Thanks and good luck with it.

Rich

From: Bowdich, David L. (DO) (FBI)
Sent: Monday, December 7, 2020 8:18 AM
To: Donoghue, Richard (ODAG) <ricdonoghue@jmd.usdoj.gov<mailto:ricdonoghue@jmd.usdoj.gov>>
Subject: FW: [EXTERNAL EMAIL] - Georgia Video Consult

This is putting us in a bad spot. We need to get this PIN issue settled as to how to proceed. I feel like we are operating under an antiquated thought process here. Everyone understood that before the election we should not do these types of inquiries, but we are in a place right now in this election cycle in which these types of allegations are important to vet out, particularly when many in the country are still questioning the results. I am no lawyer, but my interpretation of the AG's 2020 Memorandum is different from theirs. Let me know your thoughts on how to proceed. Our folks in Atlanta are prepared to begin when they receive direction from me. I am forwarding this to our General Counsel for his analysis as well.

DB

From: (FBI)
Sent: Monday, December 7, 2020 8:01 AM
To: Bowdich, David L. (DO) (FBI)
Subject: FW: [EXTERNAL EMAIL] - Georgia Video Consult

From: (FBI)
Sent: Monday, December 7, 2020 7:51 AM
To: (FBI)
Subject: FW: [EXTERNAL EMAIL] - Georgia Video Consult

FYSA.

From: (FBI)
Sent: Monday, December 07, 2020 5:19 AM
To: (FBI)
Cc:
Subject: Fwd: [EXTERNAL EMAIL] - Georgia Video Consult

Sir, guidance below from PIN in regard to the situation in GA. I have not yet provided to AT.

Introduction by Thomas Fensch

---------- Forwarded message ----------
From: "Amundson, Corey (CRM)"
Date: Dec 7, 2020 12:34 AM
Subject: [EXTERNAL EMAIL] - Georgia Video Consult
To: (FBI)

PIN understands that the FBI proposes to interview certain individuals appearing in a video depicting vote tabulation at State Farm Arena in Georgia as soon as this morning (Monday). PIN also appreciates that the Attorney General may have approved and directed the proposed steps and has ultimate decision-making authority on this issue. PIN nevertheless recognizes our continuing obligation to examine and provide input on the proposed investigative activity under the Justice Manual. Though we anticipate receiving a formal request, we recognize the need for timely input in advance of the interviews. PIN therefore provides this input now based on the information we currently have and with the understanding that additional information might change our input. As explained below, PIN does not concur in any overt investigative activity, including the proposed interviews.

Based on a review of the information provided by the FBI, including a summary of the Secretary of State (SOS) investigation, PIN concludes that the allegations here do not fall within the scope of the Attorney General's Memorandum Regarding Post-Voting Election Irregularity Inquiries (Nov. 9, 2020), which created an exception to the DOJ Election Non-Interference Policy for substantial, clear, apparently credible, and non-speculative allegations of voting and vote tabulation irregularities "that, if true, could potentially impact the outcome of a federal election in an individual State." Accordingly, any overt investigative activity (and only if sufficiently predicated) must wait until the elections in Georgia (including the forthcoming Jan. 5, 2021, special elections) are concluded, their results certified, and all recounts and election contests concluded, pursuant to the DOJ Election Non-Interference Policy (Federal Prosecution of Election Offenses, 8th ed. pp. 84-85).

The same conclusion is compelled by the Attorney General's Memorandum Regarding Election Year Sensitivities (May 15, 2020), which directs that Department employees "must be particularly sensitive to safeguarding the Department's reputation of fairness, neutrality, and nonpartisanship." SOS investigators have already conducted recorded interviews of the individuals at issue and such interviews reportedly revealed nothing to suggest nefarious activity with regard to the integrity of the election. The FBI "re-interviewing" those individuals at this point and under the current circumstances risks great damage to the Department's reputation, including the possible appearance of being motivated by partisan concerns.

Please consult again if and when your office seeks to open a full field and grand jury investigation or wants to pursue overt investigative steps after the elections in your area are concluded, certified, and uncontested. Lastly, it is our practice to note in all concurrences and certain consultations, even as to covert or future activity, that you should be aware and mindful that the Attorney General's Memorandum Regarding Election Year Sensitivities (May 15, 2020), directs, in part, that "[i]f you face an issue, or the appearance of an issue, regarding the timing of statements . . . near the time of a primary or general election, contact the Public Integrity Section of the Criminal Division for further guidance." Please consult as to any proposed press release or statement in this matter.

Corey R. Amundson
Chief | Public Integrity Section

Key Document B

Introduction by Thomas Fensch

Michael, Molly A. EOP/WHO

From:	Michael, Molly A. EOP/WHO
Sent:	Monday, December 14, 2020 4:57 PM
To:	'Jeff.Rosen38@usdoj.gov'
Subject:	From POTUS
Attachments:	Summary Doc.docx; antrim-county-forensics-report.pdf

ANTRIM COUNTY TALKING POINTS

KEY FACTS

- There was a 68% error rate in the votes cast – the Federal Election Committee allowable rate is 0.0008%
- There was an 81.96% rejection rate in the votes cast – these were sent to Adjudication
- The Adjudication files for 2020 were missing, which violates state law
- The Security records for the election software were missing - which violates state law – these also contain the internet connection records
- The election software was changed inside the 90-day Safe Harbor window, which is forbidden by state law – *this automatically decertifies the results*
- Standard security protocols were not followed – software systems were out of date by years, creating a provable security risk
- All Counties in Michigan are required to operate with the same software to guarantee consistent treatment of voters – so errors in the Antrim County software system are determinative of identical errors across the state due to the requirement to use the same software everywhere
- The Secretary of State directed the County Clerks on December 1, 2020, throughout Michigan to delete all of their electronic election records for 2020 by December 8, 2020, in violation of Michigan state law MCL 168.811 requiring retention of voting records for 22 months

TALKING POINTS - EVIDENCE OF INTENTIONAL FRAUD AND CORRUPTION OF THE VOTING MACHINES

- this is the evidence that Dominion Voting machines can and are being manipulated
- This is not human error as we have proven
- Secretary Benson lied
- Federal Law was violated – the election records were destroyed
- This is a Cover-up of voting crimes
    - **Records were missing** in violation of the legal requirements for retention
        - These records exist in this county for previous elections, but not 2020
    - Security records are missing – including the record of internet access to the machines

Introduction by Thomas Fensch

- - o Adjudication records do not exist – there is no ability to tell who or how or to where the "Adjudicated" votes were moved
        - An Administrator reviews votes sent to Adjudication and then can vote them as the wish – no oversight, no transparency, no record, no accountability
  - 68% of votes were switched in this county in error – FEC rules only allow a .0008% error rate
  - 81% of the votes were voted by an Administrator – not by the VOTER
    - o The Voter's choice was not voted by the voter – intervention happened and votes were moved
  - The same Ballots were run it three times and produced three different results
  - Laws have been Broken
  - A Cover-up is Happening regarding the voting machines in Michigan
  - We fought this for the Voters of Michigan whose votes were not accurately counted – we are here for the integrity of the voting process and the will of the People
  - Republicans and Democrats alike had their votes manipulated – all voters were impacted and we must defend their voting rights

CONCLUSIONS

- Based on the violation of law, these election results cannot be certified in Antrim County
- The vast amount of fraud in the votes here demands a review of the votes throughout Michigan
- Security on the Dominion machines was practically non-existent – this is not a secure result
- These same Dominion machines were used throughout Michigan, and the results must be discounted until all Dominion machines can be reviewed for fraudulent vote manipulation
  - o The other 48 counties have been required to use the same certified software – the error rate is a given
- Michigan cannot certify for Biden
- This is a seditious conspiracy to undermine the election process and the will of the American people

ARGUMENTS AGAINST US:

- Errors happen all the time
  - o *Counter:* Not at this massive rate

- *the software is designed to generate 68% errors, which sends the ballots to a file for bulk adjudication, and then an unknown person (or the computer itself) will mass adjudicate the ballots with no oversight*
- It wasn't significant
    - *Counter*: There was an almost 100% change of votes in one precinct alone
    - *this is an intentional design flaw to systematically create fraud*
- It was just in this one township
    - *Counter*: It's indicative of what the machines can and did do to move votes
- It didn't happen everywhere
    - *Counter*: We believe it has happened everywhere – we must review this statewide.
    - *IN fact, the constitution requires we investigate every county*
    - *the election cannot be certified*
- It didn't impact the election
    - *Counter*: It impacted offices and propositions from the President down to the School Board – every office on the ballot was impacted
- It doesn't matter
    - *Counter*: The Election Process is a vital part of the US National Critical Infrastructure – we must know that One Person One Vote is counted
- Only 3 votes for President were impacted
    - *Counter*: The vote swing between Trump and Biden moved by the 1000s
- The Forensics team was not professional
    - *Counter*: Our forensics team was led by a highly decorated military officer, who specializes in cyber security operations and data analytics, working with ta team of the highest-skilled technical cyber forensics experts

INTRODUCTION BY THOMAS FENSCH

Allied Security Operations Group

Antrim Michigan Forensics Report

REVISED PRELIMINARY SUMMARY, v2

Report Date 12/13/2020

Client: Bill Bailey

Attorney: Matthew DePerno

A. **WHO WE ARE**

1. My name is Russell James Ramsland, Jr., and I am a resident of Dallas County, Texas. I hold an MBA from Harvard University, and a political science degree from Duke University. I have worked with the National Aeronautics and Space Administration (NASA) and the Massachusetts Institute of Technology (MIT), among other organizations, and have run businesses all over the world, many of which are highly technical in nature. I have served on technical government panels.

2. I am part of the management team of Allied Security Operations Group, LLC, (ASOG). ASOG is a group of globally engaged professionals who come from various disciplines to include Department of Defense, Secret Service, Department of Homeland Security, and the Central Intelligence Agency. It provides a range of security services, but has a particular emphasis on cybersecurity, open source investigation and penetration testing of networks. We employ a wide variety of cyber and cyber forensic analysts. We have patents pending in a variety of applications from novel network security applications to SCADA (Supervisory Control and Data Acquisition) protection and safe browsing solutions for the dark and deep web. For this report, I have relied on these experts and resources.

B. **PURPOSE AND PRELIMINARY CONCLUSIONS**

1. The purpose of this forensic audit is to test the integrity of Dominion Voting System in how it performed in Antrim County, Michigan for the 2020 election.

2. We conclude that the Dominion Voting System is intentionally and purposefully designed with inherent errors to create systemic fraud and influence election results. The system intentionally generates an enormously high number of ballot errors. The electronic ballots are then transferred for adjudication. The intentional errors lead to bulk adjudication of ballots with no oversight, no transparency, and no audit trail. This leads to voter or election fraud. Based on our study, we conclude that The Dominion Voting System should not be used in Michigan. We further conclude that the results of Antrim County should not have been certified.

3. The following is a breakdown of the votes tabulated for the 2020 election in Antrim County, showing different dates for the tabulation of the same votes.

Date	Registered Voters	Total Votes Cast	Biden	Trump	Third Party	Write-In	TOTAL VOTES for President
Nov 3	22,082	16,047	7,769	4,509	145	14	12,423
Nov 5	22,082	18,059	7,289	9,783	255	20	17,327
Nov 21	22,082	16,044	5,960	9,748	241	23	15,949

4. The Antrim County Clerk and Secretary of State Jocelyn Benson have stated that the election night error (detailed above by the vote "flip" from Trump to Biden, was the result of human error caused by the failure to update the Mancelona Township tabulator prior to election night for a down ballot race. We disagree and conclude that the vote flip occurred because of machine error built into the voting software designed to create error.

5. Secretary of State Jocelyn Benson's statement on November 6, 2020 that "[t]the correct results always were and continue to be reflected on the tabulator totals tape . . . ." was false.

6. The allowable election error rate established by the Federal Election Commission guidelines is of 1 in 250,000 ballots (.0008%). We observed an error rate of 68.05%. This demonstrated a significant and fatal error in security and election integrity.

7. The results of the Antrim County 2020 election are not certifiable. This is a result of machine and/or software error, not human error.

8. The tabulation log for the forensic examination of the server for Antrim County from December 6, 2020consists of 15,676 individual events, of which 10,667 or 68.05% of the events were recorded errors. These errors resulted in overall tabulation errors or ballots being sent to adjudication. This high error rates proves the Dominion Voting System is flawed and does not meet state or federal election laws.

9. These errors occurred after The Antrim County Clerk provided a re-provisioned CF card with uploaded software for the Central Lake Precinct on November 6, 2020. This means the statement by Secretary Benson was false. The Dominion Voting System produced systemic errors and high error rates both prior to the update and after the update; meaning the update (or lack of update) is not the cause of errors.

Introduction by Thomas Fensch

10. In Central Lake Township there were 1,222 ballots **reversed** out of 1,491 total ballots cast, resulting in an 81.96% rejection rate. All reversed ballots are sent to adjudication for a decision by election personnel.

11. It is critical to understand that the Dominion system classifies ballots into two categories, 1) normal ballots and 2) adjudicated ballots. Ballots sent to adjudication can be altered by administrators, and adjudication files can be moved between different Results Tally and Reporting (RTR) terminals with no audit trail of which administrator actually adjudicates (i.e. votes) the ballot batch. This demonstrated a significant and fatal error in security and election integrity because it provides no meaningful observation of the adjudication process or audit trail of which administrator actually adjudicated the ballots.

12. A staggering number of votes required adjudication. This was a 2020 issue not seen in previous election cycles still stored on the server. This is caused by intentional errors in the system. The intentional errors lead to bulk adjudication of ballots with no oversight, no transparency or audit trail. Our examination of the server logs indicates that this high error rate was incongruent with patterns from previous years. The statement attributing these issues to human error is not consistent with the forensic evaluation, which points more correctly to systemic machine and/or software errors. The systemic errors are intentionally designed to create errors in order to push a high volume of ballots to bulk adjudication.

13. The linked video demonstrates how to cheat at adjudication:

    https://mobile.twitter.com/KanekoaTheGreat/status/1336888454538428418

14. Antrim County failed to properly update its system. A purposeful lack of providing basic computer security updates in the system software and hardware demonstrates incompetence, gross negligence, bad faith, and/or willful non-compliance in providing the fundamental system security required by federal and state law. There is no way this election management system could have passed tests or have been legally certified to conduct the 2020 elections in Michigan under the current laws. According to the National Conference of State Legislatures   Michigan requires full compliance with federal standards as determined by a federally accredited voting system laboratory.

15. Significantly, the computer system shows vote adjudication logs for prior years; but all adjudication log entries for the 2020 election cycle are missing. The adjudication process is the simplest way to manually manipulate votes. The lack of records prevents any form of audit accountability, and their conspicuous absence is extremely suspicious since the files exist for previous years using the same software. Removal of these files violates state law and prevents a meaningful audit, even if the Secretary wanted to conduct an audit. We must conclude that the 2020 election cycle records have been manually removed.

16. Likewise, all server security logs prior to 11:03 pm on November 4, 2020 are missing. This means that all security logs for the day after the election, on election day, and prior to election day are gone. Security logs are very important to an audit trail, forensics, and for detecting advanced persistent threats and outside attacks, especially on systems with outdated system files. These logs would contain domain controls, authentication failures, error codes, times users logged on and off, network connections to file servers between file accesses, internet connections, times, and data transfers. Other server logs before November 4, 2020 are present; therefore, there is no reasonable explanation for the security logs to be missing.

17. On November 21, 2020, an unauthorized user unsuccessfully attempted to zero out election results. This demonstrates additional tampering with data.

18. The Election Event Designer Log shows that Dominion ImageCast Precinct Cards were programmed with new ballot programming on 10/23/2020 and then again after the election on 11/05/2020. These system changes affect how ballots are read and tabulated, and our examination demonstrated a significant change in voter results using the two different programs. In accordance with the Help America Vote Act, this violates the 90-day Safe Harbor Period which prohibits changes to election systems, registries, hardware/software updates without undergoing re-certification. According to the National Conference of State Legislatures Michigan requires full compliance with federal standards as determined by a federally accredited voting system laboratory.

19. The only reason to change software after the election would be to obfuscate evidence of fraud and/or to correct program errors that would de-certify the election. Our findings show that the Central Lake Township tabulator tape totals were significantly altered by utilizing two different program versions (10/23/2020 and 11/05/2020), both of which were software changes during an election which violates election law, and not just human error associated with the **Dominion Election Management System.** This is clear evidence of software generated movement of votes. The claims made on the **Office of the Secretary of State** website are false.

20. The Dominion ImageCast Precinct (ICP) machines have the ability to be connected to the internet (see Image 11). By connecting a network scanner to the ethernet port on the ICP machine and creating Packet Capture logs from the machines we examined show the ability to connect to the network, Application Programming Interface (API) (a data exchange between two different systems) calls and web (http) connections to the Election Management System server. Best practice is to disable the network interface card to avoid connection to the internet. This demonstrated a significant and fatal error in security and election integrity. Because certain files have been deleted, we have not yet found origin or destination; but our research continues.

Introduction by Thomas Fensch

21. Because the intentional high error rate generates large numbers of ballots to be adjudicated by election personnel, we must deduce that bulk adjudication occurred. However, because files and adjudication logs are missing, we have not yet determined where the bulk adjudication occurred or who was responsible for it. Our research continues.

22. Research is ongoing. However, based on the preliminary results, we conclude that the errors are so significant that they call into question the integrity and legitimacy of the results in the Antrim County 2020 election to the point that the results are not certifiable. Because the same machines and software are used in 48 other counties in Michigan, this casts doubt on the integrity of the entire election in the state of Michigan.

23. DNI Responsibilities: President Obama signed Executive Order on National Critical Infrastructure on 6 January 2017, stating in Section 1. Cybersecurity of Federal Networks, "The Executive Branch operates its information technology (IT) on behalf of the American people. The President will hold heads of executive departments and agencies (agency heads) accountable for managing cybersecurity risk to their enterprises. In addition, because risk management decisions made by agency heads can affect the risk to the executive branch as a whole, and to national security, it is also the policy of the United States to manage cybersecurity risk as an executive branch enterprise." President Obama's EO further stated, effective immediately, each agency head shall use The Framework for Improving Critical Infrastructure Cybersecurity (the Framework) developed by the National Institute of Standards and Technology." Support to Critical Infrastructure at Greatest Risk. The Secretary of Homeland Security, in coordination with the Secretary of Defense, the Attorney General, the Director of National Intelligence, the Director of the Federal Bureau of Investigation, the heads of appropriate sector-specific agencies, as defined in Presidential Policy Directive 21 of February 12, 2013 (Critical Infrastructure Security and Resilience) (sector-specific agencies), and all other appropriate agency heads, as identified by the Secretary of Homeland Security, shall: (i) identify authorities and capabilities that agencies could employ to support the cybersecurity efforts of critical infrastructure entities identified pursuant to section 9 of Executive Order 13636 of February 12, 2013 (Improving Critical Infrastructure Cybersecurity), to be at greatest risk of attacks that could reasonably result in catastrophic regional or national effects on public health or safety, economic security, or national security (section 9 entities);

    This is a national security imperative. **In July 2018, President Trump strengthened President Obama's Executive Order to include requirements to ensure US election systems, processes, and its people were not manipulated by foreign meddling, either through electronic or systemic manipulation, social media, or physical changes made in hardware, software, or supporting systems.** The 2018 Executive Order. Accordingly, I hereby order:

Section 1. (a) Not later than 45 days after the conclusion of a United States election, the Director of National Intelligence, in consultation with the heads of any other appropriate executive departments and agencies (agencies), shall conduct an assessment of any information indicating that a foreign government, or any person acting as an agent of or on behalf of a foreign government, has acted with the intent or purpose of interfering in that election. The assessment shall identify, to the maximum extent ascertainable, the nature of any foreign interference and any methods employed to execute it, the persons involved, and the foreign government or governments that authorized, directed, sponsored, or supported it. The Director of National Intelligence shall deliver this assessment and appropriate supporting information to the President, the Secretary of State, the Secretary of the Treasury, the Secretary of Defense, the Attorney General, and the Secretary of Homeland Security.

We recommend that an independent group should be empaneled to determine the extent of the adjudication errors throughout the State of Michigan. This is a national security issue.

24. Michigan resident Gustavo Delfino, a former professor of mathematics in Venezuela and alumni of University of Michigan, offered a compelling affidavit [Exhibit 2] recognizing the inherent vulnerabilities in the SmartMatic electronic voting machines (software which was since incorporated into Dominion Voting Systems) during the 2004 national referendum in Venezuela (see attached declaration). After 4 years of research and 3 years of undergoing intensive peer review, Professor Delfino's paper was published in the highly respected "Statistical Science" journal, November 2011 issue (Volume 26, Number 4) with title "Analysis of the 2004 Venezuela Referendum: The Official Results Versus the Petition Signatures." The intensive study used multiple mathematical approaches to ascertain the voting results found in the 2004 Venezuelan referendum. Delfino and his research partners discovered not only the algorithm used to manipulate the results, but also the precise location in the election processing sequence where vulnerability in machine processing would provide such an opportunity. According to Prof Delfino, the magnitude of the difference between the official and the true result in Venezuela estimated at 1,370,000 votes. Our investigation into the error rates and results of the Antrim County voting tally reflect the same tactics, which have also been reported in other Michigan counties as well. This demonstrates a national security issue.

C. **PROCESS**

We visited Antrim County twice: November 27, 2020 and December 6, 2020.

On November 27, 2020, we visited Central Lake Township, Star Township, and Mancelona Township. We examined the Dominion Voting Systems tabulators and tabulator roles.

INTRODUCTION BY THOMAS FENSCH

On December 6, 2020, we visited the Antrim County Clerk's office. We inspected and performed forensic duplication of the following:

1. **Antrim County Election Management Server** running **Dominion Democracy Suite** 5.5.3-002;

2. **Compact Flash** cards used by the local precincts in their **Dominion ImageCast Precinct**;

3. **USB memory sticks** used by the **Dominion VAT** (Voter Assist Terminals); and

4. **USB memory sticks** used for the Poll Book.

Dominion voting system is a Canadian owned company with global subsidiaries. It is owned by Staple Street Capital which is in turn owned by UBS Securities LLC, of which 3 out of their 7 board members are Chinese nationals. The Dominion software is licensed from Smartmatic which is a Venezuelan owned and controlled company. Dominion Server locations have been determined to be in Serbia, Canada, the US, Spain and Germany.

D. CENTRAL LAKE TOWNSHIP

1. On November 27, 2020, part of our forensics team visited the Central Lake Township in Michigan to inspect the **Dominion ImageCast Precint** for possible hardware issues on behalf of a local lawsuit filed by Michigan attorney Matthew DePerno on behalf of William Bailey. In our conversations with the clerk of **Central Lake Township** Ms. Judith L. Kosloski, she presented to us "two separate paper totals tape" from Tabulator ID 2.

    - One dated "Poll Opened Nov. 03/2020 06:38:48" (Roll 1);
    - Another dated "Poll Opened Nov. 06/2020 09:21:58" (Roll 2).

2. We were then told by Ms. Kosloski that on November 5, 2020, Ms. Kosloski was notified by Connie Wing of the County Clerk's Office and asked to bring the tabulator and ballots to the County Clerk's office for re-tabulation. They ran the ballots and printed "Roll 2". She noticed a difference in the votes and brought it up to the clerk, but canvasing still occurred, and her objections were not addressed.

3. Our team analyzed both rolls and compared the results. Roll 1 had **1,494** total votes and Roll 2 had **1,491** votes (Roll 2 had 3 less ballots because 3 ballots were damaged in the process.)

4. "Statement of Votes Cast from Antrim" shows that only **1,491** votes were counted, and the **3** ballots that were damaged were not entered into final results.

5. Ms. Kosloski stated that she and her assistant manually refilled out the three ballots, curing them, and ran them through the ballot counting system - but the final numbers do not reflect the inclusion of those 3 damaged ballots.

6. This is the most preliminary report of serious election fraud indicators. In comparing the numbers on both rolls, *we estimate **1,474** votes changed* across the two rolls, between the first and the second time the exact same ballots were run through the County Clerk's vote counting machine - *which is almost the same number of voters that voted in total.*

   - ***742** votes were added to* **School Board Member for Central Lake Schools (3)**

   - ***657** votes were removed from* **School Board Member for Ellsworth Schools (2)**

   - **7** votes were added to the total for **State Proposal 20-1 (1)** and out of those there were **611** votes moved between the Yes and No Categories.

7. There were incremental changes throughout the rolls with some significant adjustments between the 2 rolls that were reviewed. This demonstrates conclusively that votes can be and were changed during the second machine count after the software update. That should be impossible especially at such a high percentage to total votes cast.

8. For the **School Board Member for Central Lake Schools (3)** [Image 1] there were **742 votes** added to this vote total. Since multiple people were elected, this did not change the result of both candidates being elected, but one does see a change in who had most votes. If it were a single-person election this would have changed the outcome and demonstrates conclusively that votes can be and were changed during the second machine counting. That should be impossible.

[Image 1]:

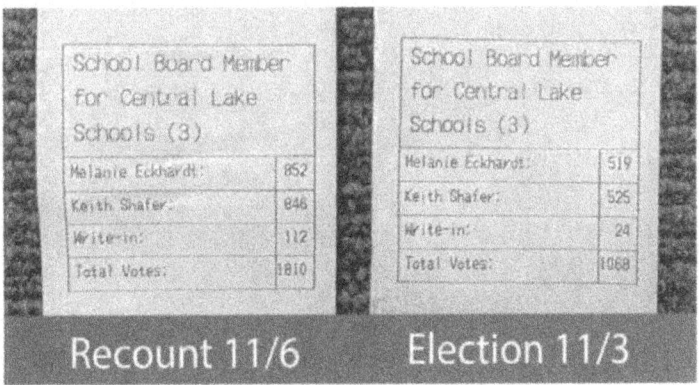

9. For the **School Board Member for Ellsworth Schools (2)** [Image 2]

   - Shows *657 votes being removed* from this election.

   - In this case, only **3** people who were eligible to vote actually voted. Since there were **2** votes allowed for each voter to cast.

   - The recount correctly shows **6** votes.

   But on election night, there was a major calculation issue:

   [Image 2]:

   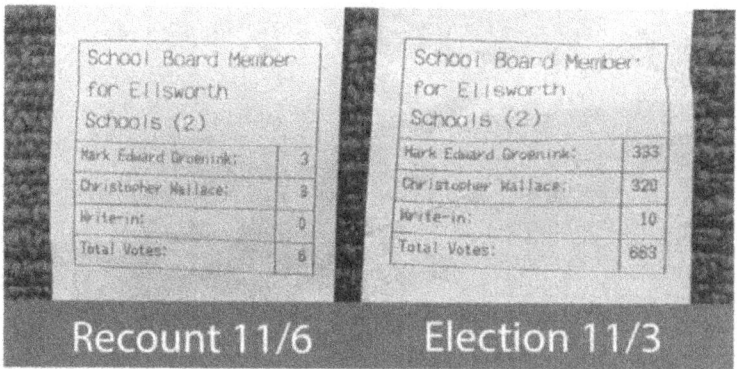

10. In **State Proposal 20-1 (1)**, [Image 3] there is a major change in votes in this category.

    - There were **774 votes for YES** during the election, to **1,083 votes for YES** on the recount a change of **309 votes**.

    - 7 votes were added to the total for **State Proposal 20-1 (1)** out of those there were **611** votes moved between the Yes and No Categories.

    [Image 3]:

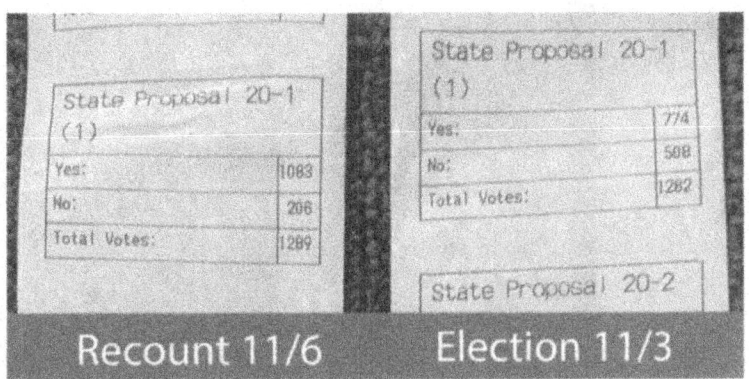

11. **State Proposal 20-1 (1)** is a fairly technical and complicated proposed amendment to the Michigan Constitution to change the disposition and allowable uses of future revenue generated from oil and gas bonuses, rentals and royalties from state-owned land. Information about the proposal: https://crcmich.org/publications/statewide-ballot- proposal-20-1-michigan-natural-resources-trust-fund

12. A Proposed Initiated **Ordinance to Authorize One (1) Marihuana (sic) Retailer Establishment Within the Village of Central Lake (1)**. [Image 4]

    - On election night, it was a tie vote.

    - Then, on the rerun of ballots 3 ballots were destroyed, but only one vote changed on the totals to allow the proposal to pass.

    When **3 ballots were not counted** and **programming change on the tabulator was installed** the proposal **passed with 1 vote being removed from the No** vote.

    [Image 4]:

INTRODUCTION BY THOMAS FENSCH

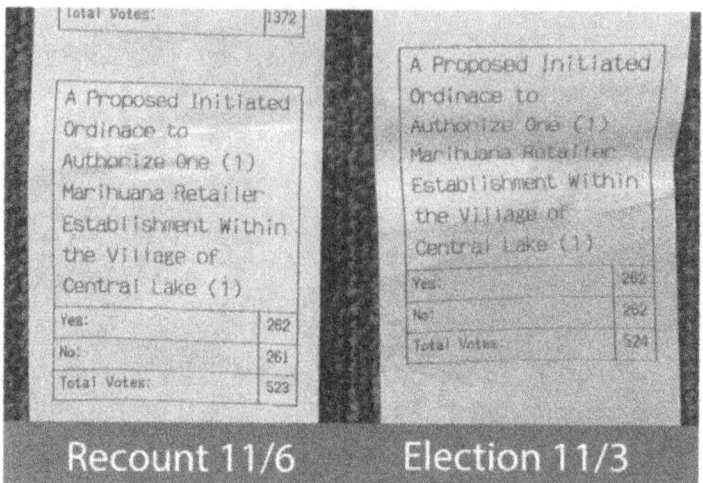

13. On Sunday December 6, 2020, our forensics team visited the Antrim County Clerk. There were two USB memory sticks used, one contained the software package used to tabulate election results on November 3, 2020, and the other was programmed on November 6, 2020 with a different software package which yielded significantly different voting outcomes. The election data package is used by the **Dominion Democracy Suite** software & election management system software to upload programming information onto the Compact Flash Cards for the **Dominion ImageCast Precinct** to enable it to calculate ballot totals.

14. This software programming should be standard across all voting machines systems for the duration of the entire election if accurate tabulation is the expected outcome as required by US Election Law. This intentional difference in software programming is a design feature to alter election outcomes.

15. The election day outcomes were calculated using the original software programming on November 3, 2020. On November 5, 2020 the township clerk was asked to re-run the Central Lake Township ballots and was given no explanation for this unusual request. On November 6, 2020 the Antrim County Clerk, Sheryl Guy issued the second version of software to re-run the same Central Lake Township ballots and oversaw the process. This resulted in greater than a 60% change in voting results, inexplicably impacting every single election contest in a township with less than 1500 voters. These errors far exceed the ballot error rate standard of 1 in 250,000 ballots (.0008%) as required by federal election law.

- The original election programming files are last dated 09/25/2020 1:24pm

- The updated election data package files are last dated 10/22/2020 10:27 am.

16. As the tabulator tape totals prove, there were large numbers of votes switched from the November 3, 2020 tape to the November 6, 2020 tape. This was solely based on using different software versions of the operating program to calculate votes, not tabulate votes. This is evidenced by using same the Dominion System with two different software program versions contained on the two different USB Memory Devices.

17. The Help America Vote Act, Safe Harbor provides a 90-day period prior to elections where no changes can be made to election systems. To make changes would require recertification of the entire system for use in the election. The Dominion User Guide prescribes the proper procedure to test machines with test ballots to compare the results to validate machine functionality to determine if the **Dominion ImageCast Precinct** was programmed correctly. If this occurred a ballot misconfiguration would have been identified. Once the software was updated to the 10/22/2020 software the test ballots should have been re-run to validate the vote totals to confirm the machine was configured correctly.

18. The November 6, 2020 note from **The Office of the Secretary of State Jocelyn Benson** states: "The correct results always were and continue to be reflected on the tabulator totals tape and on the ballots themselves. Even if the error in the reported unofficial results had not been quickly noticed, it would have been identified during the county canvass. Boards of County Canvassers, which are composed of 2 Democrats and 2 Republicans, review the printed totals tape from each tabulator during the canvass to verify the reported vote totals are correct."

    - Source: https://www.michigan.gov/sos/0,4670,7-127-1640_9150-544676--,00.html

19. The **Secretary of State Jocelyn Benson's** statement is false. Our findings show that the tabulator tape totals were significantly altered by utilization of two different program versions, and not just the **Dominion Election Management System**. This is the opposite of the claim that the **Office of the Secretary of State** made on its website. The fact that these significant errors were not caught in ballot testing and not caught by the local county clerk shows that there are major inherent built-in vulnerabilities and process flaws in the **Dominion Election Management System**, and that other townships/precincts and the entire election have been affected.

20. On Sunday December 6, 2020, our forensics team visited the Antrim County Clerk office to perform forensic duplication of the **Antrim County Election Management Server** running **Dominion Democracy Suite** 5.5.3-002.

21. Forensic copies of the **Compact Flash** cards used by the local precincts in their **Dominion ImageCast Precinct** were inspected, **USB memory sticks** used by the **Dominion VAT** (Voter Assist Terminals) and the **USB memory sticks** used for the Poll Book were forensically duplicated.

22. We have been told that the ballot design and configuration for the **Dominion ImageCast Precinct** and VAT were provided by **ElectionSource.com** which is which is owned by MC&E, Inc of Grand Rapids, MI.

E. **MANCELONA TOWNSHIP**

1. In Mancelona township, problems with software versions were also known to have been present. Mancelona elections officials understood that ballot processing issued were not accurate and used the second version of software to process votes on 4 November, again an election de-certifying event, as no changes to the election system are authorized by law in the 90 days preceding elections without re-certification.

2. Once the 10/22/2020 software update was performed on the Dominion ImageCast Precinct the test ballot process should have been performed to validate the programming. There is no indication that this procedure was performed.

F. **ANTRIM COUNTY CLERK'S OFFICE**

1. Pursuant to a court ordered inspection, we participated in an onsite collection effort at the Antrim County Clerk's office on December 6, 2020. [Image 5]:

Among other items forensically collected, the Antrim County Election Management Server (EMS) with Democracy Suite was forensically collected. [Images 6 and 7].

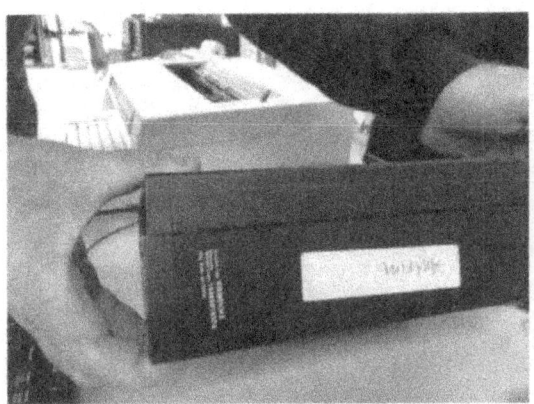 

The EMS (Election Management Server) was a:

Dell Precision Tower 3420.

Service Tag: 6NB0KH2

The EMS contained 2 hard drives in a RAID-1 configuration. That is the 2 drives redundantly stored the same information and the server could continue to operate if either of the 2 hard drives failed. The EMS was booted via the Linux Boot USB memory sticks and both hard drives were forensically imaged.

At the onset of the collection process we observed that the initial program thumb drive was not secured in the vault with the CF cards and other thumbdrives. We watched as the County employees, including Clerk Sheryl Guy searched throughout the office for the missing thumb drive. Eventually they found the missing thumb drive in an unsecured and unlocked desk drawer along with multiple other random thumb drives. This demonstrated a significant and fatal error in security and election integrity.

G. **FORENSIC COLLECTION**

We used a built for purpose Linux Boot USB memory stick to boot the EMS in a forensically sound mode. We then used Ewfacquire to make a forensic image of the 2 independent internal hard drives.

Ewfacquire created an E01 file format forensic image with built-in integrity verification via MD5 hash.

We used Ewfverify to verify the forensic image acquired was a true and accurate copy of the original disk. That was done for both forensic images.

H. **ANALYSIS TOOLS**

INTRODUCTION BY THOMAS FENSCH

X-Ways Forensics: We used X-Ways Forensics, a commercial Computer Forensic tool, to verify the image was useable and full disk encryption was not in use. In particular we confirmed that Bit locker was not in use on the EMS.

Other tools used: PassMark OSForensics, Truxton - Forensics, Cellebrite Physical Analyzer, Blackbag-Blacklight Forensic Software, Microsoft SQL Server Management Studio, Virtual Box, and miscellaneous other tools and scripts.

I. SERVER OVERVIEW AND SUMMARY

1. Our initial audit on the computer running the Democracy Suite Software showed that standard computer security best practices were not applied. These minimum-security standards are outlined the 2002 HAVA, and FEC Voting System Standards it did not even meet the minimum standards required of a government desktop computer.

2. The election data software package USB drives (November 2020 election, and November 2020 election updated) are secured with bitlocker encryption software, but they were not stored securely on-site. At the time of our forensic examination, the election data package files were already moved to an unsecure desktop computer and were residing on an unencrypted hard drive. This demonstrated a significant and fatal error in security and election integrity. Key Findings on Desktop and Server Configuration: - There were multiple Microsoft security updates as well as Microsoft SQL Server updates which should have been deployed, however there is no evidence that these security patches were ever installed. As described below, many of the software packages were out of date and vulnerable to various methods of attack.

   a) Computer initial configuration on 10/03/2018 13:08:11:911

   b) Computer final configuration of server software on 4/10/2019

   c) Hard Drive not Encrypted at Rest

   d) Microsoft SQL Server Database not protected with password.

   e) Democracy Suite Admin Passwords are reused and share passwords.

   f) Antivirus is 4.5 years outdated

   g) Windows updates are 3.86 years out of date.

   h) When computer was last configured on 04/10/2019 the windows updates were 2.11 years out of date.

   i) User of computer uses a Super User Account.

3. The hard drive was not encrypted at rest which means that if hard drives are removed or initially booted off an external USB drive the files are susceptible to manipulation directly. An attacker is able to mount the hard drive because it is unencrypted, allowing for the manipulation and replacement of any file on the system.

4. The Microsoft SQL Server database files were not properly secured to allow modifications of the database files.

5. The Democracy Suite Software user account logins and passwords are stored in the unsecured database tables and the multiple Election System Administrator accounts share the same password, which means that there are no audit trails for vote changes, deletions, blank ballot voting, or batch vote alterations or adjudication.

6. Antivirus definition is 1666 days old on 12/11/2020. Antrim County updates its system with USB drives. USB drives are the most common vectors for injecting malware into computer systems. The failure to properly update the antivirus definition drastically increases the harm cause by malware from other machines being transmitted to the voting system.

7. Windows Server Update Services (WSUS) Offline Update is used to enable updates the computer which is a package of files normally downloaded from the internet but compiled into a program to put on a USB drive to manually update server systems.

8. Failure to properly update the voting system demonstrates a significant and fatal error in security and election integrity.

9. There are 15 additional updates that should have been installed on the server to adhere to Microsoft Standards to fix known vulnerabilities. For the 4/10/2019 install, the most updated version of the update files would have been 03/13/2019 which is 11.6.1 which is 15 updates newer than 10.9.1

This means the updates installed were 2 years, 1 month, 13 days behind the most current update at the time. This includes security updates and fixes. This demonstrated a significant and fatal error in security and election integrity.

- Wed 04/10/2019 10:34:33.14 - Info: Starting WSUS Offline Update (v. 10.9.1)

- Wed 04/10/2019 10:34:33.14 - Info: Used path "D:\WSUSOFFLINE1091 2012R2 W10\cmd\" on EMSSERVER (user: EMSADMIN)

- Wed 04/10/2019 10:34:35.55 - Info: Medium build date: 03/10/2019

Introduction by Thomas Fensch

- Found on c:\Windows\wsusofflineupdate.txt
- *WSUS Offline Update (v.10.9.1) was created on 01/29/2017

*WSUS information found here https://download.wsusoffline.net/

10. Super User Administrator account is the primary account used to operate the **Dominion Election Management System** which is a major security risk. The user logged in has the ability to make major changes to the system and install software which means that there is no oversight to ensure appropriate management controls i.e. anyone who has access to the shared administrator user names and passwords can make significant changes to the entire voting system. The shared usernames and passwords mean that these changes can be made in an anonymous fashion with no tracking or attribution.

J. ERROR RATES

1. We reviewed the Tabulation logs in their entirety for 11/6/2020. The election logs for Antrim County consist of 15,676 total lines or events.

   - Of the 15,676 there were a total of 10,667 critical errors/warnings or a 68.05% error rate.
   - Most of the errors were related to configuration errors that could result in overall tabulation errors or adjudication. These 11/6/2020 tabulation totals were used as the official results.

2. For examples, there were 1,222 ballots **reversed** out of 1,491 total ballots cast, thus resulting in an 81.96% rejection rate. Some of which were reversed due to "Ballot's size exceeds maximum expected ballot size".

   - According to the NCSL, Michigan requires testing by a federally accredited laboratory for voting systems. In section 4.1.1 of the Voluntary Voting Systems Guidelines (VVSG) Accuracy Requirements a. **All systems shall achieve a report total error rate of no more than one in 125,000.**
   - https://www.eac.gov/sites/default/files/eac_assets/1/28/VVSG.1.1.VOL.1.FINAL1.pdf
   - In section 4.1.3.2 Memory Stability of the VVSG it states that **Memory devices used to retain election management data shall have demonstrated error free data retention for a period of 22 months.**
   - In section 4.1.6.1 Paper-based System Processing Requirements sub-section a. of the VVSG it states "The ability of the system to produce and receive electronic signals from the scanning of the ballot, perform logical and numerical operations upon these data, and reproduce the contents of memory when required **shall** be sufficiently free of **error** to enable

satisfaction of the system-level accuracy requirement indicated in Subsection 4.1.1."

- These are not human errors; this is definitively related to the software and software configurations resulting in error rates far beyond the thresholds listed in the guidelines.

3. A high "error rate" in the election software (in this case 68.05%) reflects an algorithm used that will weight one candidate greater than another (for instance, weight a specific candidate at a 2/3 to approximately 1/3 ratio). In the logs we identified that the RCV or Ranked Choice Voting Algorithm was enabled (see image below from the Dominion manual). This allows the user to apply a weighted numerical value to candidates and change the overall result. The declaration of winners can be done on a basis of points, not votes. [Image 8]:

choice voting results are evaluated on a district per district basis and each district has a set number of points (100). Elimination and declaration of winners is done on basis of points, not votes.

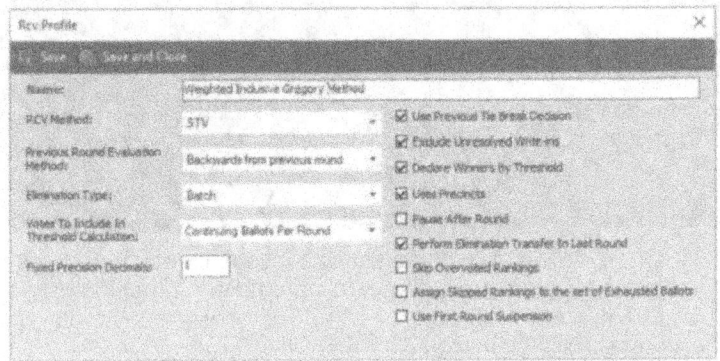

Figure 11-3: RCV Profile screen

4. The Dominion software configuration logs in the Divert Options, shows that all write-in ballots were flagged to be diverted automatically for adjudication. This means that all write-in ballots were sent for "adjudication" by a poll worker or election official to process the ballot based on voter "intent". Adjudication files allow a computer operator to decide to whom to award those votes (or to trash them).

5. In the logs all but two of the Override Options were enabled on these machines, thus allowing any operator to change those votes. [Image 9]:

6. In the logs all but two of the Override Options were enabled on these machines, thus allowing any operator to change those votes. This gives the system operators carte blanche to adjudicate ballots, in this case 81.96% of the total cast ballots with no audit trail or oversight. [Image 10]:

7. On 12/8/2020 Microsoft issued 58 security patches across 10+ products, some of which were used for the election software machine, server and programs. Of the 58 security fixes 22, were patches to remote code execution (RCE) vulnerabilities. [Image 11]:

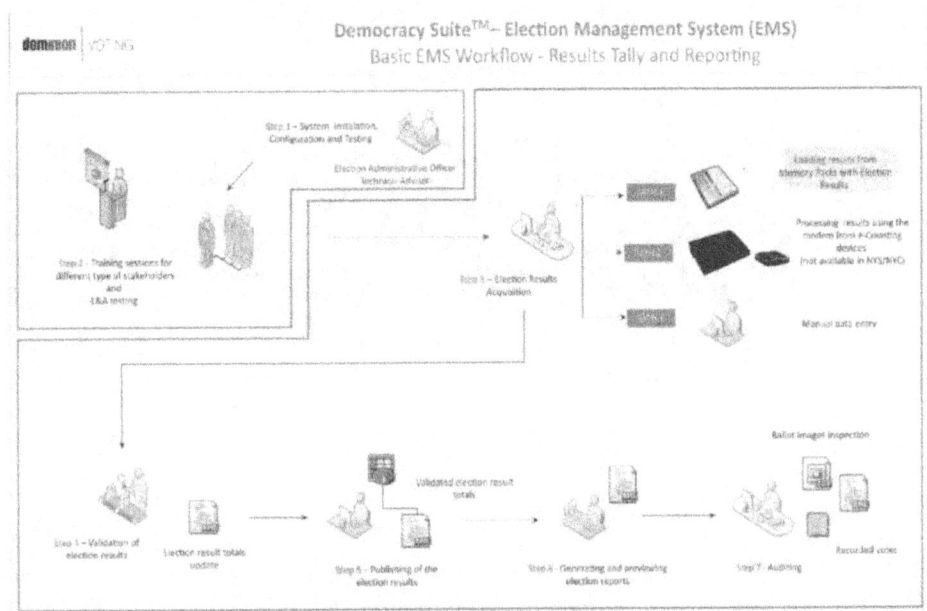

8. We reviewed the Election Management System logs (EmsLogger) in their entirety from 9/19/2020 through 11/21/2020 for the Project: Antrim November 2020. There were configuration errors throughout the set-up, election and tabulation of results. The last error for Central Lake Township, Precinct 1 occurred on 11/21/2020 at 14:35:11 System.Xml.XmlException System.Xml.XmlException: The ' ' character, hexadecimal value 0x20, cannot be included in a name. Bottom line is that this is a calibration that rejects the vote (see picture below). [Image 12]:

INTRODUCTION BY THOMAS FENSCH

Notably 42 minutes earlier on Nov 21 2020 at 13:53:09 a user attempted to zero out election results. Id:3168 EmsLogger - There is no permission to {0} - Project: User: Thread: 189. This is direct proof of an attempt to tamper with evidence.

9. The Election Event Designer Log shows that Dominion ImageCast Precinct Cards were programmed with updated new programming on 10/23/2020 and again after the election on 11/05/2020. As previously mentioned, this violates the HAVA safe harbor period.

   Source: C:\Program Files\Dominion Voting Systems\Election Event Designer\Log\Info.txt

   - Dominion Imagecast Precinct Cards Programmed with 9/25/2020 programming on 09/29/2020, 09/30/2020, and 10/12/2020.

   - Dominion Imagecast Precinct Cards Programmed with New Ballot Programming dated 10/22/2020 on 10/23/2020 and after the election on 11/05/2020

   Excerpt from 2020-11-05 showing "ProgramMemoryCard" commands.

10. Analysis is ongoing and updated findings will be submitted as soon as possible. A summary of the information collected is provided below.

```
10|12/07/20 18:52:30| Indexing completed at Mon Dec 7 18:52:30 2020
12|12/07/20 18:52:30| INDEX SUMMARY
12|12/07/20 18:52:30| Files indexed: 159312
```

```
12|12/07/20 18:52:30| Files skipped: 64799
12|12/07/20 18:52:30| Files filtered: 0
12|12/07/20 18:52:30| Emails indexed: 0
12|12/07/20 18:52:30| Unique words found: 5325413
12|12/07/20 18:52:30| Variant words found: 3597634
12|12/07/20 18:52:30| Total words found: 239446085
12|12/07/20 18:52:30| Avg. unique words per page: 33.43
12|12/07/20 18:52:30| Avg. words per page: 1503
12|12/07/20 18:52:30| Peak physical memory used: 2949 MB
12|12/07/20 18:52:30| Peak virtual memory used: 8784 MB
12|12/07/20 18:52:30| Errors: 10149
12|12/07/20 18:52:30| Total bytes scanned/downloaded: 1919289906
```

Dated: December 13, 2020

Russell Ramsland

Key Document C

Introduction by Thomas Fensch

Watson, Theresa (OAG)

From:	Watson, Theresa (OAG)
Sent:	Monday, December 14, 2020 4:59 PM
To:	Schneider, Matthew (USAMIE); Birge, Andrew B. (USAMIW)
Subject:	Documents
Attachments:	Antrim County Talking Points.pdf; Antrim Michigan Forensics Report.pdf

See attachments per Rich Donoghue.

Theresa J. Watson-Walker
Office Manager & Confidential Assistant
Office of the Attorney General
U.S. Department of Justice
Office: 202-514-9755

ANTRIM COUNTY TALKING POINTS

KEY FACTS

- There was a 68% error rate in the votes cast – the Federal Election Committee allowable rate is 0.0008%
- There was an 81.96% rejection rate in the votes cast – these were sent to Adjudication
- The Adjudication files for 2020 were missing, which violates state law
- The Security records for the election software were missing - which violates state law – these also contain the internet connection records
- The election software was changed inside the 90-day Safe Harbor window, which is forbidden by state law – *this automatically decertifies the results*
- Standard security protocols were not followed – software systems were out of date by years, creating a provable security risk
- All Counties in Michigan are required to operate with the same software to guarantee consistent treatment of voters – so errors in the Antrim County software system are determinative of identical errors across the state due to the requirement to use the same software everywhere
- The Secretary of State directed the County Clerks on December 1, 2020, throughout Michigan to delete all of their electronic election records for 2020 by December 8, 2020, in violation of Michigan state law MCL 168.811 requiring retention of voting records for 22 months

TALKING POINTS - EVIDENCE OF INTENTIONAL FRAUD AND CORRUPTION OF THE VOTING MACHINES

- this is the evidence that Dominion Voting machines can and are being manipulated
- This is not human error as we have proven
- Secretary Benson lied
- Federal Law was violated – the election records were destroyed
- This is a Cover-up of voting crimes
    - Records were missing in violation of the legal requirements for retention
        - These records exist in this county for previous elections, but not 2020
    - Security records are missing – including the record of internet access to the machines

Introduction by Thomas Fensch

- - o Adjudication records do not exist – there is no ability to tell who or how or to where the "Adjudicated" votes were moved
    - ▪ An Administrator reviews votes sent to Adjudication and then can vote them as the wish – no oversight, no transparency, no record, no accountability
  - 68% of votes were switched in this county in error – FEC rules only allow a .0008% error rate
  - 81% of the votes were voted by an Administrator – not by the VOTER
    - o The Voter's choice was not voted by the voter – intervention happened and votes were moved
  - The same Ballots were run it three times and produced three different results
  - Laws have been Broken
  - A Cover-up is Happening regarding the voting machines in Michigan
  - We fought this for the Voters of Michigan whose votes were not accurately counted – we are here for the integrity of the voting process and the will of the People
  - Republicans and Democrats alike had their votes manipulated – all voters were impacted and we must defend their voting rights

CONCLUSIONS

- Based on the violation of law, these election results cannot be certified in Antrim County
- The vast amount of fraud in the votes here demands a review of the votes throughout Michigan
- Security on the Dominion machines was practically non-existent – this is not a secure result
- These same Dominion machines were used throughout Michigan, and the results must be discounted until all Dominion machines can be reviewed for fraudulent vote manipulation
  - o The other 48 counties have been required to use the same certified software – the error rate is a given
- Michigan cannot certify for Biden
- This is a seditious conspiracy to undermine the election process and the will of the American people

ARGUMENTS AGAINST US:

- Errors happen all the time
  - o *Counter*: Not at this massive rate

Subverting Justice

- - - -
    - the software is designed to generate 68% errors, which sends the ballots to a file for bulk adjudication, and then an unknown person (or the computer itself) will mass adjudicate the ballots with no oversight
- It wasn't significant
    - *Counter*: There was an almost 100% change of votes in one precinct alone
    - this is an intentional design flaw to systematically create fraud
- It was just in this one township
    - *Counter*: It's indicative of what the machines can and did do to move votes
- It didn't happen everywhere
    - *Counter*: We believe it has happened everywhere – we must review this statewide.
    - IN fact, the constitution requires we investigate every county
    - the election cannot be certified
- It didn't impact the election
    - *Counter*: It impacted offices and propositions from the President down to the School Board – every office on the ballot was impacted
- It doesn't matter
    - *Counter*: The Election Process is a vital part of the US National Critical Infrastructure – we must know that One Person One Vote is counted
- Only 3 votes for President were impacted
    - *Counter*: The vote swing between Trump and Biden moved by the 1000s
- The Forensics team was not professional
    - *Counter*: Our forensics team was led by a highly decorated military officer, who specializes in cyber security operations and data analytics, working with ta team of the highest-skilled technical cyber forensics experts

INTRODUCTION BY THOMAS FENSCH

Allied Security Operations Group

Antrim Michigan Forensics Report
REVISED PRELIMINARY SUMMARY, v2
Report Date 12/13/2020

Client: Bill Bailey

Attorney: Matthew DePerno

A. **WHO WE ARE**

1. My name is Russell James Ramsland, Jr., and I am a resident of Dallas County, Texas. I hold an MBA from Harvard University, and a political science degree from Duke University. I have worked with the National Aeronautics and Space Administration (NASA) and the Massachusetts Institute of Technology (MIT), among other organizations, and have run businesses all over the world, many of which are highly technical in nature. I have served on technical government panels.

2. I am part of the management team of Allied Security Operations Group, LLC, (ASOG). ASOG is a group of globally engaged professionals who come from various disciplines to include Department of Defense, Secret Service, Department of Homeland Security, and the Central Intelligence Agency. It provides a range of security services, but has a particular emphasis on cybersecurity, open source investigation and penetration testing of networks. We employ a wide variety of cyber and cyber forensic analysts. We have patents pending in a variety of applications from novel network security applications to SCADA (Supervisory Control and Data Acquisition) protection and safe browsing solutions for the dark and deep web. For this report, I have relied on these experts and resources.

B. **PURPOSE AND PRELIMINARY CONCLUSIONS**

1. The purpose of this forensic audit is to test the integrity of Dominion Voting System in how it performed in Antrim County, Michigan for the 2020 election.

2. We conclude that the Dominion Voting System is intentionally and purposefully designed with inherent errors to create systemic fraud and influence election results. The system intentionally generates an enormously high number of ballot errors. The electronic ballots are then transferred for adjudication. The intentional errors lead to bulk adjudication of ballots with no oversight, no transparency, and no audit trail. This leads to voter or election fraud. Based on our study, we conclude that The Dominion Voting System should not be used in Michigan. We further conclude that the results of Antrim County should not have been certified.

3. The following is a breakdown of the votes tabulated for the 2020 election in Antrim County, showing different dates for the tabulation of the same votes.

Date	Registered Voters	Total Votes Cast	Biden	Trump	Third Party	Write-In	TOTAL VOTES for President
Nov 3	22,082	16,047	7,769	4,509	145	14	12,423
Nov 5	22,082	18,059	7,289	9,783	255	20	17,327
Nov 21	22,082	16,044	5,960	9,748	241	23	15,949

4. The Antrim County Clerk and Secretary of State Jocelyn Benson have stated that the election night error (detailed above by the vote "flip" from Trump to Biden, was the result of human error caused by the failure to update the Mancelona Township tabulator prior to election night for a down ballot race. We disagree and conclude that the vote flip occurred because of machine error built into the voting software designed to create error.

5. Secretary of State Jocelyn Benson's statement on November 6, 2020 that "[t]he correct results always were and continue to be reflected on the tabulator totals tape . . . ." was false.

6. The allowable election error rate established by the Federal Election Commission guidelines is of 1 in 250,000 ballots (.0008%). We observed an error rate of 68.05%. This demonstrated a significant and fatal error in security and election integrity.

7. The results of the Antrim County 2020 election are not certifiable. This is a result of machine and/or software error, not human error.

8. The tabulation log for the forensic examination of the server for Antrim County from December 6, 2020consists of 15,676 individual events, of which 10,667 or 68.05% of the events were recorded errors. These errors resulted in overall tabulation errors or ballots being sent to adjudication. This high error rates proves the Dominion Voting System is flawed and does not meet state or federal election laws.

9. These errors occurred after The Antrim County Clerk provided a re-provisioned CF card with uploaded software for the Central Lake Precinct on November 6, 2020. This means the statement by Secretary Benson was false. The Dominion Voting System produced systemic errors and high error rates both prior to the update and after the update; meaning the update (or lack of update) is not the cause of errors.

Introduction by Thomas Fensch

10. In Central Lake Township there were 1,222 ballots **reversed** out of 1,491 total ballots cast, resulting in an 81.96% rejection rate. All reversed ballots are sent to adjudication for a decision by election personnel.

11. It is critical to understand that the Dominion system classifies ballots into two categories, 1) normal ballots and 2) adjudicated ballots. Ballots sent to adjudication can be altered by administrators, and adjudication files can be moved between different Results Tally and Reporting (RTR) terminals with no audit trail of which administrator actually adjudicates (i.e. votes) the ballot batch. This demonstrated a significant and fatal error in security and election integrity because it provides no meaningful observation of the adjudication process or audit trail of which administrator actually adjudicated the ballots.

12. A staggering number of votes required adjudication. This was a 2020 issue not seen in previous election cycles still stored on the server. This is caused by intentional errors in the system. The intentional errors lead to bulk adjudication of ballots with no oversight, no transparency or audit trail. Our examination of the server logs indicates that this high error rate was incongruent with patterns from previous years. The statement attributing these issues to human error is not consistent with the forensic evaluation, which points more correctly to systemic machine and/or software errors. The systemic errors are intentionally designed to create errors in order to push a high volume of ballots to bulk adjudication.

13. The linked video demonstrates how to cheat at adjudication:

    https://mobile.twitter.com/KanekoaTheGreat/status/1336888454538428418

14. Antrim County failed to properly update its system. A purposeful lack of providing basic computer security updates in the system software and hardware demonstrates incompetence, gross negligence, bad faith, and/or willful non-compliance in providing the fundamental system security required by federal and state law. There is no way this election management system could have passed tests or have been legally certified to conduct the 2020 elections in Michigan under the current laws. According to the National Conference of State Legislatures – Michigan requires full compliance with federal standards as determined by a federally accredited voting system laboratory.

15. Significantly, the computer system shows vote adjudication logs for prior years; but all adjudication log entries for the 2020 election cycle are missing. The adjudication process is the simplest way to manually manipulate votes. The lack of records prevents any form of audit accountability, and their conspicuous absence is extremely suspicious since the files exist for previous years using the same software. Removal of these files violates state law and prevents a meaningful audit, even if the Secretary wanted to conduct an audit. We must conclude that the 2020 election cycle records have been manually removed.

16. Likewise, all server security logs prior to 11:03 pm on November 4, 2020 are missing. This means that all security logs for the day after the election, on election day, and prior to election day are gone. Security logs are very important to an audit trail, forensics, and for detecting advanced persistent threats and outside attacks, especially on systems with outdated system files. These logs would contain domain controls, authentication failures, error codes, times users logged on and off, network connections to file servers between file accesses, internet connections, times, and data transfers. Other server logs before November 4, 2020 are present; therefore, there is no reasonable explanation for the security logs to be missing.

17. On November 21, 2020, an unauthorized user unsuccessfully attempted to zero out election results. This demonstrates additional tampering with data.

18. The Election Event Designer Log shows that Dominion ImageCast Precinct Cards were programmed with new ballot programming on 10/23/2020 and then again after the election on 11/05/2020. These system changes affect how ballots are read and tabulated, and our examination demonstrated a significant change in voter results using the two different programs. In accordance with the Help America Vote Act, this violates the 90-day Safe Harbor Period which prohibits changes to election systems, registries, hardware/software updates without undergoing re-certification. According to the National Conference of State Legislatures – Michigan requires full compliance with federal standards as determined by a federally accredited voting system laboratory.

19. The only reason to change software after the election would be to obfuscate evidence of fraud and/or to correct program errors that would de-certify the election. Our findings show that the Central Lake Township tabulator tape totals were significantly altered by utilizing two different program versions (10/23/2020 and 11/05/2020), both of which were software changes during an election which violates election law, and not just human error associated with the **Dominion Election Management System.** This is clear evidence of software generated movement of votes. The claims made on the **Office of the Secretary of State** website are false.

20. The Dominion ImageCast Precinct (ICP) machines have the ability to be connected to the internet (see Image 11). By connecting a network scanner to the ethernet port on the ICP machine and creating Packet Capture logs from the machines we examined show the ability to connect to the network, Application Programming Interface (API) (a data exchange between two different systems) calls and web (http) connections to the Election Management System server. Best practice is to disable the network interface card to avoid connection to the internet. This demonstrated a significant and fatal error in security and election integrity. Because certain files have been deleted, we have not yet found origin or destination; but our research continues.

21. Because the intentional high error rate generates large numbers of ballots to be adjudicated by election personnel, we must deduce that bulk adjudication occurred. However, because files and adjudication logs are missing, we have not yet determined where the bulk adjudication occurred or who was responsible for it. Our research continues.

22. Research is ongoing. However, based on the preliminary results, we conclude that the errors are so significant that they call into question the integrity and legitimacy of the results in the Antrim County 2020 election to the point that the results are not certifiable. Because the same machines and software are used in 48 other counties in Michigan, this casts doubt on the integrity of the entire election in the state of Michigan.

23. DNI Responsibilities: President Obama signed Executive Order on National Critical Infrastructure on 6 January 2017, stating in Section 1. Cybersecurity of Federal Networks, "The Executive Branch operates its information technology (IT) on behalf of the American people. The President will hold heads of executive departments and agencies (agency heads) accountable for managing cybersecurity risk to their enterprises. In addition, because risk management decisions made by agency heads can affect the risk to the executive branch as a whole, and to national security, it is also the policy of the United States to manage cybersecurity risk as an executive branch enterprise." President Obama's EO further stated, effective immediately, each agency head shall use The Framework for Improving Critical Infrastructure Cybersecurity (the Framework) developed by the National Institute of Standards and Technology." Support to Critical Infrastructure at Greatest Risk. The Secretary of Homeland Security, in coordination with the Secretary of Defense, the Attorney General, the Director of National Intelligence, the Director of the Federal Bureau of Investigation, the heads of appropriate sector-specific agencies, as defined in Presidential Policy Directive 21 of February 12, 2013 (Critical Infrastructure Security and Resilience) (sector-specific agencies), and all other appropriate agency heads, as identified by the Secretary of Homeland Security, shall: (i) identify authorities and capabilities that agencies could employ to support the cybersecurity efforts of critical infrastructure entities identified pursuant to section 9 of Executive Order 13636 of February 12, 2013 (Improving Critical Infrastructure Cybersecurity), to be at greatest risk of attacks that could reasonably result in catastrophic regional or national effects on public health or safety, economic security, or national security (section 9 entities);

This is a national security imperative. **In July 2018, President Trump strengthened President Obama's Executive Order to include requirements to ensure US election systems, processes, and its people were not manipulated by foreign meddling, either through electronic or systemic manipulation, social media, or physical changes made in hardware, software, or supporting systems.** The 2018 Executive Order. Accordingly, I hereby order:

Section 1. (a) Not later than 45 days after the conclusion of a United States election, the Director of National Intelligence, in consultation with the heads of any other appropriate executive departments and agencies (agencies), shall conduct an assessment of any information indicating that a foreign government, or any person acting as an agent of or on behalf of a foreign government, has acted with the intent or purpose of interfering in that election. The assessment shall identify, to the maximum extent ascertainable, the nature of any foreign interference and any methods employed to execute it, the persons involved, and the foreign government or governments that authorized, directed, sponsored, or supported it. The Director of National Intelligence shall deliver this assessment and appropriate supporting information to the President, the Secretary of State, the Secretary of the Treasury, the Secretary of Defense, the Attorney General, and the Secretary of Homeland Security.

We recommend that an independent group should be empaneled to determine the extent of the adjudication errors throughout the State of Michigan. This is a national security issue.

24. Michigan resident Gustavo Delfino, a former professor of mathematics in Venezuela and alumni of University of Michigan, offered a compelling affidavit [Exhibit 2] recognizing the inherent vulnerabilities in the SmartMatic electronic voting machines (software which was since incorporated into Dominion Voting Systems) during the 2004 national referendum in Venezuela (see attached declaration). After 4 years of research and 3 years of undergoing intensive peer review, Professor Delfino's paper was published in the highly respected "Statistical Science" journal, November 2011 issue (Volume 26, Number 4) with title "Analysis of the 2004 Venezuela Referendum: The Official Results Versus the Petition Signatures." The intensive study used multiple mathematical approaches to ascertain the voting results found in the 2004 Venezuelan referendum. Delfino and his research partners discovered not only the algorithm used to manipulate the results, but also the precise location in the election processing sequence where vulnerability in machine processing would provide such an opportunity. According to Prof Delfino, the magnitude of the difference between the official and the true result in Venezuela estimated at 1,370,000 votes. Our investigation into the error rates and results of the Antrim County voting tally reflect the same tactics, which have also been reported in other Michigan counties as well. This demonstrates a national security issue.

C. **PROCESS**

We visited Antrim County twice: November 27, 2020 and December 6, 2020.

On November 27, 2020, we visited Central Lake Township, Star Township, and Mancelona Township. We examined the Dominion Voting Systems tabulators and tabulator roles.

INTRODUCTION BY THOMAS FENSCH

On December 6, 2020, we visited the Antrim County Clerk's office. We inspected and performed forensic duplication of the following:

1. **Antrim County Election Management Server** running **Dominion Democracy Suite** 5.5.3-002;

2. **Compact Flash** cards used by the local precincts in their **Dominion ImageCast Precinct**;

3. **USB memory sticks** used by the **Dominion VAT** (Voter Assist Terminals); and

4. **USB memory sticks** used for the Poll Book.

Dominion voting system is a Canadian owned company with global subsidiaries. It is owned by Staple Street Capital which is in turn owned by UBS Securities LLC, of which 3 out of their 7 board members are Chinese nationals. The Dominion software is licensed from Smartmatic which is a Venezuelan owned and controlled company. Dominion Server locations have been determined to be in Serbia, Canada, the US, Spain and Germany.

D. CENTRAL LAKE TOWNSHIP

1. On November 27, 2020, part of our forensics team visited the Central Lake Township in Michigan to inspect the **Dominion ImageCast Precint** for possible hardware issues on behalf of a local lawsuit filed by Michigan attorney Matthew DePerno on behalf of William Bailey. In our conversations with the clerk of **Central Lake Township** Ms. Judith L. Kosloski, she presented to us "two separate paper totals tape" from Tabulator ID 2.

   - One dated "Poll Opened Nov. 03/2020 06:38:48" (Roll 1);
   - Another dated "Poll Opened Nov. 06/2020 09:21:58" (Roll 2).

2. We were then told by Ms. Kosloski that on November 5, 2020, Ms. Kosloski was notified by Connie Wing of the County Clerk's Office and asked to bring the tabulator and ballots to the County Clerk's office for re-tabulation. They ran the ballots and printed "Roll 2". She noticed a difference in the votes and brought it up to the clerk, but canvasing still occurred, and her objections were not addressed.

3. Our team analyzed both rolls and compared the results. Roll 1 had **1,494** total votes and Roll 2 had **1,491** votes (Roll 2 had 3 less ballots because 3 ballots were damaged in the process.)

4. "Statement of Votes Cast from Antrim" shows that only **1,491** votes were counted, and the **3** ballots that were damaged were not entered into final results.

5. Ms. Kosloski stated that she and her assistant manually refilled out the three ballots, curing them, and ran them through the ballot counting system - but the final numbers do not reflect the inclusion of those **3** damaged ballots.

6. This is the most preliminary report of serious election fraud indicators. In comparing the numbers on both rolls, *we estimate **1,474** votes changed across the two rolls, between the first and the second time the exact same ballots were run through the County Clerk's vote counting machine - which is almost the same number of voters that voted in total.*

    - ***742** votes were added to* **School Board Member for Central Lake Schools (3)**

    - ***657** votes were removed from* **School Board Member for Ellsworth Schools (2)**

    - **7** votes were added to the total for **State Proposal 20-1 (1)** and out of those there were **611** votes moved between the Yes and No Categories.

7. There were incremental changes throughout the rolls with some significant adjustments between the 2 rolls that were reviewed. This demonstrates conclusively that votes can be and were changed during the second machine count after the software update. That should be impossible especially at such a high percentage to total votes cast.

8. For the **School Board Member for Central Lake Schools (3)** [Image 1] there were **742 votes** added to this vote total. Since multiple people were elected, this did not change the result of both candidates being elected, but one does see a change in who had most votes. If it were a single-person election this would have changed the outcome and demonstrates conclusively that votes can be and were changed during the second machine counting. That should be impossible.

[Image 1]:

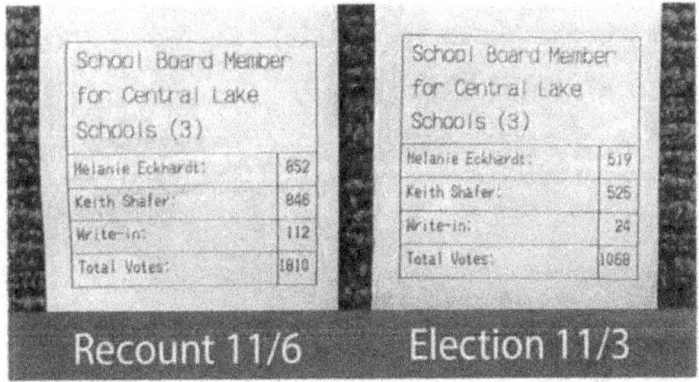

9. For the **School Board Member for Ellsworth Schools (2)** [Image 2]

    - Shows *657 votes being removed* from this election.

    - In this case, only **3** people who were eligible to vote actually voted. Since there were **2** votes allowed for each voter to cast.

    - The recount correctly shows **6** votes.

    But on election night, there was a major calculation issue:

    [Image 2]:

    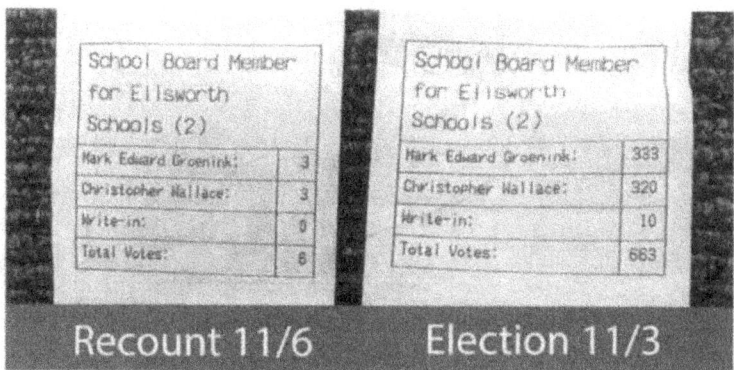

10. In **State Proposal 20-1 (1)**, [Image 3] there is a major change in votes in this category.

    - There were **774 votes for YES** during the election, to **1,083 votes for YES** on the recount a change of **309 votes**.

    - **7** votes were added to the total for **State Proposal 20-1 (1)** out of those there were **611** votes moved between the Yes and No Categories.

    [Image 3]:

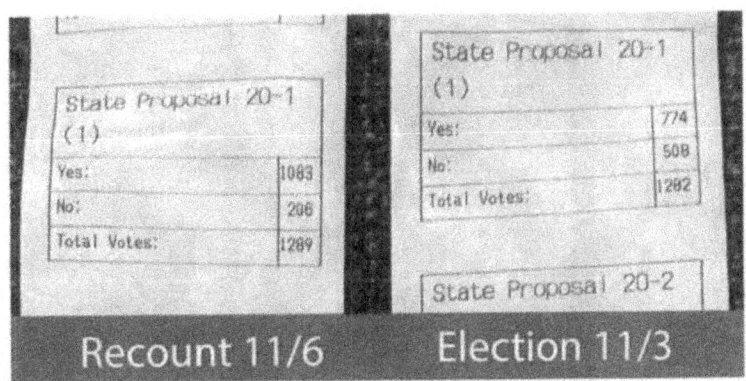

11. **State Proposal 20-1 (1)** is a fairly technical and complicated proposed amendment to the Michigan Constitution to change the disposition and allowable uses of future revenue generated from oil and gas bonuses, rentals and royalties from state-owned land. Information about the proposal: https://crcmich.org/publications/statewide-ballot- proposal-20-1-michigan-natural-resources-trust-fund

12. A Proposed Initiated **Ordinance to Authorize One (1) Marihuana (sic) Retailer Establishment Within the Village of Central Lake (1)**. [Image 4]

    - On election night, it was a tie vote.

    - Then, on the rerun of ballots 3 ballots were destroyed, but only one vote changed on the totals to allow the proposal to pass.

    When **3 ballots were not counted** and **programming change on the tabulator was installed** the proposal **passed with 1 vote being removed from the No** vote.

    [Image 4]:

Introduction by Thomas Fensch

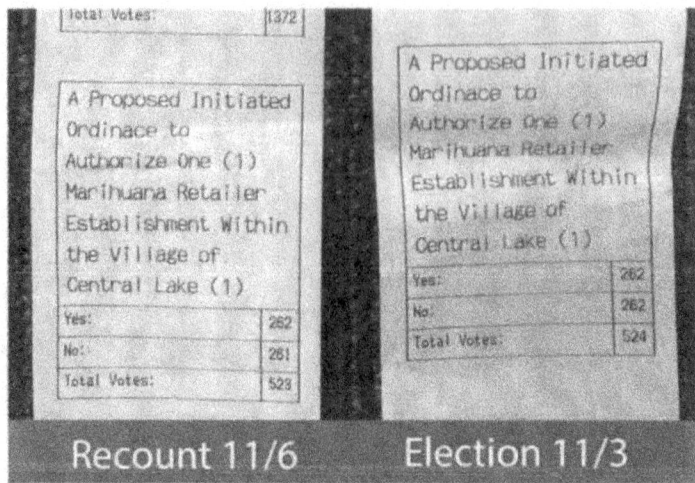

13. On Sunday December 6, 2020, our forensics team visited the Antrim County Clerk. There were two USB memory sticks used, one contained the software package used to tabulate election results on November 3, 2020, and the other was programmed on November 6, 2020 with a different software package which yielded significantly different voting outcomes. The election data package is used by the **Dominion Democracy Suite** software & election management system software to upload programming information onto the Compact Flash Cards for the **Dominion ImageCast Precinct** to enable it to calculate ballot totals.

14. This software programming should be standard across all voting machines systems for the duration of the entire election if accurate tabulation is the expected outcome as required by US Election Law. This intentional difference in software programming is a design feature to alter election outcomes.

15. The election day outcomes were calculated using the original software programming on November 3, 2020. On November 5, 2020 the township clerk was asked to re-run the Central Lake Township ballots and was given no explanation for this unusual request. On November 6, 2020 the Antrim County Clerk, Sheryl Guy issued the second version of software to re-run the same Central Lake Township ballots and oversaw the process. This resulted in greater than a 60% change in voting results, inexplicably impacting every single election contest in a township with less than 1500 voters. These errors far exceed the ballot error rate standard of 1 in 250,000 ballots (.0008%) as required by federal election law.

    - The original election programming files are last dated 09/25/2020 1:24pm
    - The updated election data package files are last dated 10/22/2020 10:27 am.

16. As the tabulator tape totals prove, there were large numbers of votes switched from the November 3, 2020 tape to the November 6, 2020 tape. This was solely based on using different software versions of the operating program to calculate votes, not tabulate votes. This is evidenced by using same the Dominion System with two different software program versions contained on the two different USB Memory Devices.

17. The Help America Vote Act, Safe Harbor provides a 90-day period prior to elections where no changes can be made to election systems. To make changes would require recertification of the entire system for use in the election. The Dominion User Guide prescribes the proper procedure to test machines with test ballots to compare the results to validate machine functionality to determine if the **Dominion ImageCast Precinct** was programmed correctly. If this occurred a ballot misconfiguration would have been identified. Once the software was updated to the 10/22/2020 software the test ballots should have been re-run to validate the vote totals to confirm the machine was configured correctly.

18. The November 6, 2020 note from **The Office of the Secretary of State Jocelyn Benson** states: "The correct results always were and continue to be reflected on the tabulator totals tape and on the ballots themselves. Even if the error in the reported unofficial results had not been quickly noticed, it would have been identified during the county canvass. Boards of County Canvassers, which are composed of 2 Democrats and 2 Republicans, review the printed totals tape from each tabulator during the canvass to verify the reported vote totals are correct."

    - Source: https://www.michigan.gov/sos/0,4670,7-127-1640_9150-544676--,00.html

19. The **Secretary of State Jocelyn Benson's** statement is false. Our findings show that the tabulator tape totals were significantly altered by utilization of two different program versions, and not just the **Dominion Election Management System**. This is the opposite of the claim that the **Office of the Secretary of State** made on its website. The fact that these significant errors were not caught in ballot testing and not caught by the local county clerk shows that there are major inherent built-in vulnerabilities and process flaws in the **Dominion Election Management System**, and that other townships/precincts and the entire election have been affected.

20. On Sunday December 6, 2020, our forensics team visited the Antrim County Clerk office to perform forensic duplication of the **Antrim County Election Management Server** running **Dominion Democracy Suite** 5.5.3-002.

21. Forensic copies of the **Compact Flash** cards used by the local precincts in their **Dominion ImageCast Precinct** were inspected, **USB memory sticks** used by the **Dominion VAT** (Voter Assist Terminals) and the **USB memory sticks** used for the Poll Book were forensically duplicated.

22. We have been told that the ballot design and configuration for the **Dominion ImageCast Precinct** and VAT were provided by **ElectionSource.com** which is which is owned by MC&E, Inc of Grand Rapids, MI.

E. **MANCELONA TOWNSHIP**

1. In Mancelona township, problems with software versions were also known to have been present. Mancelona elections officials understood that ballot processing issued were not accurate and used the second version of software to process votes on 4 November, again an election de-certifying event, as no changes to the election system are authorized by law in the 90 days preceding elections without re-certification.

2. Once the 10/22/2020 software update was performed on the Dominion ImageCast Precinct the test ballot process should have been performed to validate the programming. There is no indication that this procedure was performed.

F. **ANTRIM COUNTY CLERK'S OFFICE**

1. Pursuant to a court ordered inspection, we participated in an onsite collection effort at the Antrim County Clerk's office on December 6, 2020. [Image 5]:

Among other items forensically collected, the Antrim County Election Management Server (EMS) with Democracy Suite was forensically collected. [Images 6 and 7].

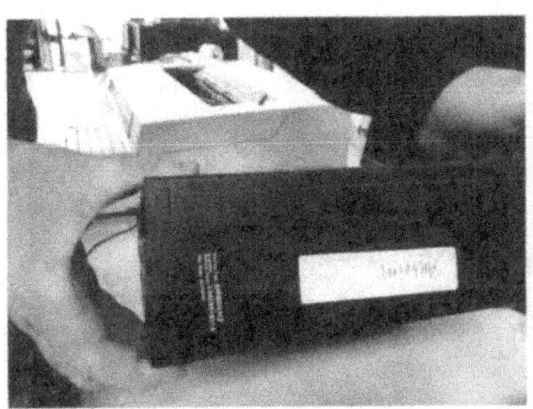 

The EMS (Election Management Server) was a:

Dell Precision Tower 3420.

Service Tag: 6NB0KH2

The EMS contained 2 hard drives in a RAID-1 configuration. That is the 2 drives redundantly stored the same information and the server could continue to operate if either of the 2 hard drives failed. The EMS was booted via the Linux Boot USB memory sticks and both hard drives were forensically imaged.

At the onset of the collection process we observed that the initial program thumb drive was not secured in the vault with the CF cards and other thumbdrives. We watched as the County employees, including Clerk Sheryl Guy searched throughout the office for the missing thumb drive. Eventually they found the missing thumb drive in an unsecured and unlocked desk drawer along with multiple other random thumb drives. This demonstrated a significant and fatal error in security and election integrity.

G. **FORENSIC COLLECTION**

We used a built for purpose Linux Boot USB memory stick to boot the EMS in a forensically sound mode. We then used Ewfacquire to make a forensic image of the 2 independent internal hard drives.

Ewfacquire created an E01 file format forensic image with built-in integrity verification via MD5 hash.

We used Ewfverify to verify the forensic image acquired was a true and accurate copy of the original disk. That was done for both forensic images.

H. **ANALYSIS TOOLS**

X-Ways Forensics: We used X-Ways Forensics, a commercial Computer Forensic tool, to verify the image was useable and full disk encryption was not in use. In particular we confirmed that Bit locker was not in use on the EMS.

Other tools used: PassMark – OSForensics, Truxton - Forensics, Cellebrite – Physical Analyzer, Blackbag-Blacklight Forensic Software, Microsoft SQL Server Management Studio, Virtual Box, and miscellaneous other tools and scripts.

I. SERVER OVERVIEW AND SUMMARY

1. Our initial audit on the computer running the Democracy Suite Software showed that standard computer security best practices were not applied. These minimum-security standards are outlined the 2002 HAVA, and FEC Voting System Standards – it did not even meet the minimum standards required of a government desktop computer.

2. The election data software package USB drives (November 2020 election, and November 2020 election updated) are secured with bitlocker encryption software, but they were not stored securely on-site. At the time of our forensic examination, the election data package files were already moved to an unsecure desktop computer and were residing on an unencrypted hard drive. This demonstrated a significant and fatal error in security and election integrity. Key Findings on Desktop and Server Configuration: - There were multiple Microsoft security updates as well as Microsoft SQL Server updates which should have been deployed, however there is no evidence that these security patches were ever installed. As described below, many of the software packages were out of date and vulnerable to various methods of attack.

   a) Computer initial configuration on 10/03/2018 13:08:11:911

   b) Computer final configuration of server software on 4/10/2019

   c) Hard Drive not Encrypted at Rest

   d) Microsoft SQL Server Database not protected with password.

   e) Democracy Suite Admin Passwords are reused and share passwords.

   f) Antivirus is 4.5 years outdated

   g) Windows updates are 3.86 years out of date.

   h) When computer was last configured on 04/10/2019 the windows updates were 2.11 years out of date.

   i) User of computer uses a Super User Account.

3. The hard drive was not encrypted at rest – which means that if hard drives are removed or initially booted off an external USB drive the files are susceptible to manipulation directly. An attacker is able to mount the hard drive because it is unencrypted, allowing for the manipulation and replacement of any file on the system.

4. The Microsoft SQL Server database files were not properly secured to allow modifications of the database files.

5. The Democracy Suite Software user account logins and passwords are stored in the unsecured database tables and the multiple Election System Administrator accounts share the same password, which means that there are no audit trails for vote changes, deletions, blank ballot voting, or batch vote alterations or adjudication.

6. Antivirus definition is 1666 days old on 12/11/2020. Antrim County updates its system with USB drives. USB drives are the most common vectors for injecting malware into computer systems. The failure to properly update the antivirus definition drastically increases the harm cause by malware from other machines being transmitted to the voting system.

7. Windows Server Update Services (WSUS) Offline Update is used to enable updates the computer – which is a package of files normally downloaded from the internet but compiled into a program to put on a USB drive to manually update server systems.

8. Failure to properly update the voting system demonstrates a significant and fatal error in security and election integrity.

9. There are 15 additional updates that should have been installed on the server to adhere to Microsoft Standards to fix known vulnerabilities. For the 4/10/2019 install, the most updated version of the update files would have been 03/13/2019 which is 11.6.1 which is 15 updates newer than 10.9.1

This means the updates installed were 2 years, 1 month, 13 days behind the most current update at the time. This includes security updates and fixes. This demonstrated a significant and fatal error in security and election integrity.

- Wed 04/10/2019 10:34:33.14 - Info: Starting WSUS Offline Update (v. 10.9.1)

- Wed 04/10/2019 10:34:33.14 - Info: Used path "D:\WSUSOFFLINE1091_2012R2_W10\cmd\" on EMSSERVER (user: EMSADMIN)

- Wed 04/10/2019 10:34:35.55 - Info: Medium build date: 03/10/2019

- Found on c:\Windows\wsusofflineupdate.txt
- *WSUS Offline Update (v.10.9.1) was created on 01/29/2017

*WSUS information found here https://download.wsusoffline.net/

10. Super User Administrator account is the primary account used to operate the **Dominion Election Management System** which is a major security risk. The user logged in has the ability to make major changes to the system and install software which means that there is no oversight to ensure appropriate management controls – i.e. anyone who has access to the shared administrator user names and passwords can make significant changes to the entire voting system. The shared usernames and passwords mean that these changes can be made in an anonymous fashion with no tracking or attribution.

J. ERROR RATES

1. We reviewed the Tabulation logs in their entirety for 11/6/2020. The election logs for Antrim County consist of 15,676 total lines or events.

    - Of the 15,676 there were a total of 10,667 critical errors/warnings or a 68.05% error rate.

    - Most of the errors were related to configuration errors that could result in overall tabulation errors or adjudication. These 11/6/2020 tabulation totals were used as the official results.

2. For examples, there were 1,222 ballots **reversed** out of 1,491 total ballots cast, thus resulting in an 81.96% rejection rate. Some of which were reversed due to "Ballot's size exceeds maximum expected ballot size".

    - According to the NCSL, Michigan requires testing by a federally accredited laboratory for voting systems. In section 4.1.1 of the Voluntary Voting Systems Guidelines (VVSG) Accuracy Requirements a. **All systems shall achieve a report total error rate of no more than one in 125,000.**

    - https://www.eac.gov/sites/default/files/eac_assets/1/28/VVSG.1.1.VOL.1.FINAL1.pdf

    - In section 4.1.3.2 Memory Stability of the VVSG it states that **Memory devices used to retain election management data shall have demonstrated error free data retention for a period of 22 months.**

    - In section 4.1.6.1 Paper-based System Processing Requirements subsection a. of the VVSG it states "The ability of the system to produce and receive electronic signals from the scanning of the ballot, perform logical and numerical operations upon these data, and reproduce the contents of memory when required **shall** be sufficiently free of **error** to enable satisfaction of the system-level accuracy requirement indicated in Subsection 4.1.1."

- These are not human errors; this is definitively related to the software and software configurations resulting in error rates far beyond the thresholds listed in the guidelines.

3. A high "error rate" in the election software (in this case 68.05%) reflects an algorithm used that will weight one candidate greater than another (for instance, weight a specific candidate at a 2/3 to approximately 1/3 ratio). In the logs we identified that the RCV or Ranked Choice Voting Algorithm was enabled (see image below from the Dominion manual). This allows the user to apply a weighted numerical value to candidates and change the overall result. The declaration of winners can be done on a basis of points, not votes. [Image 8]:

choice voting results are evaluated on a district per district basis and each district has a set number of points (100). Elimination and declaration of winners is done on basis of points, not votes.

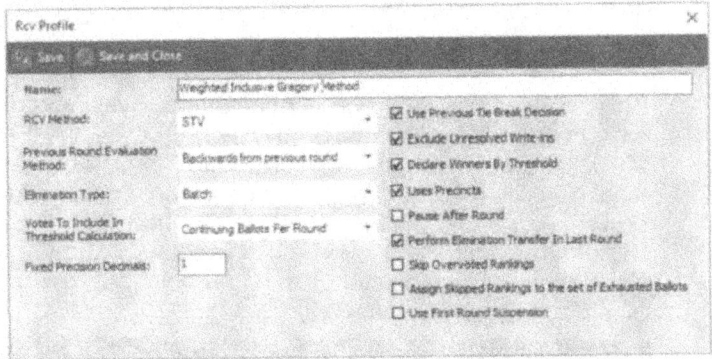

Figure 11-3: RCV Profile screen

4. The Dominion software configuration logs in the Divert Options, shows that all write-in ballots were flagged to be diverted automatically for adjudication. This means that all write-in ballots were sent for "adjudication" by a poll worker or election official to process the ballot based on voter "intent". Adjudication files allow a computer operator to decide to whom to award those votes (or to trash them).

5. In the logs all but two of the Override Options were enabled on these machines, thus allowing any operator to change those votes. [Image 9]:

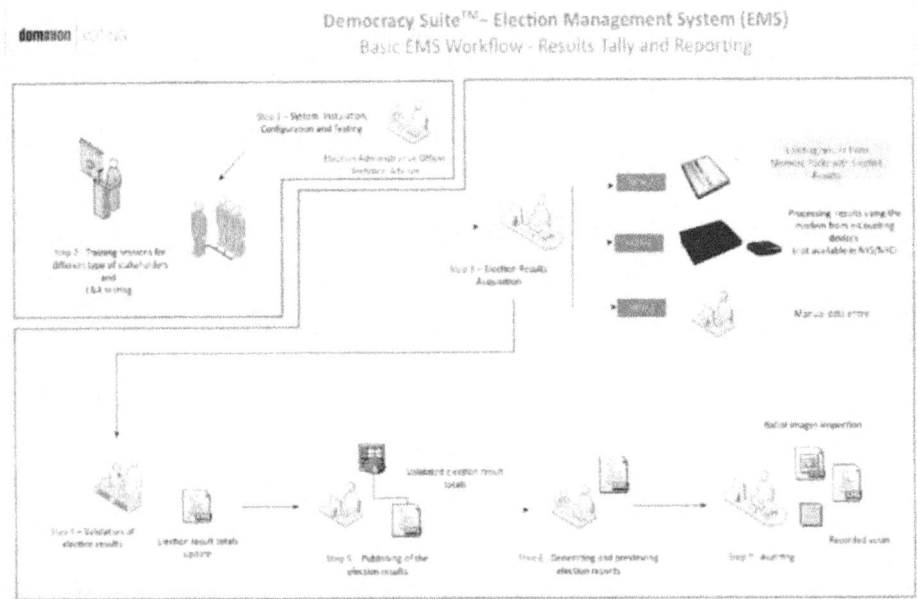

8. We reviewed the Election Management System logs (EmsLogger) in their entirety from 9/19/2020 through 11/21/2020 for the Project: Antrim November 2020. There were configuration errors throughout the set-up, election and tabulation of results. The last error for Central Lake Township, Precinct 1 occurred on 11/21/2020 at 14:35:11 System.Xml.XmlException System.Xml.XmlException: The ' ' character, hexadecimal value 0x20, cannot be included in a name. Bottom line is that this is a calibration that rejects the vote (see picture below). [Image 12]:

Notably 42 minutes earlier on Nov 21 2020 at 13:53:09 a user attempted to zero out election results. Id:3168 EmsLogger - There is no permission to {0} - Project: User: Thread: 189. This is direct proof of an attempt to tamper with evidence.

9. The Election Event Designer Log shows that Dominion ImageCast Precinct Cards were programmed with updated new programming on 10/23/2020 and again after the election on 11/05/2020. As previously mentioned, this violates the HAVA safe harbor period.

Source: C:\Program Files\Dominion Voting Systems\Election Event Designer\Log\Info.txt

- Dominion Imagecast Precinct Cards Programmed with 9/25/2020 programming on 09/29/2020, 09/30/2020, and 10/12/2020.

- Dominion Imagecast Precinct Cards Programmed with New Ballot Programming dated 10/22/2020 on 10/23/2020 and after the election on 11/05/2020

Excerpt from 2020-11-05 showing "ProgramMemoryCard" commands.

10. Analysis is ongoing and updated findings will be submitted as soon as possible. A summary of the information collected is provided below.

10|12/07/20 18:52:30| Indexing completed at Mon Dec 7 18:52:30 2020
12|12/07/20 18:52:30| INDEX SUMMARY
12|12/07/20 18:52:30| Files indexed: 159312

```
12|12/07/20 18:52:30| Files skipped: 64799
12|12/07/20 18:52:30| Files filtered: 0
12|12/07/20 18:52:30| Emails indexed: 0
12|12/07/20 18:52:30| Unique words found: 5325413
12|12/07/20 18:52:30| Variant words found: 3597634
12|12/07/20 18:52:30| Total words found: 239446085
12|12/07/20 18:52:30| Avg. unique words per page: 33.43
12|12/07/20 18:52:30| Avg. words per page: 1503
12|12/07/20 18:52:30| Peak physical memory used: 2949 MB
12|12/07/20 18:52:30| Peak virtual memory used: 8784 MB
12|12/07/20 18:52:30| Errors: 10149
12|12/07/20 18:52:30| Total bytes scanned/downloaded: 1919289906
```

Dated: December 13, 2020

_____
Russell Ramsland

INTRODUCTION BY THOMAS FENSCH

Key Document D

From:	Ken Cuccinelli Email Address
Sent:	Friday, December 18, 2020 2:54 PM
To:	Donoghue, Richard (ODAG)
Cc:	Early, Emily
Subject:	Follow up
Attachments:	MI Report Summary.pdf

Rich,

Brandon is doing three briefings today, among other things, so rather than wait for him to resurface, I thought we should get this back to you.

Please note that this is based only on publicly available information and is effectively a high level summary of the concerns with the report as requested   it is not a full white paper.

I hope it is useful, though as it relates to the particular county, the hand recount would seem to have addressed matters in that jurisdiction.

Sincerely,
Ken Cuccinelli

Introduction by Thomas Fensch

MI Report Summary.pdf for Printed Item: 4 (Attachment 1 of 1)

Voters in Antrim County, Michigan, voted on paper ballots. Those records were reviewed yesterday and recounted by hand. This verification, independent of the software and hardware systems in question, returned results that indicates the consistency of the systems, with a 12 vote difference from the previous final tally.

The Allied Security Operations Group Antrim Michigan Forensics Report was issued prior to yesterday's hand recount. The report draws conclusions based upon descriptions of software that it is our understanding Antrim County does not own, and for versions of the software we understand to be incompatible with the version of the voting system Antrim County owns.

- The Dominion Voting System's (DVS) Democracy Suite (D-Suite) 5.5 that is used in Antrim County, Michigan was certified by the United States (U.S.) Election Assistance Commission (EAC) on September 14, 2018.[2] The D-Suite 5.5 voting system is comprised of multiple software, hardware, and firmware components. The back-end computer server system, known as the Election Management System (EMS), is a suite of multiple independent software applications. Antrim County only uses a subset of those software applications.

- It is our understanding that Antrim County does not use the ballot adjudication application software addressed in the report, and does not have compatible systems, mainly the ImageCast Central tabulator and thus has no forensic logs of such systems. The lack of such logs is raised in the report, but given that Antrim County does not use the adjudication application, there would be no logs of such use.

- When hand-marked paper ballots are scanned by a machine, the machine will alert election officials to things like write-in voting, damaged ballots, overvotes, undervotes, and stray marks. The evidence provided in the report that shows screenshots of logs and file settings describe situations where the machine performed the intended processes based on the configuration settings. Counting programmed machine alerts that are for common occurrences in an election does not demonstrate error on the part of the machine, yet the report appears to treat such occurrences as errors for their compilation purposes.

- Discussion of the possibility that Ranked Choice Voting may have been enabled is not applicable given the systems in use in Antrim County. It is our understanding that Dominion Voting System's (DVS) Democracy Suite (D-Suite) 5.5 does not have Ranked Choice Voting capability the screenshot provided is for D-Suite 5.11.[3]

Discussion in the report is inconsistent with the current voting system certification process in the US Election Assistance Commission's Voluntary Voting System Guidelines.[4] Finally, we would leave to the Department of Justice evaluation of the references to the Help America Votes Act.

Hendrickson, Clara and Paul Egan, "Antrim County hand tally affirms certified election results." Detroit Free Press. Dec. 17, 2020. "Previous final tally" references the fact that there were acknowledged errors in earlier counts explained as being related to how the machines were used, not errors by the machines themselves.

[2] https://www.eac.gov/sites/default/files/voting_system/files/DSuite55_CertConf_Scope%28FINAL%29.pdf (last accessed on December 15, 2020)

[3] Ibid

[4] https://www.eac.gov/sites/default/files/eac_assets/1/28/VVSG.1.0_Volume_1.PDF (last accessed on December 15, 2020)

Donoghue, Richard (ODAG)

From:	Donoghue, Richard (ODAG)
Sent:	Friday, December 18, 2020 3:05 PM
To:	Ken Cuccinelli Email Address
Subject:	RE: Follow up

I agree about the hand count in Antrim. Understand the limited scope of this and will be sure the AG knows that. Thanks very much.

From: Ken Cuccinelli Email Address
Sent: Friday, December 18, 2020 2:54 PM
To: Donoghue, Richard (ODAG) <ricdonoghue@jmd.usdoj.gov>
Cc: Early, Emily (b) (6) >
Subject: Follow up

Rich,

Brandon is doing three briefings today, among other things, so rather than wait for him to resurface, I thought we should get this back to you.

Please note that this is based only on publicly available information and is effectively a high level summary of the concerns with the report as requested - it is not a full white paper.

I hope it is useful, though as it relates to the particular county, the hand recount would seem to have addressed matters in that jurisdiction.

Sincerely,
Ken Cuccinelli

INTRODUCTION BY THOMAS FENSCH

Donoghue, Richard (ODAG)

From:	Donoghue, Richard (ODAG)
Sent:	Friday, December 18, 2020 3:11 PM
To:	Watson, Theresa (OAG)
Subject:	FW: Follow up
Attachments:	MI Report Summary.pdf

Theresa,

Please forward this attachment to the AG.

Thanks,

Rich

From: Ken Cuccinelli Email Address
Sent: Friday, December 18, 2020 2:54 PM
To: Donoghue, Richard (ODAG) <ricdonoghue@jmd.usdoj.gov>
Cc: Early, Emily (b)(6) >
Subject: Follow up

Rich,

Brandon is doing three briefings today, among other things, so rather than wait for him to resurface, I thought we should get this back to you.

Please note that this is based only on publicly available information and is effectively a high level summary of the concerns with the report as requested - it is not a full white paper.

I hope it is useful, though as it relates to the particular county, the hand recount would seem to have addressed matters in that jurisdiction.

Sincerely,
Ken Cuccinelli

Key Document E

Introduction by Thomas Fensch

12/27/20

DAG call - on w/ POTUS + wants to
conference me in

P - County is up in arms over the corruption

Scott Perry (PA) + Senator fr
PA - Guy Ustriano - some of the ones
calling

205K votes - more than reg. voters - PA
- flooded the market w/ ballots

- 600K votes added
- 570K - for Biden
- few for me + lots of blanks

0332 - flooded the market - all at
once
- multiple states

Jim Jordan: fighter - will like
3rd World coup.

Detroit - look at districts in MI
- was very close but not
Wayne Cty (Detroit)

- Call dropped ... ~ 3 voicemails

- We have thousands of people who went in to vote + were told you already voted by absentee ballot

- people are angry - blaming DOJ for inaction
- Statistically - election night it was a done deal
   - Somehow, overnight the outcome changed bc all these ballots showed up
- AZ, GA, PA ...

People won't have confidence in the GA Senate races

GA, NV, AZ, MI - all corrupted elections

People are complaining to him constantly

Thousands of people called their USAOs + FBI

Introduction by Thomas Fensch

DOJ failing to respond to legitimate complaints/reports of crimes

PA - 5M voters in the state
(possibly true?) - but 5.25M votes - clearly fraud

GA - tape that shows fraud, election
- Ruby Freeman - Huckster - closed the facility + then came back w/ hidden ballots, under table...
- networks magnified the tape + saw them running the tapes repeatedly

"You guys may not be following the internet the way I do"

Detroit - threw the "poll watchers out

Don't even look at the alleged abuses - don't need to, it's obvious

FBI will always say nothing there
- leaders there oppose me, SAs support me

(TW) — that whole thing, crazy...
- hand to no SenT[?] tries DJ
- also upset

FBI — I made some bad decision on leadership there, but it was being under an illegal investigation — special tho. should never have been convened
- You figure out what to do w/ Biden — people will criticize the DOJ if He's not investigated for real.

- GA Leg is on our side — they want to bring a case but the Gov won't let them

- Statistically impossible for me to lose
- Predicts had me at 100% on election night — dropped to 32% in 4 or 5 hours — never happens

- DAG — will look at whether more ballots in PA than registered voters — should be able to check on that quickly but understand that the DOJ can't + won't snap its fingers + change the outcome of the election, doesn't work that way
- P: "Don't expect you to do

"...no, just say that the election was was corrupt + leave the rest to me and the R. Congressmen."

- (DOJ) - Sir, we have done dozens of investig., hundreds of interview Major allegations are not supported by evid. developed.
  - GA/PA/MI/NV
- We are doing our jobs. Much of the info you're getting is false.
  - eg MI - report says 68% error vote - but realify is it was .0063% error vote - less than 1 in 15k.
  - Ok fine - but what about the others?
- PA Truck Driver - we interviewed on both ends - no ballots & couldn't even ID the envelope
  - ok, so he didn't watch that one - what about the others?
- GA - looked at the tape, interviewed the W, no suitcases (ok - but they looked like that), cutters legit, no multiple scanning of ballots

Subverting Justice

- Double voting, dead people, Indians getting paid. Lots of fraud.

- AZ - d any lead by 9K - clearly more fraud than that.

- Judges keep saying - where is the DOJ? Why are they not filing in these cases?
  - DAG/ODAG - bc. we are not in a position based on the evidence - we can only act on the actual evidence developed.

- Told him flat out that much of the info he is getting is false, +/or just not supported by the evidence
  - we look at allegations but they don't pan out
  - P - this is election-turning fraud

"We have an obligation to tell people that this was an illegal, corrupt election."

- People tell me Jeff Clark is great, I should put him
- People want me to replace DOJ leadership
- DAG - fine, but won't change the Dept's position
- you should have the leadership you want

Introduction by Thomas Fensch

- You, Rich, should go to Fulton Cty + do a signature verification and you'll see how illegal it is. You'll find tens of thousands.
- More votes than voters.
  - I told him in WI they were comparing the 2020 votes cast to 2016 registration #s – not a valid complaint

- "Nobody trusts the FBI" – need others to corroborate this

- "I'd like to request" – Fulton Cty, GA clerk signatures against years prior – not this year
- DHS responds: we will take into account

- These people who saying that the election isn't corrupt are corrupt

- Not much time left

- Asked for cell # – provided (he had it anyway) – may have elected officials w/ relevant info call

SJC-Pre-CertificationEvents-07292021-000741

- Sen Johnson has done great job getting to bottom of things
  - and that's done in public unlike DOJ investigations

NV - forensic accounting shows we won by 200k votes

Mark Martin - NC SC Justice - retired, scholar

"Ballot drops" day of the election

INTRODUCTION BY THOMAS FENSCH

Key Document F

Cong. Perry (PA) – 12/28/20

~1500
EVT Car
en route to DC

- POTUS asked him to call

- Concerned about the election
- Thinks DOJ hasn't done its job on election result

- On Foreign Affairs Committee
  - can't understand why DOJ said no to voting about H. Biden investigation — its ongoing

- Likes Jeff Clark a lot – thinks he would do something about this

e.g. — Aiken Brokers – Hq RTT Scandal
  - IG find – we asked FBI to interview her – told her to not bring anything.
  - She felt like she was the one under investigation.
  - FBI doesn't do the right thing in all instances

- Forensic plaintiff who is State Rep — looking at open source info — all counties but 3 (still working on too)
  - 205K more votes than voters – clear fraud

asked to set up
email address
he will send info
on this

- Told him we would, of course, be willing to look at that but, thus far, we haven't seen fraud on scale to change outcome in404

INTRODUCTION BY THOMAS FENSCH

Key Document G

Donoghue, Richard (ODAG)

From:	Donoghue, Richard (ODAG)
Sent:	Sunday, December 27, 2020 10:05 PM
To:	Brady, Scott (USAPAW)
Subject:	Fwd: Report for Voter Deficit
Attachments:	Summary PA Election Issues 12222020.pdf; ATT00001.htm; Letter Reply to Sec. Boockvar Lancaster County.pdf; ATT00002.htm; Election Timeline for Butler County - Kim Geyer.pdf; ATT00003.htm; Final Letter to Sen Johnson and Congressman Perry 12222020A(1).pdf; ATT00004.htm

JFYI regarding allegations about PA voting irregularities, for whatever it may be worth.

Begin forwarded message:

> **From:** Scott Perry <scott@patriotsforperry.com>
> **Date:** December 27, 2020 at 8:42:38 PM EST
> **To:** "Donoghue, Richard (ODAG)" <ricdonoghue@jmd.usdoj.gov>
> **Subject: Fwd: Report for Voter Deficit**
>
> Sir, as discussed.
>
> Sent from my iPhone
>
> Begin forwarded message:
>
>> **From:** Frank Ryan <(b) (6) com>
>> **Date:** December 22, 2020 at 5:46:53 PM EST
>> **To:** "Downey, Brian (HSGAC)" <brian_Downey@hsgac.senate.gov>, scott@patriotsforperry.com, "Aument, Ryan" <ryanaument@pasen.gov>, rboop@pasen.gov, bcutler@pahousegop.com, kbenning@pahousegop.com, Jake Smeltz <jsmeltz@pahousegop.com>, bnye@pahousegop.com, Bill Dougherty (b) (6), Heather Honey (b) (6)
>> **Cc:** Frank Ryan <fryan@pahousegop.com>, Rod Corey <rcorey@pahousegop.com>
>> **Subject: Re: Report for Voter Deficit**
>>
>> I would ask you to use the following materials. One page was inadvertently not scanned in for the Final Letter to Sen. Johnson and Congressman Perry. Everything else is perfect.

Introduction by Thomas Fensch

I apologize for the inconvenience and truly appreciate your understanding.

Semper fi,

Frank

On Tue, Dec 22, 2020 at 2:55 PM Frank Ryan (b) (6) > wrote:
Please see attached report for inclusion in the U. S. Senate Report as well as the update on the Voter Deficit in the 2020 General Election for President.

Semper fi,

Frank

--

Francis X. Ryan, KM
Colonel, USMCR (ret)
(b) (6)
(b) (6) (cell)
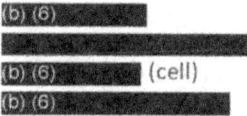

Life Lessons Learned Book - www.colfrankryan.com
Revolutionizing Accounting for Decision Making - www.leanabc.com

CONFIDENTIALITY NOTE: THIS EMAIL MESSAGE, INCLUDING ANY ATTACHMENT(S) CONTAINS INFORMATION THAT MAY BE CONFIDENTIAL, PROTECTED BY THE ATTORNEY CLIENT OR OTHER LEGAL PRIVILEGE, AND/OR PROPRIETARY NON PUBLIC INFORMATION. IF YOU ARE NOT AN INTENDED RECIPIENT OF THIS MESSAGE OR AN AUTHORIZED ASSISTANT TO AN INTENDED RECIPIENT, PLEASE NOTIFY THE SENDER BY REPLYING TO THIS MESSAGE AND THEN DELETE IT FROM YOUR SYSTEM. USE, DISSEMINATION, DISTRIBUTION OR REPRODUCTION OF THIS MESSAGE AND/OR ANY OF ITS ATTACHMENTS (IF ANY) BY UNINTENDED RECIPIENTS IS NOT AUTHORIZED AND MAY BE UNLAWFUL.

--

Francis X. Ryan, KM
Colonel, USMCR (ret)
(b) (6)
(b) (6) (cell)
(b) (6)

Life Lessons Learned Book - www.colfrankryan.com
Revolutionizing Accounting for Decision Making - www.leanabc.com

CONFIDENTIALITY NOTE: THIS EMAIL MESSAGE, INCLUDING ANY ATTACHMENT(S) CONTAINS INFORMATION THAT MAY BE CONFIDENTIAL, PROTECTED BY THE ATTORNEY CLIENT OR OTHER LEGAL PRIVILEGE, AND/OR PROPRIETARY NON PUBLIC INFORMATION. IF YOU ARE NOT AN INTENDED RECIPIENT OF THIS MESSAGE OR AN AUTHORIZED ASSISTANT TO AN INTENDED RECIPIENT, PLEASE NOTIFY THE SENDER BY REPLYING TO THIS MESSAGE AND THEN DELETE IT FROM YOUR SYSTEM. USE, DISSEMINATION, DISTRIBUTION OR REPRODUCTION OF THIS MESSAGE AND/OR ANY OF ITS ATTACHMENTS (IF ANY) BY UNINTENDED RECIPIENTS IS NOT AUTHORIZED AND MAY BE UNLAWFUL.

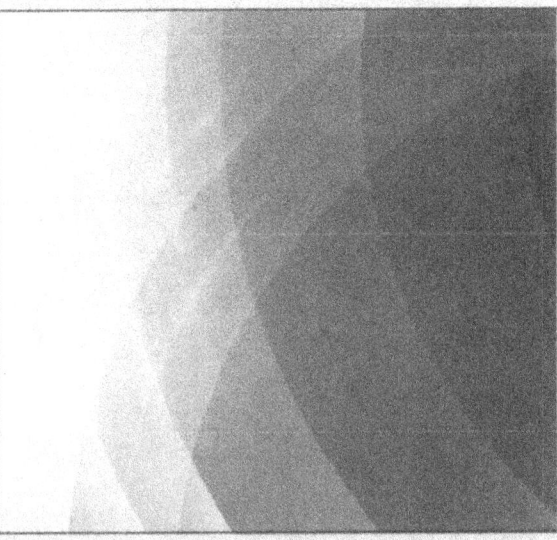

PA 2020 ELECTION ISSUES SUMMARY

ELECTION ISSUES

- **MORE VOTES COUNTED THAN VOTERS WHO VOTED**
  - MAIL IN
  - IN PERSON
- **DUPLICATE VOTERS:** PEOPLE IN SURE MORE THAN ONCE
  - EXAMPLE: SAME NAME & DOB BUT DIFFERENT ID #
- **DUPLICATE BALLOTS:** REQUESTED AND RETURNED

INTRODUCTION BY THOMAS FENSCH

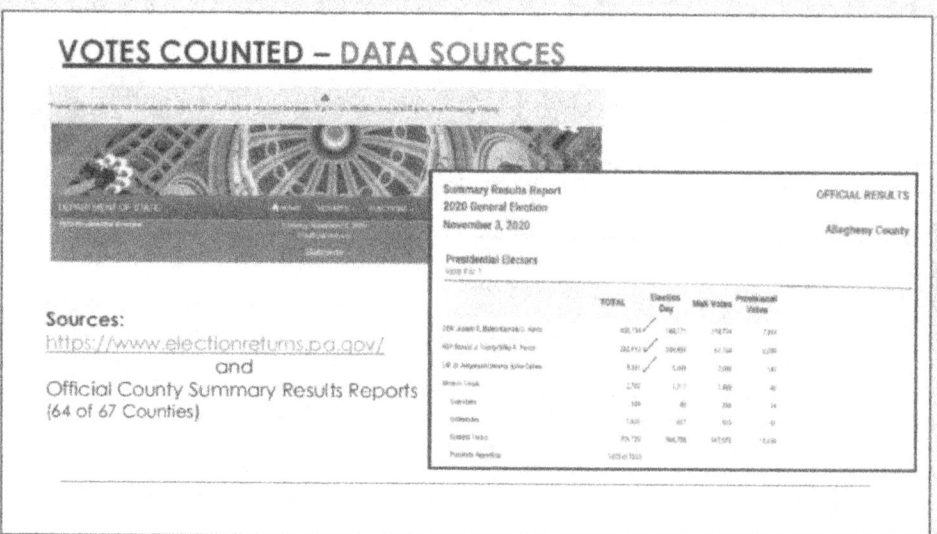

VOTERS WHO VOTED – DATA SOURCES

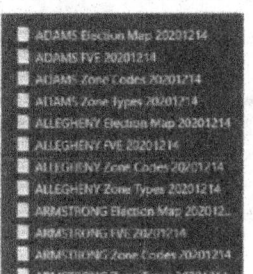

Sources:
https://www.pavoterservices.pa.gov/pages/purchasepafullvoterexport.aspx
and
Official County FVE files directly from the County Dated 12/14/2020

DATA FILE DEFINITIONS

- **Total Votes for President** – Sum of all votes counted for Biden, Trump, Jorgensen and all write in votes
- **Total Ballots Cast** – Total number of ballots cast in the county
- **Over-Votes** – Ballots cast with more than one selection for President
- **Under-Votes** – Ballots cast with no selection made for President
- **Write-In Votes** – Ballots cast with one write in vote for President
- **Total Voters SURE** – Total number of voters in the FVE who voted in the 2020 General Election 11/3/2020 (files updated 12/14/2020)
- **Voter Deficit** – Difference between the Total Ballots Cast and Total Voters recorded as voting on 11/3/2020 in SURE

INTRODUCTION BY THOMAS FENSCH

12/20/2020

COUNTY	TOTAL VOTES 3 MAJOR CANDIDATES	NOTE	TOTAL WRITE IN	TOTAL VOTES FOR PRESIDENT	OVER & UNDER VOTES	TOTAL BALLOTS CAST	TOTAL VOTERS SURE	TOTAL VOTER DEFICIT
	DOS DATA		COUNTY DATA				FVE	
CAMERON	2,434		6	2440	15	2455	2450	-5

SAMPLE COUNTY DATA - CAMERON

Cameron County has a voter deficit of 5 — meaning that there were 5 more ballots cast than the number of voters in SURE FVE for Cameron County as of 12/14/2020

TIMELINESS OF SURE FVE RECORDS

- Secretary of State certified the election results on 11/24/20.

- SURE FVE Files used for this analysis are dated 12/14/2020, 20 days after the certification

Department Of State Certifies Presidential Election Results

11/24/2020

Harrisburg, PA - Following certifications of the presidential vote submitted by all 67 counties late Monday, Secretary of State Kathy Boockvar today certified the results of the November 3 election in Pennsylvania for president and vice president of the United States.

Shortly thereafter, as required by federal law, Governor Tom Wolf signed the Certificate of Ascertainment for the slate of electors for Joseph R. Biden as president and Kamala D. Harris as vice president of the United States. The certificate was submitted to the Archivist of the United States.

INTERIM REPORT TOTALS AS OF 12-20-2020

- Report contains full data from **64 counties**
- Write In Votes and Over/Undervotes were not available for all counties. Updates pending.
- Data is not included for over/undervotes or total ballots cast for the following counties: Clarion, Crawford & Sullivan
- 24 of 67 Counties had vote totals that <u>did not</u> match the Department of State Results

INTERIM REPORT TOTALS AS OF 12-20-2020

COUNTY	TOTAL VOTES 3 MAJOR CANDIDATES	TOTAL WRITE IN	TOTAL VOTES FOR PRESIDENT	OVER & UNDER VOTES	TOTAL BALLOTS CAST	TOTAL VOTERS SURE	TOTAL VOTER DEFICIT	TOTAL VOTER SURPLUS
	DOS DATA	COUNTY DATA				FVE		
64/67	6,915,283	18,580	6,931,060	29,077	6,962,607	6,760,230	-205,122	2,532

Using the sources and data described in the previous slides, there is a VOTER DEFICIT in Pennsylvania. **205,122** more votes were counted than total number of voters who voted.

SURE IS THE OFFICIAL VOTER RECORD IN PA

- If SURE data was correct, the election could not be certified due to the discrepancies.
- If SURE data was incorrect, the election could not be certified due to discrepancies.

By Statute, the SURE System is the official voter record in Pennsylvania. This record includes the date last voted. Total voters who voted in the General Election on 11/3/2020 was **6,760,230**. Secretary of State Boockvar certified **6,915,283** votes for just the three major candidates. That alone is a **voter deficit of 155,053 voters**.

This does not include write in votes or over/under votes which all increase the voter deficit.

VOTER SURPLUS

Some counties have more voters than votes counted which is a normal variance. This is a result of several issues including:
- Rejected Provisional Ballots
- Mail-In Ballots Received after 8pm on Election Day
- Naked Ballots
- Mail Ballots with no Signature

The expectation would be that every county would have some votes that were not counted. In PA, **only 18 counties reported a voter surplus**. Despite the fact that every county had some ballots that were rejected.

COUNTY	TOTAL VOTES 3 MAJOR CANDIDATES	NOTE	TOTAL WRITE IN	TOTAL VOTES FOR PRESIDENT	OVER & UNDER VOTES	TOTAL BALLOTS CAST	TOTAL VOTERS SURE	TOTAL VOTER DEFICIT	TOTAL VOTER SURPLUS
	DOS DATA			COUNTY DATA			FVE		
ADAMS	56,540	*	174	56,809	121	56,930	56,853	77	
ALLEGHENY	719,733	*	2,767	724,800	1,920	726,720	605,754	120,966	
ARMSTRONG	36,370	*	55	36,426	45	36,471	36,147	324	
BEAVER	94,122		275	94,397	248	94,645	94,387	258	
BEDFORD	27,574	*	0	27,610	67	27,677	27,564	113	
BERKS	205,540		584	206,124	1,452	207,576	207,587		11
BLAIR	63,595		153	63,748	141	63,889	63,834	55	
BRADFORD	30,159	*	60	30,232	156	30,388	30,349	39	
BUCKS	396,234		1,057	397,291	1,506	398,797	396,877	1,920	
BUTLER	113,305	*	349	111,309	227	113,899	113,914		15
CAMBRIA	70,574		177	70,751	244	70,995	50,058	20,937	
CAMERON	2,434		6	2,440	15	2,455	2,450	5	
CARBON	33,629	*	38	33,689	64	33,753	33,716	37	
CENTRE	77,493		398	77,891	203	78,094	77,328	766	

COUNTY	TOTAL VOTES 3 MAJOR CANDIDATES	NOTE	TOTAL WRITE IN	TOTAL VOTES FOR PRESIDENT	OVER & UNDER VOTES	TOTAL BALLOTS CAST	TOTAL VOTERS SURE	TOTAL VOTER DEFICIT	TOTAL VOTER SURPLUS
CHESTER	314,502		1,251	315,753	833	316,586	313,543	-3,043	
CLARION	19,493		31	19,524			19,525		
CLEARFIELD	39,422		74	39,496	114	39,610	39,247	-363	
CLINTON	17,625		36	17,661	55	17,716	17,478	-238	
COLUMBIA	31,171		87	31,258	187	31,445	31,481		36
CRAWFORD	42,004	*	98	42,104			42,301		
CUMBERLAND	141,595		592	142,187	545	142,732	142,845		113
DAUPHIN	147,368		533	147,901	487	148,388	149,096		708
DELAWARE	327,331	*	1,075	328,329	1,821	330,150	326,142	-4,008	
ELK	16,906		40	16,946	89	17,035	17,077		42
ERIE	137,083	*	347	137,451	453	137,944	138,240		296
FAYETTE	62,139	*	91	62,258	117	62,375	61,952	423	
FOREST	2,646	*	8	2,621	10	2,631	2,666		35
FRANKLIN	80,783		242	81,025	183	81,208	81,143	-65	
FULTON	7,977		13	7,990	44	8,034	8,016	-18	
GREENE	17,669		0	17,669	0	17,776	17,760	-16	

INTRODUCTION BY THOMAS FENSCH

12/20/2020

COUNTY	TOTAL VOTES 3 MAJOR CANDIDATES	NOTE	TOTAL WRITE IN	TOTAL VOTES FOR PRESIDENT	OVER & UNDER VOTES	TOTAL BALLOTS CAST	TOTAL VOTERS SURE	TOTAL VOTER DEFICIT	TOTAL VOTER SURPLUS
HUNTINGDON	22,792		51	22,843	63	22,906	22,872	-34	
INDIANA	41,198		91	41,289	140	41,429	41,026	-403	
JEFFERSON	22,824	*	39	22,800	51	22,851	22,576	-275	
JUNIATA	12,043		29	12,072	36	12,108	12,072	-36	
LACKAWANNA	115,410		285	115,695	338	116,033	116,391		358
LANCASTER	280,239		1,136	281,375	1,163	282,538	281,117	-1,421	
LAWRENCE	46,076		111	46,187	132	46,319	46,023	-296	
LEBANON	71,652		206	71,858	202	72,060	71,524	-536	
LEHIGH	184,713	*	563	185,655	572	186,227	185,450	-777	
LUZERNE	153,321	*	99	153,499	635	154,134	149,877	-4,257	
LYCOMING	59,254		143	59,397	84	59,481	59,367	-114	
McKEAN	19,466		44	19,510	88	19,598	19,569	-29	
MERCER	57,954		163	58,117	178	58,295	58,308		13
MIFFLIN	21,502		45	21,547	56	21,603	21,538	-65	
MONROE	83,829	*	205	82,484	493	82,977	82,765	-212	
MONTGOMERY	510,157		0	510,157	3,238	513,395	508,084	-5,311	
MONTOUR	9,771		46	9,817	31	9,848	9,846	-2	

COUNTY	TOTAL VOTES 3 MAJOR CANDIDATES	NOTE	TOTAL WRITE IN	TOTAL VOTES FOR PRESIDENT	OVER & UNDER VOTES	TOTAL BALLOTS CAST	TOTAL VOTERS SURE	TOTAL VOTER DEFICIT	TOTAL VOTER SURPLUS
NORTHAMPTON	170,942		457	171,399	762	172,161	171,962	-199	
NORTHUMBERLAND	42,283		100	42,383	209	42,592	42,408	-184	
PERRY	24,652		76	24,728	54	24,782	24,894		112
PHILADELPHIA	741,377	*	2,067	743,966	5,351	749,317	719,024	-30,293	
PIKE	32,554	*		32,616	127	32,743	32,645	-98	
POTTER	9,064		21	9,085	3	9,088	9,119		31
SCHUYLKILL	70,605	*	152	69,672	1,237	70,909	70,974		65
SNYDER	19,140		41	19,181	57	19,238	19,237	-1	
SOMERSET	40,545		83	40,626	90	40,716	40,738		22
SULLIVAN	3,595		3	3,598			3,613		
SUSQUEHANNA	21,752	*	61	21,325	118	21,443	21,536		93
TIOGA	21,075	*		21,126	81	21,207	21,115	-92	
UNION	20,115		77	20,192	80	20,272	20,221	-51	
VENANGO	26,528		73	26,601	52	26,653	26,606	-49	
WARREN	20,650	*	56	20,345	129	20,474	21,012		538
WASHINGTON	118,478		278	118,756	383	119,139	117,156	-1,983	
WAYNE	28,089		58	28,147	88	28,235	28,231	-4	
WESTMORELAND	204,697	*	486	205,330	758	206,088	202,143	-3,945	
WYOMING	14,858		42	14,900	38	14,938	14,982		44
YORK	238,471	*	582	239,052	613	239,665	238,877	788	

RELIABILITY OF DATA FROM DEPARTMENT OF STATE

Candidate	Election Day	Mail	Provisional	Math Total	Certified Electors	Difference
Biden	1409341	1995691	53168	3458200	3458229	29
Jorgensen	53318	24783	1277	79378	79380	2
Trump	2731230	595538	50874	3377642	3377674	32
Write In	0	0	0	0	0	0
Totals	4193889	2616012	105319	6915220	6915283	63

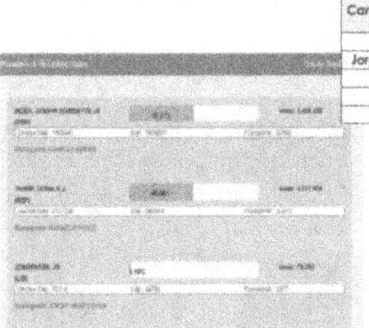

- Source: https://www.electionreturns.pa.gov/

- The DOS Data is not using equations or formulas to populate. This is demonstrated by the mathematical errors on the dashboard.
- Based on the Dashboard, **PA actually certified the <u>incorrect number of electors</u>**
- Data downloaded from the DOS website does not match data reported

---

RELIABILITY OF DATA FROM DEPARTMENT OF STATE

Candidate	Election Day	Mail	Provisional	Math Total	Certified Electors	Difference
Biden	1409341	1995691	53168	3458200	3458229	29
Jorgensen	53318	24783	1277	79378	79380	2
Trump	2731230	595538	50874	3377642	3377674	32
Write In	0	0	0	0	0	0
Totals	4193889	2616012	105319	6915220	6915283	63

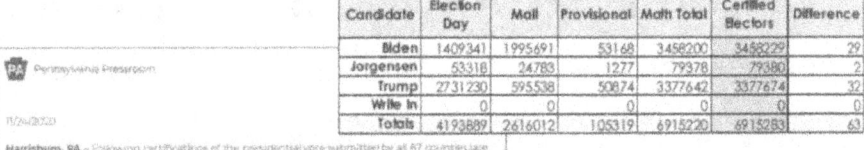

Due to mathematical errors, the Secretary of State **actually certified the incorrect number of electors**

Source: https://www.media.pa.gov/pages/State-details.aspx?newsid=435

DUPLICATE VOTERS
Individuals in SURE With Multiple ID Numbers-
Both IDs Shown as Voted 11-3-2020

POSSIBLE DUPLICATE VOTERS

USING THE STATEWIDE FVE, A QUERY OF ALL RECORDS WHERE THE FIRST NAME, LAST NAME AND DATE OF BIRTH MATCHED AND WHERE BOTH RECORDED A VOTE ON 11/3/2020 – PRODUCED **4241 RECORDS**. THESE RECORDS WARRANT INVESTIGATION TO DETERMINE HOW MANY PEOPLE VOTED TWO OR MORE TIMES.

*THESE RECORDS HAVE BEEN REFERRED TO LAW ENFORCEMENT FOR INVESTIGATION

DUPLICATE BALLOTS
Requested & Returned

DUPLICATE MAIL IN BALLOT APPLICATIONS

- County election officials were inundated with duplicate mail in ballot applications
- It was up to the county to review each new application and make a judgement call about whether to send a second mail in ballot
- There was no accounting of the excess mailed ballots.

Source: https://www.post-gazette.com/news/politics-state/2020/10/16/pennsylvania-rejected-mail-ballot-applications-duplicates-voters/stories/202010160153

"Overall, one out of every five requests for mail ballots is being rejected in Pennsylvania. An estimated 208,000 Pennsylvania voters sent in the spurned requests, some submitting them multiple times. Although the state's email rejecting the requests describes them as duplicates, it doesn't explain why, prompting some people to reapply. ProPublica and The Inquirer identified hundreds of voters who submitted three or more duplicate applications; one voter appears to have submitted 11 duplicates."

INTRODUCTION BY THOMAS FENSCH

12/20/2020

DUPLICATE APPLICATIONS

County	Total MIB Requests Approved	Duplicate Requests Rejected
ADAMS	9,695	2,001
ALLEGHENY	190,557	49,025
ARMSTRONG	3,995	1,347
BEAVER	16,893	5,362
BEDFORD	2,906	384
BERKS	42,084	7,544
BLAIR	7,578	2,993
BRADFORD	3,948	500
BUCKS	104,236	21,607
BUTLER	16,718	4,468
CAMBRIA	6,865	1,292
CAMERON	310	98
CARBON	5,670	1,011
CENTRE	17,952	3,483
CHESTER	88,236	24,433
CLARION	2,265	364
CLEARFIELD	4,894	897
CLINTON	2,229	332
COLUMBIA	5,264	693
CRAWFORD	6,584	782
CUMBERLAND	31,206	5,703
DAUPHIN	32,778	7,247
DELAWARE	71,523	15,779
ELK	2,075	472
ERIE	26,985	4,183
FAYETTE	7,965	1,680
FOREST	547	6
FRANKLIN	11,108	1,443
FULTON	784	128
GREENE	2,278	317
HUNTINGDON	1,674	202
INDIANA	8,676	
JEFFERSON	2,464	249
JUNIATA	1,116	281
LACKAWANNA	24,748	7,794
LANCASTER	53,245	9,984
LAWRENCE	7,379	1,113
LEBANON	13,613	2,205
LEHIGH	46,091	9,279
LUZERNE	34,077	11,254
LYCOMING	7,922	1,128
MCKEAN	9,691	460
MERCER	2,468	320
MIFFLIN	21,455	3,661
MONROE	138,758	32,407
MONTGOMERY	1,975	438
MONTOUR	2,292	343
MORTOUR	2,292	240
NORTHAMPTON	42,284	6,890
NORTHUMBERLAND	5,494	1,047
PERRY	3,304	545
PHILADELPHIA	230,594	48,727
PIKE	8,355	1,059
POTTER	842	92
SCHUYLKILL	6,813	443
SNYDER	2,223	423
SOMERSET	4,390	359
SULLIVAN	375	39
SUSQUEHANNA	2,833	392
TIOGA	2,561	444
UNION	3,185	508
VENANGO	2,653	747
WARREN	3,032	336
WASHINGTON	21,829	4,567
WAYNE	3,124	654
WESTMORELAND	34,103	12,871
WYOMING	2,313	304
YORK	42,677	10,191
TOTAL		**336,301**

as of 10/16/2020

Department of State released data showing the number of duplicate MIB Applications that had been rejected as of 10/16/2020.
DOS did not release the number of duplicates that were approved & mailed.

EXAMPLE: LEBANON COUNTY DUPLICATES

- Lebanon County has 92,637 registered voters.
- As of 10/16/2020, Lebanon had already received 2205 duplicate mail in ballot applications.
- County election officials had to review and evaluate each application to determine if a second mail in ballot should be mailed
- 804 duplicate ballots were sent to voters in Lebanon County.
- The location of the additional 804 mail in ballots is unknown.

Third Party Access - SURE
Recap of Previous Issues Raised

Department of State Granted Access & Authority to Third Party Entities

- Third Party Access to SURE using Web API
- Allowing Third Party Entities authority to use Web API to request Mail In Ballots
- Illegal Use of Voter Registration Data – posting on the internet

CHAPTER 183. ESTABLISHMENT, IMPLEMENTATION AND ADMINISTRATION OF THE STATEWIDE UNIFORM REGISTRY OF ELECTORS (SURE System)

4 Pa. Code § 183.14. Public information lists

(i) Within 10 days of receiving a written request accompanied by the payment of the cost of reproduction and postage, the Department or a commission will distribute the public information list to any registrant in this Commonwealth for a reasonable fee, determined by the office providing the copies, as provided by section 1404(c)(1) of the act (relating to public information lists).

(j) The Department and a commission will supply the public information list in a paper copy or in an electronic format.

(k) The list may not be published on the Internet.

DOS Expanded Third Party Entities Access to Include Mail-In Ballot Requests

On March 5 2020, The Department of State issued an update to the PA OVR Web API Specification document. In that update, they reveal that Posting Entities would be granted access and authority to allow the use of their apps to not only create voter registrations but also to add them to **permanent mail-in list.**

MAIL-IN BALLOT REQUEST OPTION (ACT 77 OF 2019)

As a part of Act 77 of 2019, a new ballot option was introduced for Pennsylvania voters, the mail-in ballot option. This is another option for voters to receive a ballot in the mail and it does not require an excuse to vote. Additionally, a voter who is requesting a mail-in ballot may also request to be added to a permanent mail-in voter list, which is otherwise known as an annual mail-in ballot request. If they opt for the permanent option, they will then receive ballots automatically for the remainder of the calendar year for eligible elections. Then, they will be asked to renew this request each year from the county election office to continue to receive ballots for eligible election.

The process begins with the voter electing to submit a mail-in ballot application. Once their application is completed, processed and approved by the county, the voter will be begin to receive their ballots via the address

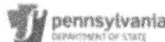

pennsylvania
DEPARTMENT OF STATE

Page 14

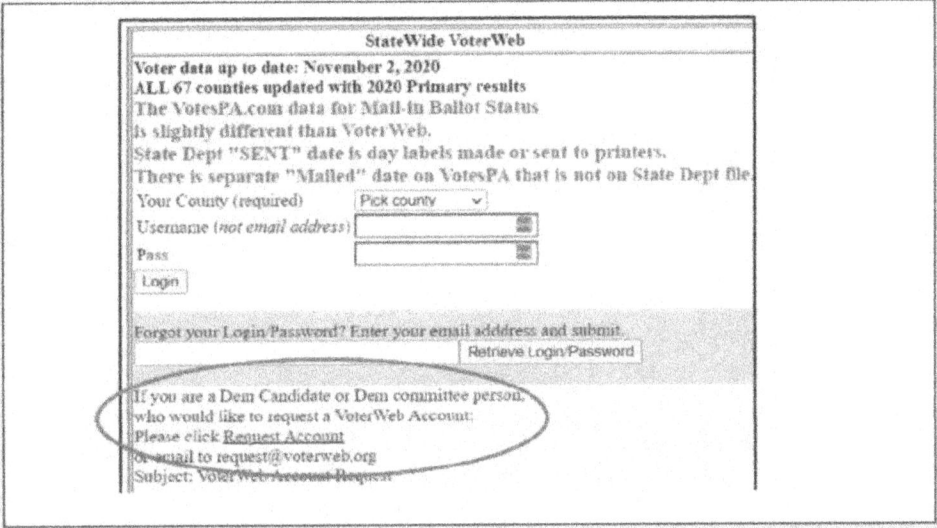

INTRODUCTION BY THOMAS FENSCH

County Commissioners
Joshua G. Parsons, Chairman
Ray D'Agostino, Vice-Chairman
Craig E. Lehman

Office of the Commissioners

150 North Queen Street
Suite #715
Lancaster, PA 17603
Phone: 717-299-8300
Fax: 717-293-7208
www.co.lancaster.pa.us

Hon. Kathy Boockvar
Secretary of the Commonwealth
Pennsylvania Department of State
North Office Building, Suite 302
401 North Office Building
Harrisburg, PA 17120
Via email

Dear Secretary Boockvar:

As you know Act 77 of 2019, which was signed into law by Governor Wolf, created a new mail in ballot option for voters in Pennsylvania. The law as passed by the legislature and signed by the Governor requires that all mailed ballots be received by 8:00 PM on election day.

Subsequently, the Pennsylvania Supreme Court created its own new rule. It ordered that ballots are to be accepted if they are postmarked on or before election day and are received within three days after polls close. Further, a ballot with no postmark or an illegible postmark must also be accepted if it is received by that same date.

That ruling has been appealed to the United States Supreme Court. In the U.S. Supreme Court's denial of a motion to expedite the case, the court appears to have relied on information from your department that you would provide guidance to counties to segregate ballots that come in after election day. It said:

"[W]e have been informed by the Pennsylvania Attorney General that the Secretary of the Commonwealth issued guidance today directing county boards of elections to segregate ballots received between 8:00 p.m. on November 3, 2020, and 5:00 p.m. on November 6, 2020."

On October 28th, 2020, Lancaster County received an email from Jonathan Marks, Deputy Secretary for Elections & Commissions, stating the following:

"Yesterday the Secretary issued the attached guidance related to mail-in and absentee ballots received from the United States Postal Service after 8:00 p.m. on Tuesday November 3, 2020. The guidance referenced that a motion to expedite a petition for a writ of certiorari related to the three-day extension was pending in

INTRODUCTION BY THOMAS FENSCH

the United States Supreme Court. After the Secretary issued the guidance yesterday, the United States Supreme Court denied the pending motion to expedite consideration of the petition for a writ of certiorari. In doing so, three Justices of the Supreme Court joined in a statement that referenced the guidance that the Secretary issued yesterday directing county boards of elections to segregate ballots received between 8:00 p.m. on November 3, 2020 and 5:00 p.m. on November 6, 2020. Though the Secretary continues to strongly defend the 3 day extension to ensure that every timely and validly cast mail-in and absentee ballot is counted, to ensure uniformity and to respect the United States Supreme Court's consideration of the issues still before it, the Secretary strongly encourages each county board of elections to affirmatively confirm that it will comply with the attached guidance."

The attached "guidance" read:

"The county boards of elections **shall not pre-canvass or canvass any mail-in or civilian absentee ballots** received between 8:00 p.m. on Tuesday, November 3, 2020 and 5:00 p.m. on Friday, November 6, 2020 until further direction is received. These ballots shall be maintained by the county board in a secure, safe and sealed container separate from other voted ballots." [Emphasis added.]

By law, counties have eight days to complete the canvas. We have been informed by our elections office staff that once ballots are canvassed, it is logistically impossible to later remove those ballots from the total count. Thus, the guidance to keep these ballots separate and not canvass them immediately makes sense as they are likely the subject of litigation.

However, on November 1st, 2020, we received new "guidance" from Mr. Marks.

Strangely the new "guidance" has suddenly been changed to the following statement, which is in direct conflict with the earlier "guidance."

"The county board of elections **shall canvass** segregated absentee and mail-in ballots received after 8:00 P.M. on Tuesday November 3, 2020, and before 5:00 P.M. on Friday November 6, 2020 **as soon as possible upon receipt of the ballots** and within the period specified by law for the canvass. The canvass meeting shall continue until all segregated absentee and mail-in ballots have been canvassed." [Emphasis added.]

The new guidance is essentially asking us to add any ballots that come in after election day to our total count. In fact, the new "guidance" is strangely asking us to do this as "soon as possible." I anticipate that you would know full well that those contested votes cannot then be removed if the Commonwealth is ordered to do so by the United States Supreme Court.

This is in contravention to your earlier guidance and appears to be in contravention to what the United States Supreme Court relied on from your department. That court, in refusing to expedite the case, surely did not anticipate that you would make those votes impossible to remove from the total count.

As a result, at our Board of Elections meeting on November 2nd, 2020 a majority of the board exercised our legal authority to comply with the law and your first set of guidance and wait to canvass any ballots that come in after election day. We will make further decisions at a future board meeting and, of course, intend to continue to fully comply with the law, including the canvass deadline.

I remain, however, deeply concerned about this strange change in guidance by your department and what it means for the integrity of the election.

Sincerely,

Joshua G. Parsons
Chairman, Board of Commissioners

CC: Senator Joe Scarnati, President Pro Tempore, Pennsylvania Senate
    Via email
    Representative Bryan Cutler, Speaker of the Pennsylvania House of Representatives
    Via email

INTRODUCTION BY THOMAS FENSCH

Election Timeline for Butler County, Pennsylvania/November 12, 2020

In 2016, Butler County had a 72% voter support for Donald J. Trump in comparison to Hilary Clinton at 28%. Pennsylvania ranks 25th for voter participation with 51 percent of the eligible population voting in the 2018 election. Butler County was a stronghold for President Trump in the past as well as other Republican Candidates, I believe, our County was specifically targeted by external forces such as Governor Tom Wolf, Secretary of Commonwealth and State Election Director Kathy Boockvar, Mark Zuckerberg/ Media/ Tech, as well as, Progress PA and Democrats statewide, to name just a few. There is no doubt these entities used their positions to influence the overall outcome of the Pennsylvania 2020 election. Often times this was done under the Covid guise of safeguarding the health, safety, and accessibility of Pennsylvania voters. As a Butler County Commissioner, I witnessed first hand these ongoing efforts made by these entities to chip away preceding and post election through a variety of tactics with the purpose of creating confusion, chaos, and instilling fear...all implemented by design. Changes made "on the fly" to election laws intentionally without our elected state legislature, left Pennsylvania counties isolated and at the mercy of edicts by State officials with no recourse. Counties were left to their own devices and fortitude to determine what was occurring and push back as we did multiple times. What was even more tragic, these changes were most often accomplished under the guise and cover of the Covid pandemic that was used to influence the behavior of the public voter who fell for it hook, line, and sinker by the mail in ballot system which encompassed early voting. One by one, our own Pennsylvania Democratic State Officials stripped each of the previously established safeguards and firewall requirements that protect the integrity of the voter system. It was astonishing the extent and effort these aforementioned entities went to, to influence and marginalize the 2020 vote in any way to the advantage of Presidential Candidate Joe Biden. Progressive entities well understood it would not take much to manipulate and alter the playing field in what was predetermined to be a race separated by less than a 100,000 votes. Secretary Kathy Boockvar went as far as requesting King Bench provisions to be used as a mechanism by the Pennsylvania State Supreme Court, as State Officials were struggling to get Counties to comply with over zealous state edicts and guidance in lieu of laws. Governor Wolf signed a second renewal of his 90 day disaster for the Covid 19 pandemic that would extend beyond the November 3, 2020 election. Naturally, as expected, Covid hype despite evidence would begin to surge prior to and during the election with the intent to keep senior citizens from venturing out to the polls. Democrats were whole heartedly supportive of mail in balloting and they knew Republicans would prefer to vote in person at the polls. Bad weather or a pandemic, could possibly persuade some elderly or unhealthy individuals to stay at home? Hopefully, the Butler County timeline will illuminate a much needed light into the workings of these forces and how they can influence our local, state, and national elections. The data, numbers, and dubious actions compiled in the Butler County timeline demonstrate repeatedly as to the Governor and his Election Administration's great reluctance to follow existing election law and processes, their lack of respect for the Constitution, and the Governor's own defiance to govern with the elected Pennsylvania General

Introduction by Thomas Fensch

Assembly who represent the voice of and by the people. The people of Pennsylvania deserve to know to the extent and effort made by various entities to marginalize the existing laws and processes governing our Commonwealth's election system in an effort to alter and/or influence a Presidential Election. After all, if our laws and Constitution do not mean or stand for anything and we allow anyone, even a Governor, to over ride laws, even under the conditions of a pandemic, then why have a Constitution? Moving forward we must learn how we must work in each of our own capacities, whether, we are a working man or an elected county commissioner to stand up and protect not only our election system nationwide for the greater good of democracy and our country as a whole. Our future generations of voters and our country depend upon it.

Kimberly D. Geyer, Vice Chairman of the Butler County Commissioners

- Coming into office in 2016, Butler County, like many in PA, were in the process of researching state certified vendors of election equipment and investing into new voter equipment with a paper trail to replace existing equipment which was a touch screen technology and no paper trail. In April 2018, the Department of State informed counties they must select the new voting systems by the end of 2019 and voters must use the new system no later than the April 2020 primary election. At least 52 counties, or 78 percent, have taken official action toward selecting a new voting system. And 46 counties, or 68 percent, plan to use their new voting system in the November 2019 election. Because Butler County had begun the process of interviewing and acquiring new election equipment prior to the state mandate by the Governor, we felt in a better prepared position prior to our fellow counties who, some, had only begun the process after the 2018 mandate.
- October 31, 2019 Governor Tom Wolf made voting more convenient by signing PA Act 77 of 2019 into law. Without state legislature input, Governor Wolf removed straight party ballot voting. Governor Wolf established the ability for counties to set up temporary polling locations as early voting stations.

Some of the provisions of PA Act 77 of 2019 are as follows: (prior to last minute changes)

- **No excuse mail-in voting**
  The law creates a new option to vote by mail without providing an excuse, which is currently required for voters using absentee ballots. Pennsylvania joins 31 other states and Washington, D.C. with mail in voting that removes barriers to elections.
- **50-day mail-in voting period**
  All voters can request and submit their mail in or absentee ballot up to 50 days before the election, which is the longest vote by mail period in the country.

- **Permanent mail-in and absentee ballot list**
  Voters can request to receive applications for mail in or absentee ballots for all primary, general and special elections held in a given year. Counties will mail applications to voters on the list by the first Monday of each February. Voters who return an application will receive ballots for each election scheduled through the next February. Pennsylvania is the 12th state to provide voters with the automatic option.
- **15 more days to register to vote**
  The deadline to register to vote is extended to 15 days from 30 days before an election. Cutting the current deadline by half enables more people to participate in elections. The new more flexible and voter friendly deadlines provide more time to register to vote than 24 other states.
- **Creates Early Voting**
  Perhaps without full legislative awareness, Act 77 also creates early voting, which many state legislators did not fully understand as it was not clear in the act. This suddenly created long lines of voters in County election bureau offices in the week(s) leading up to the election, further distracting and hampering the ability to effectively execute actual mail ballot processing and election preparations. (See attached article from Philadelphia 3.0 PAC)
- **Extends mail-in and absentee submission deadlines**
  Voters can submit mail in and absentee ballots until 8:00 p.m. on Election Day. (Later extended to three days post Election Day). The current deadline is 5:00 p.m. on the Friday before an election, which is the most restrictive in the country. Pennsylvanians submitted 195,378 absentee ballots in 2018, but 8,162 more than four percent missed the deadline and were rejected. The national average is only two percent.
- The law also authorizes the governor to pursue a $90 million bond to reimburse counties for 60 percent of their actual costs to replace voting systems. The new systems have enhanced security to help guard against hacking and produce an anonymous paper record so voters can verify their ballot is correctly marked when casting it. Paper records also allow officials to conduct the most accurate recounts and audits of election results.
- 3/6/20 Covid 19 made its presence known in Butler County. Meanwhile, PA Department of Health Secretary Rachel Levine was providing Pennsylvanians daily televised updates on the Covid pandemic and statewide stay at home, school, and business closures began to be implemented across regions of the PA Commonwealth.
- 3/27/20 Governor Wolf signed Senate Bill 422, which rescheduled Pennsylvania's primary election from April 28 to June 2 due to the COVID 19 emergency.
- 4/22/20 Governor closed Commonwealth with the exception of life sustaining businesses. Schools and childcare facilities closed. Stay at home orders in place.
- 4/22/20 Butler County election director resigns approximately one month ahead of what was to be the May 2020 Presidential Primary before the State

Introduction by Thomas Fensch

extended it to June 2, 2020. This would be a pattern reoccurring statewide due to frustration by State changes being made on the fly, and increased workloads related to the mail in ballot requirements. More than a 19 of PA's County Election Directors or Deputies resigned or left, that is one in every 3.5 counties. Butler County deputized two long time workers to split the position until posting the job vacancy after the June 2nd Primary.

- 4/28/20 Updated DOS (Dept. of State) guidance began occurring to all counties in regards to preparation of elections (2020 Presidential Primary) and HEIGHTENING Covid 19.
- 5/1/20 DOS asked counties to participate in a technology program called Albert Sensors to have counties connect into and to provide multi state information sharing and analytics. Butler County declined to participate as a pilot county. Butler County had just invested in new technology enhancements and did not want to that to interfere with our new internal technologies and security. (This request will come around again by DOS in the weeks leading to the Fall November election).
- 5/5/20 Butler County represented by two Republican County Commissioners (Osche & Geyer) filed petition for amicus brief for the Friends of Danny Devito case v. Governor Tim Wolf and Rachel Levine, Secretary of Health (respondents) for the statewide business closures and the Constitutional violations represented by Attorney Thomas W. King III.
- 5/7/20 (2:30p.m.) Butler County (Osche & Geyer) files lawsuit in federal district court on behalf of Butler County, and joining counties, Greene, Fayette, and Washington Counties v. Governor Tom Wolf and Rachel Levine, Secretary of Health for violating the constitutional rights of businesses and for the subjective process in determining business closures statewide.
- 5/7/20 Governor Wolf extends Stay at Home order for Counties in the Red to June 4th, two days AFTER the scheduled June 2nd primary further confusing voters, discouraging in person voting, and challenging Counties' ability to recruit adequate numbers of poll workers.
- 5/12/ 5/14/20 Poll Worker Training Occurred over these days with four sessions, two each morning and two each afternoon and one evening. Consider the changes since that time prior to the June 2 Primary and all of the changes that the DOS implemented between the Primary and November 3rd election. The constant barrage of DOS changes made it extremely challenging for Judges of Elections and poll workers to keep abreast of accurate information they needed to operate for election day. See attached letter from a Judge of Election.
- 5/2020 the two Republican county commissioners worked feverishly to equip all 89 precincts with trained poll workers, PPE, and locate new sites for those closed due to the Covid pandemic and the media narrative instilling wide spread fear into former poll workers. It was extremely challenging to get each and every poll open and staffed by those less fearful and willing to work under these conditions. Many older poll workers could not work due to compromised immune systems and it caused us to up our

game on recruiting and training new poll workers. i.e. Former precincts located in churches and schools closed due to the Governor's stay at home orders was in conflict with us as elected officials trying to get the public to understand that elections was a constitutional right and we had to open facilities for voting.

- The State stated they would send PPE to all the counties for their polling sites, such as hand sanitizer and masks. Despite that promise, Butler County went ahead and ordered our own PPE and Plexiglas partitions for the polls and it is a good thing we did, as the State's masks and hand sanitizers arrived the day before the election after we had delivered all the voting equipment to the polls for the June 2nd Primary.
- Training for poll workers was extremely challenging as per trying to secure a county site such as a school or facility that would allow us to hold training during a Covid pandemic and Governor ordered statewide closures. Thankfully, Butler School District and Cranberry Twp. Municipal Building each provided us a physical space to hold poll worker and Judge of Elections trainings. The next challenge was adhering to the Covid compliance while trying to conduct and provide training with masking and people fearful due to the nationwide and statewide narrative coming from the news sources. It certainly created extensive work above and beyond for everyone involved.
- Mid May, Counties received DOS guidance advising Counties may have drop boxes and drop off locations. This last minute change was one that the Butler County Republican Commissioners voted not to implement due to the lack of security issues. May 31st and onward, Butler County had daily protests across from the courthouse in Diamond Park and along Main Street by BLM.
- 5/29/20 Counties received a court order by the DOS to require accessible mail in ballots for ADA individuals and to make arrangements.
- 5/29/20 Counties received DOS guidance on privacy envelopes. All of these guidance's issued by DOS, required all counties to adapt and create changes with their operations and procedures. Another implication was the inability to train our poll workers and Judges of Elections due to the late and daily guidance changes in preparation for and leading up to the June 2nd election.
- 5/29/20 DOS issued guidance no longer requiring voter identification for ballots to be dropped off a drop off sites and drop box locations. Butler County was requiring ID for ballots being dropped off at the Election Bureau.
- 6/1/20 At 6pm Pittsburgh Media News Channels announced publicly that Governor Wolf used executive order to extend the deadline for receiving mail in ballots the night before the June 2nd Primary Election. I watched this announcement in my own living room that evening when I returned home from being at the county all day working. The Governor never bothered to reach out to the counties about this during the workday. Governor Wolf also announced the set up of additional drop boxes for only six of sixty seven counties statewide. This strategic move all added to the public's existing confusion 12 hours before the June 2, 2020 Presidential Election.

INTRODUCTION BY THOMAS FENSCH

- 6/1/20 Governor Wolf also announced on the 6pm television news that ballots must be post marked by June 2nd, but received no later than June 9th for some counties, but not all counties. Again, adding additional public confusion and fear.
- 6/3/20 Governor Wolf amended stay at home order
- 6/5/20 Butler County was one of 12 counties to move to the yellow phase.
- 6/10/20 PA General Assembly passed a concurrent resolution directing Governor Wolf to issue a proclamation or executive order ending his issuance of the March 6 Covid 19 Disaster Emergency which was renewed June 3. Governor follows with statement that any concurrent resolution needs to come to the Governor for approval or disapproval and that orders will remain in place and that the legislature did nothing to end them.
- 6/16/20 Governor Wolf edicts: School Safety & Security Committee and Etc.
- 6/25/20 Governor Wolf and Secretary Levine sign 12 counties moving to the green phase effective the following day.
- 6/29/20 Governor Wolf announces that Lebanon County will move to the green phase of reopening on July 3, putting all counties in green.
- 6/29/20 Governor Wolf announces all businesses across PA can apply for grants to offset lost revenue associated with Covid 19.
- 7/1/20 Governor Wolf signs new order signed by Dr. Rachel Levine that mandates mask wearing directive at all times effective immediately.
- 7/ /20 Received state association communications regarding Trump Campaign and RNC filed law suit pursuant to Governor and DOS Secretary.
- 7/9/20 Governor Wolf signs an executive order protecting renters from evictions or foreclosures in the event they have not received assistance.
- 7/10/20 Governor Wolf signs an executive order authorizing state agencies to conduct administrative proceedings and hearings remotely.
- 7/16/20 Governor Tom Wolf releases federal CARES funding to PA Counties with the exception of Lebanon County who had opened their county despite the Covid associated closures moving from yellow to green on their own.
- 7/16/20 Butler County hires a new Election Director with extensive technical experience and local experience of working at the polls.
- 7/17/20 Federal Court in Pittsburgh, Judge William Stickman IV hears Butler County v. Governor Tom Wolf and Rachel Levine, Secretary of Health
- 7/22/20 Declaratory Judgment Hearing in Federal Court, Pittsburgh by Judge William Stickman
- 7/31/20 DOS announces that the State will provide the entire commonwealth's counties with prepaid postage for their envelopes, so voters would have no excuse for not mailing them. What they didn't tell county officials or the public, is typically, prepaid postage is not automatically postmarked. The State would use federal CARES funding (Covid 19 Relief Funds) to pay for postage. Postmarks matter to prove voters cast their vote on time.

Subverting Justice

- 8/14/20 Governor Tom Wolf finally concedes and releases federal CARES funding to Lebanon County after with holding it for a month. There is a timeline on these funds to be used before December 30, 2020.
- 8/27/20 The DOS contacted counties about additional second round funding being made available for election system equipment through the $90 million bond amortization pursuant to Act 77 voting system reimbursements.
- 8/31/20 Governor Wolf signed a second renewal of his 90 day disaster for the Covid 19 pandemic that would extend beyond the November 3, 2020 election.
- 9/2/20 DOS contacts all county commissioners announcing that the non profit Center for Tech and Civic Life has expanded its Covid response grant program to offer all local election jurisdictions in the United States to apply for grants to help ensure staffing, training and equipment for the November 2020 election. The expansion is thanks to a $250 million contribution from Mark Zuckerberg and his wife, Pricilla Chan, who also made a $50 million contribution to the Center for Election Innovation and Research, which will offer additional grants to states. Butler County declined to accept these funds to protect the integrity of their election system in Butler County from being influenced by a private/public entity.
- Butler County Election Director informs us that Barbara Smotherman has been assigned to Butler County as the state election liaison. Deputy Smotherman is the Deputy Chief of Staff to DOS Secretary Kathy Boockvar.
- 9/8/20 Governor Wolf puts out an edict that restaurants must have self certification documents in order to open September 21st at 50% occupancy.
- 9/11/20 DOS issues guidance concerning examination of absentee and mail in ballot return envelopes as well as addressing signatures or lack of.
- 9/14/20 Federal Judge William Stickman IV rules that Governor Wolfs orders violated three clauses of the U.S. Constitution, the right of assembly, due process, and equal protection clause. Butler County wins suit.
- 9/14/20 PA State Supreme Court rules that signature verification on a ballot Vs the one in the voter's file no longer matters.
- 9/15/20 Governor and Secretary Levine turn up the news narrative on Covid and Butler County.
- 9/16/20 PA Attorney General issues a stay on judicial decision on federal decision striking down Governor Tom Wolf's business closures.
- 9/17/20 PA State Supreme Court rules ballots mailed back without secrecy envelopes will not be counted in the general election. Known as "naked ballots".
-
- 9/17/20 PA Supreme Court (Democratic Majority) issued the following: **Majority opinion in PA Democratic Party et al. v. Boockvar et al. holding as follows:**
    - The Election Code permits county boards of election to accept hand-delivered mail-in ballots at locations other than their office addresses including drop-boxes

INTRODUCTION BY THOMAS FENSCH

- Adopts a three-day extension of the absentee and mail-in ballot received by deadline to allow for the tabulation of ballots mailed by voters via USPS and postmarked by 8:00 pm on Election Day
- Holds that voters are not entitled to notice and an opportunity to cure minor defects resulting from failure to comply with statutory requirements for vote by mail (Yet the DOS made this request on Election Day to Counties with naked ballots) See: 11/3/20
- Holds that a mail-in elector's failure to enclose a ballot in a secrecy envelope renders the ballot invalid
- Finds that the poll watcher residency requirement does not violate the state or federal constitutions
- **Order in Crossey et al v. Boockvar**
  - Dismisses the request to extend the received-by deadline for mail-in ballots as moot based on the decision in PA Democratic Party v. Boockvar
  - Dismisses the request that prepaid postage be provided on mail-in provide funding to county boards of election for postage on mail-in ballots
  - Denies the request that voters be permitted to obtain third-party assistance in return of mail in ballots
  - PA Supreme Court also ruled that the Green Party's candidate for president did not strictly follow procedures for getting on November's ballot and cannot appear on it, <u>and the Department of State has now certified the ballot*.</u>

- *What is important for the public to understand that as of 9 17 20, Counties were unable to print and prepare ballots prior to 9 17 20 due to the lack of a ruling on the Green Party candidate. <u>The ballot was not state certified until this legal decision occurred.</u> Now, counties in PA were racing to print their ballots and get them mailed out to all those who requested mail in ballots which were in the thousands.
- 9/24/2020 Commissioner Osche receives email from an overseas voter in Switzerland who is a dual resident of Butler County who claims she did not receive her email ballot. The election director reported that he had communication from the state indicating this was a "glitch" in the state system related to the secure email. She is a member of a group called "PA Abroad" and claims suspicion as that group believes that only Butler and Cumberland Counties did not send the ballots. After being called out on her reports, she replies that she did subsequently receive her ballot. And so begins the mass reports of voters "not receiving" ballots.
- Butler County began to mail out their ballots to mail in requesters beginning the week of September 28, 2020 and worked 7 days a week to begin to mail out and simultaneously accept applications. Butler County continually hired additional temporary staff and extended hours of service to keep up with all the changes and timelines.
- 10/1/20 Governor Wolf issued an executive order amending the previous order Directing Mitigation Measures, which would go into

- effect the following day and would continue to until rescinded or amended in writing.
- 10/8/20 Governor Wolf issues an executive order amending the previous order related to Directing Mitigation Measures which would go into effect the following day until rescinded or amended in writing.
- 10/8/20 We became aware of a problem originating at the Department of State in the SURE System, which is the state's 15 20 year old data election's system and software. Voters who are monitoring the status of their ballot online are suddenly seeing it was mailed out in early September (before the ballot was state certified). Someone at the state level changed something in SURE early October that populated the "Ballot Mailed On" date with the same date his or her application was processed. A similar situation occurred in the Primary. It's happened across the state, and both the SURE helpdesk and DOS are aware of it. This has generated a high volume of calls to the County of folks monitoring their ballot process online.
- Butler County will come to learn from their Election Director that there were several glitches with the SURE system preceding the election.
- Butler County did an extensive mail drop to the U.S. Post Office of approximately 10,000 ballots October 13, 2020, the day after Columbus Day which was observed as a national holiday but in which the elections department worked and another 7,000 mailed out later that week.
- Week of 10/13/20 Democratic Commissioner hears from Governor's Southwest Regional Director about Albert Sensor Technology Pilot and pushes for our County's participation to which we again, decline.
- The week of October 19, 2020, the County began to get calls and complaints by public not receiving their mail in ballot despite requests made in September. The public was told that the ballots were not state certified until 9/17 and printed and mailed out until the 28th.
- 10/19/20 Election Director reports receiving the following memo from PA SURE regarding a "system performance" issue where a permanent mail voter approved for the primary did not have a general election application or label in SURE. It was determined that the permanent record was created after and not at the same time that the record was processed which resulted in no general election application being created for the voter, therefore the voter received no mail in ballot. Counties had no way to identify which voters this affected.
- Week of 10/19/20, PA Department of Health Officials contact the County Commissioners informing them they will be coming into Butler County to set up multiple pop up Covid testing sites throughout the county to begin Covid testing of up to 440 people at each site free

Introduction by Thomas Fensch

of charge. This process would begin in two days from the call and site locations would not be disclosed until they arrived and set up. Butler County Republican Commissioners pushed back and said NO as our positivity rate was 3.2% the lowest in Western PA at that point in time and with zero patients in our local Butler Health System Hospital. State Dept. of Health staff were insistent and aggressively pushing and informed us that within a day DOH was planning to release a report to the public similar to the one they compiled for Centre County. This report would call for enforcement measures on businesses and state recommendations, as well as, recommend ways in which the State wanted us as a County to spend our federal CARES funding. We delayed DOH's momentum by insisting that surrounding counties given their Covid numbers would see greater benefit than Butler County and are a better use of tax dollars. We had a follow up call on October 26th and when the conversation initiated again, DOH was told this was nothing more than a political attempt to come into Butler County, drive up numbers via testing, and put out a report that misleads our county with misinformation when our positivity rate is only 3.2% in contrast to other counties, such as Westmoreland that had three times our numbers. We communicated that they were attempting to create more chaos in our county to suppress voter turnout by instilling fear and misinformation. We clearly called them out telling them this was political. We suggested they place their pop up site on Slippery Rock University's campus if they were so moved by trying to help their students? Dept. of Health declined and wanted testing sites implemented throughout the county in undisclosed sites. We communicated the upcoming Election was the county priority at that point in time given our extremely low Covid numbers based on the DOH's state dashboard of statewide data.

- 10/22 23/20 Butler County fielded ten thousand calls over the course of weeks leading up to the election from people saying they did not receive their mail in ballot. Hired six additional people to set up a county phone bank ASAP. Worked 18 hour days to call back each and every voter to provide options so they could exercise their right to vote. This included mailing new ballots and voiding the originals and in some cases, over nighting out of state applicants. We also had sheriff deputies deliver ballots to disabled and to those shut in their homes with no recourse. The majority came to the Election Bureau and cast their vote in person via a new mail in ballot. Lines began to form from that day on and we extended our evening hours to accommodate those who worked beyond normal business hours and had weekend hours available on Saturdays.
- 10/26/20 DOS contacts Butler County Election Director of numerous complaints made to DOS and delay of mail concerns specifically for Butler and York County ballots mailed out two weeks ago. DOS, even

communicating that Governor Wolf and his wife's ballots were delayed in the York County mail system arriving a week apart from one and other. 50 minutes later, Western PA USPS Manager Jason Graney requests for our Election Director to call him to discuss matter.

- 10/26/20 Butler County Election Director reports to the Butler County Commissioners that same day, Mr. Graney will investigate the matter with the US Post Office.
- 10/26/20 Continue to field calls from the public and work to enable them to vote by presenting one of four options: going to polls, coming to Election Bureau, mailing a new ballot and voiding the original, or over nighting out of state or to a college or hospital. In the latter days of that same week leading up to the election, people were still calling to say they had not received our new ballot or over night ballot in the mail. We checked to verify their mailing and confirm with callers, that the new ballots were mailed. Confirmed that they were mailed or over nighted.
- Throughout this process, we are still receiving a high volume of requests for mail ballots, many of which are duplicate requests due to the high number of third party mailers voters are receiving at their homes, which is making them, think that their request was not processed. In addition, because of another glitch in the state's SURE system, people are not seeing their ballots being recorded in a timely fashion. This is yet another issue that is consuming staff time and slowing down the mail process.
- Butler County did not use a third party mailing company, as we believe the chain of custody of these ballots is critical. We have a check and balance system in place to be sure that all voters are receiving the correct ballot for their district and/or precinct. We have hired twenty additional temporary staff to assist.
- 10/23/20 Commissioners meet with the Sheriff, District Attorney, and Emergency Services Director to finalize security plan for the county at the polling locations and review our safety plan.
- 10/23/20 ACLU serves the County Elections with a cease and desist order pertaining to our requiring ID when voters turn in ballots at the Election Bureau located in the Government Center on Friday, the 23rd, after work hours. They set a deadline for Monday for a response.
- 10/23/20 PA Supreme Court rules that a voter's absentee or mail in ballot cannot be rejected based solely on a comparison of the signature on the ballot with the voter's signature on their registration form. The ruling came as a result of a King's Bench petition by Kathy Boockvar Secretary of Commonwealth and Elections who used this as a mechanism to get counties to comply as she was struggling with challenges by counties as per guidance vs. law.

Introduction by Thomas Fensch

- 10/23/20 PA Supreme Court ruled against President Trump and the RNC challenging Secretary Boockvar's interpretation of the election code.
- 10/26/20 Voter Intimidation Guidelines sent by Ali Doyle of Southwest Deputy Director to Governor Wolf
- 10/26/20 Ironically, we received hundreds of intimidating calls about counting "all votes" beginning November 3rd in lieu of November 4th that was inaccurately portrayed by Progress PA and Ben Forstate's inaccurate maps depicting Butler County as the only county in Western PA not counting votes until the day after Election Day. Several numbers coming from a call bank located in Pittsburgh and Northeastern PA were pushing out text messages and social media messages. People statewide were reacting to these messages and harassing our office staff and two Republican Commissioners making demands and threats. Progress PA had our names and phone numbers posted on their Facebook page instructing people to call and pressure the two Republican Commissioners, County Solicitor, and Office Assistant by name and instructed them to "take no prisoners". This is a tactic of technology and there is no recourse for providing accurate information, as that is not the goal. This tactic demonstrated to me how technology and external entities could be used in influencing the election's system, adding to chaos and distraction. Despite that difficult day, we "knew the game being played" and we stayed focus on what really mattered.
- 10/28/20 PA State Supreme Court rules that the time frame for submitting ballots would be extended three days after the election as long as there was a postmark, and if any ballots arrive post election without a postmark, it should be assumed that ballot was cast on time. So, why the rule of a postmark if not now necessary? Or even followed? Please see 7/31/20
- 10/28/20 DOS sends clarifications on Examinations of Absentee and Mail In Envelopes and ID Verification for Ballot Requests
- 10/28/20 DOS sends guidance on Voter ID Not Required for Verification for ballots handed into polling sites and drop boxes
- 10/28/20 DOS sends voter ID requirements
- 10/30/20 DOS sends PA Election Day Communication
- 10/31/20 Secretary Boockvar sends out Important Election Day Reminders
- 11/1/20 DOS sends guidance on canvassing and segregating ballots received post election day.
- 11/2/20 Butler County held an afternoon poll worker training.
- 11/2/20 DOS requesting mock elections to test election results import process. Again, Butler County declined. Another tactic.
- 11/3/20 On Election Day, DOS issues guidance on voters in quarantine related to Covid.

Subverting Justice

- 11/3/20 On Election Day, mid day, DOS contacts Election Director and County Solicitor asks if the commissioners want those who submitted naked ballots (ballots with no secrecy envelope) to be provided to each political party, so those parties can contact individuals to redo ballot, so it can be counted? Pennsylvania is the first and only state to disqualify ballots received without a required secrecy envelope giving voters no recourse to fix the mistake. Some PA counties allowed this and others did not. It was not consistent statewide.
- 11/3/20 On Election Day, Butler County's 850 ES&S High Speed Scanner breaks and cannot be repaired by a state certified technician. It is brand new, $100,00 machine has only been used once for the June 2nd Primary Election.
- 11/3/20 On Election Day, We field multiple calls throughout the day requesting tallies and turn out from the State. We provide DOS no information other than to tell them our scanner is down. Our county election team works all day into the night to address scanning without the bigger scanner by using smaller scanning devices.
- 11/3/20 On Election Day, many of our polling locations are running out of ballots, as many people showed up surrendering their mail in ballot and wanting to vote. The costs associated with the mail in debacle have to be exorbitant due to the fact we are printing each person with an additional ballot who does this? Pennsylvania taxpayers should be furious and demanding better.
- 11/4/20 The day after the election we begin to field multiple calls from people demanding their ballots to be counted that are received after 8pm on Election Day threatening to call the ACLU & Authorities.
- 11/4/20 We announce on the 6pm news stations that Butler County is going to segregate ballots coming in after 8pm on Election Day on a daily basis and we are not going to open them, and keep them safe and secure until we receive further guidance from the DOS, to which we were promised ahead of time we would receive, but, had not.
- 11/5/20 DOS reissues guidance on ballot segregation requiring ID verification
- 11/5/20 Based on the news interviews of 11/4/20, people again begin demanding "all ballots to be counted" and for them to be integrated into the official tabulations. Again, we press back. Many of whom I spoke from, were not even from Butler County. Callers were simply reacting to text messages pushed out by anomonyous call centers and social media postings.
- 11/5/20 Commonwealth Court Order petitions requiring segregation of all provisional ballots cast on Election Day by voters who also submitted a timely mail in or absentee ballot. These court ordered segregated ballots would be subject to review and validation.
- 11/6/20 Justice Alito issues Order that any ballots received after 8pm on Election Day in PA be segregated and secured and if counted,

Introduction by Thomas Fensch

counted separately. There is a petition before SCOYTUS. Alito orders opposing side to reply by 2pm Saturday, November 7.

- Third Party entities and major political parties such as the Center for Voter Information purchased older, county voter rolls and mailed out mass distribution via the USPS thousands of unsolicited ballot applications to households and individuals. These mass mailings went to deceased voters, to former homeowners of a current homeowner, and to unregistered voters, to name a few scenarios. In some instances in Butler County, individuals filled out up to 15 different voter applications requesting a mail ballot per person. Each one of these 15 requests for a mail in ballot has to be processed through checks and balances for verification and to prevent duplication, as if it is the only and original request. These third party mailing entities also are generating hundreds of additional phone calls and taking time away from those applications needing to be processed. Adding insult to injury, often times, these third party entities utilize the County's Bureau of Election's return address as printed on the envelope in lieu of their own. This is misleading to the recipient who is led to believe that our county is mass distributing these mailers out? Taxpayers are led to believe we are using tax dollars to mail these mailers out, they are calling to verify that they are already registered as a voter and have been for years? This tactic is costing our taxpayers enormous tax dollars through time, effort, and manpower and distracting counties away from the focus of addressing applications in a timely and efficient manner. These same mailers have added to the confusion and anxiety of every voter wanting to do the right thing and that is, exercise their right to vote. This is a real problem that needs to be addressed.

- Finally, the US Postal Service needs to be addressed for the delay of processing and delivering mail in a timely and efficient manner. Butler County voters experienced many delays in receiving and returning ballots that took up to three to four weeks one way. This created thousands of phone calls. We have many accounts of ballots being mailed at the Butler Post Office across the street from the Bureau of Elections housed in Government Center that took 3 4 weeks and sometimes not at all to be returned to the Election Department. When inquired about, we were told they were considered "lost" in the mail system.
- This timeline is not inclusive of all the Governor's Orders pertaining to the Red Green, and Yellow Phases and Business Closures.

Evidence seems to point to a deliberate attempt to create confusion for voters and local election officials including local Judges of Elections, and to delay ballot delivery to voters through SURE system issues, social media campaigns that encouraged voters to flood election bureaus with phone calls and emails, and early voting in election offices, all which hindered getting mail ballots to voters and forcing our office to cancel many initial mail ballots and issue new ballots. I can't say what happened in other Counties, but it appears Butler County may have been specifically and deliberately targeted by the state in this effort.

The Counties lack of control over mail ballots once they leave our chain of custody is problematic as we have no way of truly knowing what happens with that ballot before it comes back to the bureau. While there has always been absentee balloting, perhaps the early voting process provides a better solution than no excuse mail since it is done in person. Voting by mail, while intended to increase access, unfortunately creates an opportunity for those in power to manipulate and take advantage of vulnerable populations since we truly cannot ensure that it takes place without influence or intimidation. Empowering all to seek the truth about elections and candidates and to exercise their right to vote in person as much as possible should be our message to "disenfranchised" voters. It means that they get to feed their own vote into the scanner and essentially watch it be tallied, vs. relying on someone else to scan your ballot into the system or losing chain of custody of your own ballot. Pennsylvania has a lot of explaining to do and even more work to do to protect future elections from this embarrassing debacle.

Leslie Osche
Chairman, Board of Commissioners
Butler County, PA

INTRODUCTION BY THOMAS FENSCH

FRANCIS X. RYAN, MEMBER
101ST LEGISLATIVE DISTRICT

Harrisburg Office:
P.O. Box 202101
Harrisburg, PA 17120-2101
(717) 783-1815

House of Representatives
Commonwealth of Pennsylvania
Harrisburg

District Office:
1044 E. Main Street
Palmyra, PA 17078
(717) 838-3823

Email: fryan@pahousegop.com
www.RepFrankRyan.com

December 22, 2020

Senator Ron Johnson, Chairman
Committee on Homeland Security and
Governmental Affairs
328 Hart Senate Office Building
Washington, DC 20510

Congressman Scott Perry
1207 Longworth House Office
Building Washington, DC 20515

Dear Senator Johnson and Congressman Perry,

Once again, I thank you for the opportunity to present to your committee at the United States Senate on December 16, 2020. The following report and attachments are submitted as supplemental materials for the record.

Our concern is and has been the accuracy, transparency, and soundness of the election systems in the Commonwealth of Pennsylvania. Comments from the Secretary of State of the Commonwealth received during the hearing of December 16, 2020 cause additional concern since the ability to review the election results have been hampered by delays in data requests, systems shutdowns, and inaccessibility to the records needed to put to a rationale conclusion the concerns that millions have about this 2020 election ballot irregularities.

In light of our concerns, we researched additional inconsistencies to address more specifically the irregularities that we observed. The irregularities are well beyond any claims that could reasonably be made that it is a lack of experience with the systems that caused the concerns and instead points to significantly defective processes at various points of the vote tabulation from county level to the state level. Systems established to ensure that each voter can have only one vote failed on many levels which prevents any type of verification or reconciliation.

After the more detailed micro analysis of the data, we are still forced to conclude that the general election of 2020 in Pennsylvania was fraught with inconsistencies and documented irregularities associated with mail-in balloting, pre-canvassing, and canvassing to the point that the reliability of voting in the Commonwealth of Pennsylvania is impossible to rely upon.

Introduction by Thomas Fensch

Matter of judicial and administrative re-write election law:

1. Actions from the PA Supreme Court which undermined the controls inherent in Act 77 of 2019. The controls which were undermined include:
    a. On September 17, 2020, unilaterally extended the deadline for mail-in ballots to be received to three days after the election, mandated that ballots mailed without a postmark would be presumed to be received, and allowed the use of drop boxes for collection votes.
    b. On October 23, 2020, upon a petition from the Secretary of the Commonwealth, ruled that mail-in ballots need not authenticate signatures for mail-in ballots thereby treating in-person and mail-in voters dissimilarly and eliminating a critical safeguard against potential election crime
2. Actions and inactions by the Secretary of State which undermined the consistency and controls of the election process during the weeks preceding the General Election of November 3, 2020. The attached detailed letter of concerns from Butler County is but one example of the problems found at the County caused by the Secretary of State.

In addition to the concerns of the actions of the Secretary of State and the legislative overreach by the Pennsylvania Supreme Court, the inaccuracies of the actual results themselves call into question the accuracy of the SURE system, the consistency of the application of voting laws throughout the counties.

Errors in Controls

All of our previous concerns provided during our original testimony remain, but the following analysis of "Voter Deficit" illustrates that beyond the election law issue, there are sufficient numbers of ballots unaccounted for in the data available from the state and county systems to render certifying the election problematic at best.

Election Issues:

More Votes Counted than voters who voted

INTERIM REPORT TOTALS AS OF 12-20-2020

COUNTY	TOTAL VOTES 3 MAJOR CANDIDATES	TOTAL WRITE IN	TOTAL VOTES FOR PRESIDENT	OVER & UNDER VOTES	TOTAL BALLOTS CAST	TOTAL VOTERS SURE	TOTAL VOTER DEFICIT	TOTAL VOTER SURPLUS
	DOS DATA		COUNTY DATA			FVE		
64/67	6,915,283	18,580	6,931,060	29,077	6,962,607	6,760,230	-205,122	2,532

Using the sources and data described in the previous slides, there is a VOTER DEFICIT in Pennsylvania. **205,122** more votes were counted than total number of voters who voted.

Introduction by Thomas Fensch

People who possibly voted more than once

POSSIBLE DUPLICATE VOTERS

Using the Statewide FVE, a query of all records where the First Name, Last Name and Date of Birth matched AND where both recorded a Vote on 11/3/2020 – produced **4241 Records**. These records warrant investigation to determine how many people voted two or more times.

Duplicate Ballots: Requested and returned

DUPLICATE MAIL IN BALLOT APPLICATIONS

- County election officials were inundated with duplicate mail in ballot applications
- It was up to the county to review each new application and make a judgement call about whether to send a second mail in ballot
- There was no accounting of the excess mailed ballots.

"Overall, one out of every five requests for mail ballots is being rejected in Pennsylvania. An estimated 208,000 Pennsylvania voters sent in the spurned requests, some submitting them multiple times. Although the state's email rejecting the requests describes them as duplicates, it doesn't explain why, prompting some people to reapply. ProPublica and The Inquirer identified hundreds of voters who submitted three or more duplicate applications; one voter appears to have submitted 11 duplicates."

DUPLICATE APPLICATIONS

Department of State released data showing the number of duplicate MIB Applications that had been rejected as of 10/16/202. DOS did not release the number of duplicates that were mailed.

The evidence presented in the attached report clearly shows that there was no review of the validity of votes and there was no reconciliation of the votes. The review of the data provided in this report, which was available to the Secretary of State, clearly illustrates that the results in PA should not have been certified.

INTRODUCTION BY THOMAS FENSCH

SURE IS THE OFFICIAL VOTER RECORD IN PA

- If SURE data was correct, the election could not be certified due to the discrepancies.
- If SURE data was incorrect, the election could not be certified due to discrepancies.

> By Statute, the SURE System is the official voter record in Pennsylvania. This record includes the date last voted. Total voters who voted in the General Election on 11/3/2020 was **6,760,230**. Secretary of State Boockvar certified **6,915,283** Votes for just the three major candidates. That alone is a voter **deficit of 155,053 voters**.
>
> (This does not include write-in votes or over/under votes)

The hotline designated for PA voters to report election issues was not working in the days following the election. The web form to report election issues was not functioning in the days following the election. Data that is supposed to be available to PA voters was removed from the data.pa.gov eliminating statutory requirements for transparency making any challenge to the Secretary of State's assertions a herculean task. We welcome the opportunity to work with the Secretary of State to resolve these concerns and the lack of transparency and inherent weaknesses in the control environment.

The report includes the detailed report of Voter Deficit and a Department of State timeline prepared by officials from Butler County, PA.

In light of the above, the inconsistencies and irregularities in the election process in the Commonwealth of Pennsylvania in the 2020 General Election raise questions about whether the selection of presidential electors for the Commonwealth is in dispute.

SUBVERTING JUSTICE

Francis X. Ryan, Member
101st Legislative District

David Rowe, Member
85th Legislative District

Mike Puskaric, Member
39th Legislative District

Jim Cox, Member
129th Legislative District

Kathy Rapp, Member
65th Legislative District

Russ Diamond, Member
102nd Legislative District

David Maloney, Member
130th Legislative District

Stephanie Borowicz, Member
76th Legislative District

Daryl Metcalfe, Member
12th Legislative District

Barbara Gleim
199th Legislative District

Cris Dush, Senator-Elect
25th Legislative District

Eric Nelson, Member
57th Legislative District

Rob Kauffman, Member
89th Legislative District

Brett Miller, Member
41st Legislative District

Dawn Keefer, Member
92nd Legislative District

INTRODUCTION BY THOMAS FENSCH

Key Document H

Introduction by Thomas Fensch

Clark, Jeffrey (ENRD)

From: Clark, Jeffrey (ENRD)
Sent: Monday, December 28, 2020 4:40 PM
To: Rosen, Jeffrey A. (ODAG); Donoghue, Richard (ODAG)
Subject: Two Urgent Action Items
Attachments: Draft Letter JBC 12 28 20.docx

Jeff and Rich:

(1) I would like to have your authorization to get a classified briefing tomorrow from ODNI led by DNI Radcliffe on foreign election interference issues. I can then assess how that relates to activating the IEEPA and 2018 EO powers on such matters (now twice renewed by the President). If you had not seen it, white hat hackers have evidence (in the public domain) that a Dominion machine accessed the Internet through a smart thermostat with a net connection trail leading back to China. ODNI may have additional classified evidence.

(2) Attached is a draft letter concerning the broader topic of election irregularities of any kind. The concept is to send it to the Governor, Speaker, and President pro temp of each relevant state to indicate that in light of time urgency and sworn evidence of election irregularities presented to courts and to legislative committees, the legislatures thereof should each assemble and make a decision about elector appointment in light of their deliberations. I set it up for signature by the three of us. I think we should get it out as soon as possible. Personally, I see no valid downsides to sending out the letter. I put it together quickly and would want to do a formal cite check before sending but I don't think we should let unnecessary moss grow on this

(As a small matter, I left open me signing as AAG Civil — after an order from Jeff as Acting AG designating me as actual AAG of Civil under the Ted Olson OLC opinion and thus freeing up the Acting AAG spot in ENRD for Jon Brightbill to assume. But that is a comparatively small matter. I wouldn't want to hold up the letter for that. But I continue to think there is no downside with as few as 23 days left in the President's term to give Jon and I that added boost in DOJ titles.)

I have a 5 pm internal ca [Non-Responsive] . But I am free to talk on either or both of these subjects circa 6 pm+.

Or if you want to reach me after I reset work venue to home, my cell # (b) (6)

Jeff

Pre-Decisional & Deliberative/Attorney-Client or Legal Work Product
Georgia Proof of Concept

[LETTERHEAD]

The Honorable Brian P. Kemp
Governor
111 State Capitol
Atlanta, Georgia 30334

The Honorable David Ralston
Speaker of the House
332 State Capitol
Atlanta, Georgia 30334

The Honorable Butch Miller
President *Pro Tempore* of the Senate
321 State Capitol
Atlanta, Georgia 30334

December 28, 2020

Dear Governor Kemp, Mr. Speaker, and Mr. President *Pro Tempore*:

The Department of Justice is investigating various irregularities in the 2020 election for President of the United States. The Department will update you as we are able on investigatory progress, but at this time we have identified significant concerns that may have impacted the outcome of the election in multiple States, including the State of Georgia. No doubt, many of Georgia's state legislators are aware of irregularities, sworn to by a variety of witnesses, and we have taken notice of their complaints. *See, e.g.*, The Chairman's Report of the Election Law Study Subcommittee of the Standing Senate Judiciary Committee Summary of Testimony from December 3, 2020 Hearing, http://www.senatorligon.com/THE_FINAL%20REPORT.PDF (Dec. 17, 2020) (last visited Dec. 28, 2020); Debra, Heine, *Georgia State Senate Report: Election Results Are 'Untrustworthy;' Certification Should Be Rescinded*, THE TENNESSEE STAR (Dec. 22, 2020), available at https://tennesseestar.com/2020/12/22/georgia-state-senate-report-election-results-are-untrustworthy-certification-should-be-rescinded/ (last visited Dec. 28, 2020).

Introduction by Thomas Fensch

Pre-Decisional & Deliberative/Attorney-Client or Legal Work Product

In light of these developments, the Department recommends that the Georgia General Assembly should convene in special session so that its legislators are in a position to take additional testimony, receive new evidence, and deliberate on the matter consistent with its duties under the U.S. Constitution. Time is of the essence, as the U.S. Constitution tasks Congress with convening in joint session to count Electoral College certificates, *see* U.S. Const., art. II, § 1, cl. 3, consider objections to any of those certificates, and decide between any competing slates of elector certificates, and 3 U.S.C. § 15 provides that this session shall begin on January 6, 2021, with the Vice President presiding over the session as President of the Senate.

The Constitution mandates that Congress must set the day for Electors to meet to cast their ballots, which Congress did in 3 U.S.C. § 7, and which for this election occurred on December 14, 2020. The Department believes that in Georgia and several other States, both a slate of electors supporting Joseph R. Biden, Jr., and a separate slate of electors supporting Donald J. Trump, gathered on that day at the proper location to cast their ballots, and that both sets of those ballots have been transmitted to Washington, D.C., to be opened by Vice President Pence. The Department is aware that a similar situation occurred in the 1960 election. There, Vice President Richard Nixon appeared to win the State of Hawaii on Election Day and Electors supporting Vice President Nixon cast their ballots on the day specified in 3 U.S.C. § 7, which were duly certified by the Governor of Hawaii. But Senator John F. Kennedy also claimed to win Hawaii, with his Electors likewise casting their ballots on the prescribed day, and that by January 6, 1961, it had been determined that Senator Kennedy was indeed the winner of Hawaii, so Congress accordingly accepted only the ballots cast for Senator Kennedy. *See* Jack M. Balkin, *Bush v. Gore and the Boundary Between Law and Politics*, 110 YALE L.J. 1407, 1421 n.55 (2001).

The Department also finds troubling the current posture of a pending lawsuit in Fulton County, Georgia, raising several of the voting irregularities pertaining to which candidate for President of the United States received the most lawfully cast votes in Georgia. *See Trump v. Raffensperger*, 2020cv343255 (Fulton Cty. Super. Ct.). Despite the action having been filed on December 4, 2020, the trial court there has not even scheduled a hearing on matter, making it difficult for the judicial process to consider this evidence and resolve these matters on appeal prior to January 6. Given the urgency of this serious matter, including the Fulton County litigation's sluggish pace, the Department believes that a special session of the Georgia General Assembly is warranted and is in the national interest.

Pre-Decisional & Deliberative/Attorney-Client or Legal Work Product

The Electors Clause of the U.S. Constitution provides that "[e]ach State shall appoint, in such Manner as the Legislature thereof may direct," electors to cast ballots for President and Vice President. *See* U.S. Const., art. II, § 1, cl. 2. Many State Legislatures originally chose electors by direct appointment, but over time each State Legislature has chosen to do so by popular vote on the day appointed by Congress in 3 U.S.C. § 1 to be the Election Day for Members of Congress, which this year was November 3, 2020. However, Congress also explicitly recognizes the power that State Legislatures have to appoint electors, providing in 3 U.S.C. § 2 that "[w]henever any State has held an election for the purpose of choosing electors, and has failed to make a choice on the day prescribed by [3 U.S.C. § 1], the electors may be appointed on a subsequent day in such a manner as the legislature of such State may direct."

The purpose of the special session the Department recommends would be for the General Assembly to (1) evaluate the irregularities in the 2020 election, including violations of Georgia election law judged against that body of law as it has been enacted by your State's Legislature, (2) determine whether those violations show which candidate for President won the most legal votes in the November 3 election, and (3) whether the election failed to make a proper and valid choice between the candidates, such that the General Assembly could take whatever action is necessary to ensure that one of the slates of Electors cast on December 14 will be accepted by Congress on January 6.

While the Department of Justice believes the Governor of Georgia should immediately call a special session to consider this important and urgent matter, if he declines to do so, we share with you our view that the Georgia General Assembly has implied authority under the Constitution of the United States to *call itself into special session* for the limited purpose of considering issues pertaining to the appointment of Presidential Electors. The Constitution specifies that Presidential Electors shall be appointed by the *Legislature* of each State. And the Framers clearly knew how to distinguish between a state legislature and a state executive, so their disparate choices to refer to one (legislatures), the other (executive), or both, must be respected.[1] Additionally,

---

[1] *See, e.g.,* U.S.C., art. IV, § 4 ("The United States shall guarantee to every State in this Union a Republican Form of Government, and shall protect each of them against Invasion; and on Application of *the Legislature, or of the Executive (when the Legislature cannot be convened)* against domestic Violence.") (emphases added); *id.* art. VI ("The Senators and Representatives before mentioned, and the Members of the *several State Legislatures, and all executive and judicial Officers,* both of the United States and of the several States, shall be bound by Oath or Affirmation, to support this Constitution ....") (emphasis added); *id.* XVII amend. ("When vacancies happen in the representation of any State in the Senate, *the executive authority of such State* shall issue writs of election to fill such vacancies: Provided, That *the legislature of any State* may empower

Introduction by Thomas Fensch

when the Constitution intends to refer to laws enacted by the Legislature and signed by the Governor, the Constitution refers to it simply as the "State." *See, e.g.,* U.S. Const., art. I, § 8 ("[Congress may] exercise exclusive Legislation in all Cases whatsoever, over such District (not exceeding ten Miles square) as may, *by Cession of particular States,* and the Acceptance of Congress, become the Seat of the Government of the United States, and to exercise like Authority over all Places purchased by the Consent of *the Legislature of the State* in which the Same shall be, for the Erection of Forts, Magazines, Arsenals, dock-Yards and other needful Buildings") (emphasis added) (distinguishing between the "State," writ large, and the "Legislature of the State"). The Constitution also makes clear when powers are forbidden to any type of state actor. *See, e.g.,* U.S. Const., art. I, § 10, cl. 1 ("No State shall enter into any Treaty, Alliance, or Confederation ...."). Surely, this cannot mean that a State Governor could enter into such a Treaty but a State Legislature could not, or *vice versa*.

Clearly, however, some provisions refer explicitly to state legislatures — and there the Framers must be taken at their word. One such example is in Article V, which provides that a proposed Amendment to the Constitution is adopted "when ratified by the Legislatures of three fourths of the several States," which is done by joint resolution or concurrent resolution. Supreme Court precedent makes clear that the Governor has no role in that process, and that his signature or approval is not necessary for ratification. *See, e.g., Coleman v. Miller,* 307 U.S. 433 (1939). So too, Article II requires action only by the Legislature in appointing Electors, and Congress in 3 U.S.C. § 2 likewise recognizes this Constitutional principle.

The Supreme Court has explained that the Electors Clause "leaves it to the legislature exclusively to define the method" of appointing Electors, vesting the Legislature with "the broadest possible power of determination." *McPherson v. Blecker,* 146 U.S. 1, 27 (1892). This power is "placed absolutely and *wholly* with legislatures." *Id.* at 34-35 (emphasis added). In the most recent disputed Presidential election to reach the Supreme Court, the 2000 election, the Supreme Court went on to hold that when a State Legislature appoints Presidential Electors—which it can do either through statute or through direct action—the Legislature is not acting "solely under the authority given by the people of the State, but by virtue of a direct grant of authority made under Art. II, § 1, cl. 2, of the United States Constitution." *Bush v. Palm Beach Cty. Canvassing Bd.,* 531 U.S.

---

the executive thereof to make temporary appointments until the people fill the vacancies by election *as the legislature may direct*.") (emphases added).

Pre-Decisional & Deliberative/Attorney-Client or Legal Work Product

70, 76 (2000). The State Legislature's authority to appoint Electors is "plenary." *Bush v. Gore*, 531 U.S. 98, 104 (2000) (per curiam). And a State Legislature cannot lose that authority on account of enacting statutes to join the National Election. "Whatever provisions may be made by statute, or by the state constitution, to choose electors by the people, there is no doubt of the right of the legislature to resume the power an any time, for it can neither be taken away nor abdicated." *McPherson*, 146 U.S. at 125.

The Georgia General Assembly accordingly must have inherent authority granted by the U.S. Constitution to come into session to appoint Electors, regardless of any purported limit imposed by the state constitution or state statute requiring the Governor's approval. The "powers actually granted [by the U.S. Constitution] must be such as are expressly given, or given by necessary implication." *Martin v. Hunter's Lessee*, 14 U.S. (1 Wheat.) 304, 326 (1816). And the principle of necessary implication arises because our Constitution is not prolix and thus does not "provide for minute specification of its powers, or to declare the means by which those powers should be carried into execution." *Id.* Otherwise, in a situation like this one, if a Governor were aware that the Legislature of his State was inclined to appoint Electors supporting a candidate for President that the Governor opposed, the Governor could thwart that appointment by refusing to call the Legislature into session before the next President had been duly elected. The Constitution does not empower other officials to supersede the state legislature in this fashion.

Therefore whether called into session by the Governor or by its own inherent authority, the Department of Justice urges the Georgia General Assembly to convene in special session to address this pressing matter of overriding national importance.

Sincerely,

Jeffrey A. Rosen	Richard Donoghue	Jeffrey Bossert Clark
Acting Attorney General	Acting Deputy Attorney General	(Acting) Assistant Attorney General
		Civil Division

Introduction by Thomas Fensch

Key Document I

Donoghue, Richard (ODAG)

From: Donoghue, Richard (ODAG)
Sent: Monday, December 28, 2020 5:50 PM
To: Clark, Jeffrey (ENRD)
Cc: Rosen, Jeffrey A. (ODAG)
Subject: RE: Two Urgent Action Items

Jeff,

I have only had a few moments to review the draft letter and, obviously, there is a lot raised there that would have to be thoroughly researched and discussed. That said, there is no chance that I would sign this letter or anything remotely like this.

While it may be true that the Department "is investigating various irregularities in the 2020 election for President" (something we typically would not state publicly), the investigations that I am aware of relate to suspicions of misconduct that are of such a small scale that they simply would not impact the outcome of the Presidential Election. AG Barr made that clear to the public only last week, and I am not aware of intervening developments that would change that conclusion. Thus, I know of nothing that would support the statement, "we have identified significant concerns that may have impacted the outcome of the election in multiple states." While we are always prepared to receive complaints and allegations relating to election fraud, and will investigate them as appropriate, we simply do not currently have a basis to make such a statement. Despite dramatic claims to the contrary, we have not seen the type of fraud that calls into question the reported (and certified) results of the election. Also the commitment that "the Department will update you as we are able on investigatory progress" is dubious as we do not typically update non-law enforcement personnel on the progress of any investigations.

More importantly, I do not think the Department's role should include making recommendations to a State legislature about how they should meet their Constitutional obligation to appoint Electors. Pursuant to the Electors Clause, the State of Georgia (and every other state) has prescribed the legal process through which they select their Electors. While those processes include the possibility that election results may "fail[ ] to make a choice", it is for the individual State to figure out how to address that situation should it arise. But as I note above, there is no reason to conclude that any State is currently in a situation in which their election has failed to produce a choice. As AG Barr indicated in his public comments, while I have no doubt that some fraud has occurred in this election, I have not seen evidence that would indicate that the election in any individual state was so defective as to render the results fundamentally unreliable. Given that, I cannot imagine a scenario in which the Department would recommend that a State assemble its legislature to determine whether already-certified election results should somehow be overridden by legislative action. Despite the references to the 1960 Hawaii situation (and other historical anomalies, such as the 1876 Election), I believe this would be utterly without precedent. Even if I am incorrect about that, this would be a grave step for the Department to take and it could have tremendous Constitutional, political and social ramifications for the country. I do not believe that we could even consider such a proposal without the type of research and discussion that such a momentous step warrants. Obviously, OLC would have to be involved in such discussions.

I am available to discuss this when you are available after 6:00 pm but, from where I stand, this is not even within the realm of possibility.

Rich

From: Clark, Jeffrey (ENRD) <JClark@ENRD.USDOJ.GOV>
Sent: Monday, December 28, 2020 4:40 PM

Introduction by Thomas Fensch

To: Rosen, Jeffrey A. (ODAG) <jarosen@jmd.usdoj.gov>; Donoghue, Richard (ODAG) <ricdonoghue@jmd.usdoj.gov>
Subject: Two Urgent Action Items

Jeff and Rich:

(1) I would like to have your authorization to get a classified briefing tomorrow from ODNI led by DNI Radcliffe on foreign election interference issues. I can then assess how that relates to activating the IEEPA and 2018 EO powers on such matters (now twice renewed by the President). If you had not seen it, white hat hackers have evidence (in the public domain) that a Dominion machine accessed the Internet through a smart thermostat with a net connection trail leading back to China. ODNI may have additional classified evidence.

(2) Attached is a draft letter concerning the broader topic of election irregularities of any kind. The concept is to send it to the Governor, Speaker, and President pro temp of each relevant state to indicate that in light of time urgency and sworn evidence of election irregularities presented to courts and to legislative committees, the legislatures thereof should each assemble and make a decision about elector appointment in light of their deliberations. I set it up for signature by the three of us. I think we should get it out as soon as possible. Personally, I see no valid downsides to sending out the letter. I put it together quickly and would want to do a formal cite check before sending but I don't think we should let unnecessary moss grow on this

(As a small matter, I left open me signing as AAG Civil after an order from Jeff as Acting AG designating me as actual AAG of Civil under the Ted Olson OLC opinion and thus freeing up the Acting AAG spot in ENRD for Jon Brightbill to assume. But that is a comparatively small matter. I wouldn't want to hold up the letter for that. But I continue to think there is no downside with as few as 23 days left in the President's term to give Jon and I that added boost in DOJ titles.)

I have a 5 pm internal ca [Non-Responsive]. But I am free to talk on either or both of these subjects circa 6 pm+.

Or if you want to reach me after I reset work venue to home, my cell # (b) (6)

Jeff

Key Document J

Introduction by Thomas Fensch

Donoghue, Richard (ODAG)

From: Donoghue, Richard (ODAG)
Sent: Monday, December 28, 2020 11:41 PM
To: Engel, Steven A. (OLC)
Subject: Tomorrow

Steve,

I think you'll be at the 0900 meeting tomorrow. If you can make it there about 10 minutes early, please come by my office so I can read you into some antics that could potentially end up on your radar. If you're not in by then, no big deal, we can just talk after the meeting.

Thanks,

Rich

Key Document K

Introduction by Thomas Fensch

kurtols

From: kurtols
Sent: Tuesday, December 29, 2020 10:57 AM
To: jeffrey.b.wall@usdoj.gov
Subject: AG Rosen

Dear SG Wall,

I represented Texas in the action filed in the SCT against Pennsylvania et al. Last night, the President directed me to meet with AG Rosen today to discuss a similar action to be brought by the United States. I have not been able to reach him despite multiple calls/texts. This is an urgent matter. Please call me at (b) (6) or ask AG Rosen to contact me asap. Thank you.

Sincerely,

Kurt B. Olsen

Sent with ProtonMail Secure Email.

Key Document L

Introduction by Thomas Fensch

Michael, Molly A. EOP/WHO

From:	Michael, Molly A. EOP/WHO
Sent:	Tuesday, December 29, 2020 11:17 AM
To:	Richard.Donoghue2@usdoj.gov; Jeffrey.B.Wall@usdoj.gov; Jeff.Rosen38@usdoj.gov
Subject:	USA v. Pennsylvania draft complaint Dec 28 2 pm.docx
Attachments:	USA v. Pennsylvania draft complaint Dec 28 2 pm.docx

Good morning,

The President asked me to send the attached draft document for your review. I have also shared with Mark Meadows and Pat Cipollone. If you'd like to discuss with POTUS, the best way to reach him in the next few days is through the operators: 202-456-1414

Thanks and Happy New Year!

Molly

Sent from my iPhone

No. _____, Original

In the Supreme Court of the United States

THE UNITED STATES OF AMERICA

Plaintiff,

v.

COMMONWEALTH OF PENNSYLVANIA, STATE OF STATE OF GEORGIA, STATE OF MICHIGAN, STATE OF WISCONSIN, STATE OF ARIZONA, AND STATE OF NEVADA

Defendants.

BILL OF COMPLAINT

INTRODUCTION BY THOMAS FENSCH

i
TABLE OF CONTENTS

Pages

BILL OF COMPLAINT

Our Country is deeply divided in a manner not seen in well over a century. More than 77% of Republican voters believe that "widespread fraud" occurred in the 2020 general election while 97% of Democrats say there was not.[1] On December 7, 2020, the State of Texas filed an action with this Court, *Texas v. Pennsylvania, et al.*, alleging the same constitutional violations in connection with the 2020 general election pled herein. Within three days *eighteen* other states sought to intervene in that action or filed supporting briefs. On December 11, 2020, the Court summarily dismissed that action stating that Texas lacked standing under Article III of the Constitution. The United States therefore brings this action to ensure that the U.S. Constitution does not become simply a piece of parchment on display at the National Archives.

Two issues regarding this election are not in dispute. First, about eight months ago, a few non-legislative officials in the states of Georgia, Michigan, Wisconsin, Arizona, Nevada and the Commonwealth of Pennsylvania (collectively, "Defendant States") began using the COVID-19 pandemic as an excuse to unconstitutionally revise or violate their states' election laws. Their actions all had one effect: they uniformly weakened security measures put in place *by legislators* to protect the integrity of the vote. These

---

[1] https://www.courant.com/politics/hc-pol-q-poll-republicans-believe-fraud-20201210-pcie3uqqvrhyvnt7geohhsyepe-story.html

changes squarely violated the Electors Clause of Article II, Section 1, Clause 2 vesting state legislatures with plenary authority to make election law. These same government officials then flooded the Defendant States with millions of ballots to be sent through the mails, or placed in drop boxes, with little or no chain of custody.[2] Second, the evidence of illegal or fraudulent votes, with outcome changing results, is clear—and growing daily.

Since *Marbury v. Madison* this Court has, on significant occasions, had to step into the breach in a time of tumult, declare what the law is, and right the ship. This is just such an occasion. In fact, it is situations precisely like the present—when the Constitution has been cast aside unchecked—that leads us to the current precipice. As one of the Country's Founding Fathers, John Adams, once said, "You will never know how much it has cost my generation to preserve your freedom. I hope you will make a good use of it." In times such as this, it is the duty of Court duty to act as a "faithful guardian[] of the Constitution." THE FEDERALIST NO. 78, at 470 (C. Rossiter, ed. 1961) (A. Hamilton).

Against that background, the United States of America brings this action against Defendant States based on the following allegations:

NATURE OF THE ACTION

1. The United States challenges Defendant States' administration of the 2020 election under the

---

[2] https://georgiastarnews.com/2020/12/05/dekalb-county-cannot-find-chain-of-custody-records-for-absentee-ballots-deposited-in-drop-boxes-it-has-not-been-determined-if-responsive-records-to-your-request-exist/

3

Electors Clause of Article II, Section 1, Clause 2, and the Fourteenth Amendment of the U.S. Constitution.

2. This case presents a question of law: Did Defendant States violate the Electors Clause (or, in the alternative, the Fourteenth Amendment) by taking—or allowing—non-legislative actions to change the election rules that would govern the appointment of presidential electors?

3. Those unconstitutional changes opened the door to election irregularities in various forms. The United States alleges that each of the Defendant States flagrantly violated constitutional rules governing the appointment of presidential electors. In doing so, seeds of deep distrust have been sown across the country. In *Marbury v. Madison*, 5 U.S. 137 (1803), Chief Justice Marshall described "the duty of the Judicial Department to say what the law is" because "every right, when withheld, must have a remedy, and every injury its proper redress."

4. In the spirit of *Marbury v. Madison*, this Court's attention is profoundly needed to declare what the law is and to restore public trust in this election.

5. As Justice Gorsuch observed recently, "Government is not free to disregard the [Constitution] in times of crisis. ... Yet recently, during the COVID pandemic, certain States seem to have ignored these long-settled principles." *Roman Catholic Diocese of Brooklyn, New York v. Cuomo*, 592 U.S. ___ (2020) (Gorsuch, J., concurring). This case is no different.

6. Each of Defendant States acted in a common pattern. State officials, sometimes through pending litigation (*e.g.*, settling "friendly" suits) and sometimes unilaterally by executive fiat, announced

new rules for the conduct of the 2020 election that were inconsistent with existing state statutes defining what constitutes a lawful vote.

7. Defendant States also failed to segregate ballots in a manner that would permit accurate analysis to determine which ballots were cast in conformity with the legislatively set rules and which were not. This is especially true of the mail-in ballots in these States. By waiving, lowering, and otherwise failing to follow the state statutory requirements for signature validation and other processes for ballot security, the entire body of such ballots is now constitutionally suspect and may not be legitimately used to determine allocation of the Defendant States' presidential electors.

8. The rampant lawlessness arising out of Defendant States' unconstitutional acts is described in a number of currently pending lawsuits in Defendant States or in public view including:

- *Dozens of witnesses testifying under oath about*: the physical blocking and kicking out of Republican poll challengers; thousands of the same ballots run multiple times through tabulators; mysterious late night dumps of thousands of ballots at tabulation centers; illegally backdating thousands of ballots; signature verification procedures ignored;[3]

- *Videos of*: poll workers erupting in cheers as poll challengers are removed from vote counting centers; poll watchers being blocked from entering

---

[3]Complaint (Doc. No. 1), *Donald J. Trump for President, Inc. v. Benson*, 1:20-cv-1083 (W.D. Mich. Nov. 11, 2020) at ¶¶ 26-55 & Doc. Nos. 1-2, 1-4.

vote counting centers—despite even having a court order to enter; suitcases full of ballots being pulled out from underneath tables after poll watchers were told to leave.

- *Facts for which no independently verified reasonable explanation yet exists*: On October 1, 2020, in Pennsylvania a laptop and several USB drives, used to program Pennsylvania's Dominion voting machines, were mysteriously stolen from a warehouse in Philadelphia. The laptop and the USB drives were the *only* items taken, and potentially could be used to alter vote tallies; In Michigan, which also employed the same Dominion voting system, on November 4, 2020, Michigan election officials have admitted that a purported "glitch" caused 6,000 votes for President Trump to be wrongly switched to Democrat Candidate Biden. A flash drive containing tens of thousands of votes was left unattended in the Milwaukee tabulations center in the early morning hours of Nov. 4, 2020, without anyone aware it was not in a proper chain of custody.

9. Nor was this Court immune from the blatant disregard for the rule of law. Pennsylvania itself played fast and loose with its promise to this Court. In a classic bait and switch, Pennsylvania used guidance from its Secretary of State to argue that this Court should not expedite review because the State would segregate potentially unlawful ballots. A court of law would reasonably rely on such a representation. Remarkably, before the ink was dry on the Court's 4-4 decision, Pennsylvania changed that guidance, breaking the State's promise to this Court. *Compare Republican Party of Pa. v. Boockvar*, No. 20-542, 2020

U.S. LEXIS 5188, at *5-6 (Oct. 28, 2020) ("we have been informed by the Pennsylvania Attorney General that the Secretary of the Commonwealth issued guidance today directing county boards of elections to segregate [late-arriving] ballots") (Alito, J., concurring) *with Republican Party v. Boockvar*, No. 20A84, 2020 U.S. LEXIS 5345, at *1 (Nov. 6, 2020) ("this Court was not informed that the guidance issued on October 28, which had an important bearing on the question whether to order special treatment of the ballots in question, had been modified") (Alito, J., Circuit Justice).

10. Expert analysis using a commonly accepted statistical test further raises serious questions as to the integrity of this election.

11. The probability of former Vice President Biden winning the popular vote in four of the Defendant States—Georgia, Michigan, Pennsylvania, and Wisconsin—independently given President Trump's early lead in those States as of 3 a.m. on November 4, 2020, is less than one in a quadrillion, or 1 in 1,000,000,000,000,000. For former Vice President Biden to win these four States collectively, the odds of that event happening decrease to less than one in a quadrillion to the fourth power (*i.e.*, 1 in 1,000,000,000,000,000^4). *See* Decl. of Charles J. Cicchetti, Ph.D. ("Cicchetti Decl.") at ¶¶ 14-21, 30-31. *See* App.   a-   a.[4]

12. Mr. Biden's *underperformance* in the Top-50 urban areas in the Country relative to former Secretary Clinton's performance in the 2016 election reinforces the unusual statistical improbability of Mr.

---

[4] All exhibits cited in this Complaint are in the Appendix to the United States' forthcoming motion to expedite ("App. 1a   ").

Biden's vote totals in the five urban areas in these four Defendant States, where he overperformed Secretary Clinton in all but one of the five urban areas. *See* Supp. Cicchetti Decl. at ¶¶ 4-12, 20-21. (App.   a-   a).

13. The same less than one in a quadrillion statistical improbability of Mr. Biden winning the popular vote in these four Defendant States—Georgia, Michigan, Pennsylvania, and Wisconsin— independently exists when Mr. Biden's performance in each of those Defendant States is compared to former Secretary of State Hilary Clinton's performance in the 2016 general election and President Trump's performance in the 2016 and 2020 general elections. Again, the statistical improbability of Mr. Biden winning the popular vote in these four States collectively is 1 in 1,000,000,000,000,000[5]. *Id.* 10-13, 17-21, 30-31.

14. Put simply, there is substantial reason to doubt the voting results in the Defendant States.

15. By purporting to waive or otherwise modify the existing state law in a manner that was wholly *ultra vires* and not adopted by each state's legislature, Defendant States violated not only the Electors Clause, U.S. CONST. art. II, § 1, cl. 2, but also the Elections Clause, *id.* art. I, § 4 (to the extent that the Article I Elections Clause textually applies to the Article II process of selecting presidential electors).

16. Voters who cast lawful ballots cannot have their votes diminished by states that administered their 2020 presidential elections in a manner where it is impossible to distinguish a lawful ballot from an unlawful ballot.

17. The number of absentee and mail-in ballots that have been handled unconstitutionally in

8

Defendant States greatly exceeds the difference between the vote totals of the two candidates for President of the United States in each Defendant State.

18. In December 2018, the Caltech/MIT Voting Technology Project and MIT Election Data & Science Lab issued a comprehensive report addressing election integrity issues.[5] The fundamental question they sought to address was: "How do we know that the election outcomes announced by election officials are correct?"

19. The Caltech/MIT Report concluded: "Ultimately, the only way to answer a question like this is to rely on procedures that independently review the outcomes of elections, to detect and correct material mistakes that are discovered. In other words, elections need to be audited." *Id.* at iii. The Caltech/MIT Report then set forth a detailed analysis of why and how such audits should be done for the same reasons that exist today—a lack of trust in our voting systems.

20. In addition to injunctive relief sought for this election, the United States seeks declaratory relief for all presidential elections in the future. This problem is clearly capable of repetition yet evading review. The integrity of our constitutional democracy requires that states conduct presidential elections in accordance with the rule of law and federal constitutional guarantees.

---

[5]Summary Report, Election Auditing, Key Issues and Perspectives attached at   (the "Caltech/MIT Report") (App. a -- a).

JURISDICTION AND VENUE

21. This Court has original and exclusive jurisdiction over this action because it is a "controvers[y] between the United States and [Defendant] State[s]" under Article III, § 2, cl. 2 of the U.S. Constitution and 28 U.S.C. § 1251(b)(2) (2018).

22. In a presidential election, "the impact of the votes cast in each State is affected by the votes cast for the various candidates in other States." *Anderson v. Celebrezze*, 460 U.S. 780, 795 (1983). The constitutional failures of Defendant States injure the United States as *parens patriae* for all citizens because "'the right of suffrage can be denied by a debasement or dilution of the weight of a citizen's vote just as effectively as by wholly prohibiting the free exercise of the franchise.'" *Bush v. Gore*, 531 U.S. 98, 105 (2000) (quoting *Reynolds v. Sims*, 377 U. S. 533, 555 (1964)) (*Bush II*). In other words, United States is acting to protect the interests of *all* citizens—including not only the citizens of Defendant States but also the citizens of their sister States—in the fair and constitutional conduct of elections used to appoint presidential electors.

23. Although the several States may lack "a judicially cognizable interest in the manner in which another State conducts its elections," *Texas v. Pennsylvania*, No. 22O155 (U.S. Dec. 11, 2020), the same is not true for the United States, which has *parens patriae* for the citizens of each State against the government apparatus of each State. *Alfred L. Snapp & Son v. Puerto Rico*, 458 U.S. 592, 610 n.16 (1982) ("it is the United States, and not the State, which represents them as *parens patriae*") (interior quotation omitted). For *Bush II*-type violations, the

10

United States can press this action against the Defendant States for violations of the voting rights of Defendant States' own citizens.

24. This Court's Article III decisions limit the ability of citizens to press claims under the Electors Clause. *Lance v. Coffman*, 549 U.S. 437, 442 (2007) (distinguishing citizen plaintiffs from citizen relators who sued in the name of a state); *cf. Massachusetts v. EPA*, 549 U.S. 497, 520 (2007) (courts owe states "special solicitude in standing analysis"). Moreover, redressability likely would undermine a suit against a single state officer or State because no one State's electoral votes will make a difference in the election outcome. This action against multiple State defendants is the only adequate remedy to cure the Defendant States' violations, and this Court is the only court that can accommodate such a suit.

25. As federal sovereign under the Voting Rights Act, 52 U.S.C. §§10301-10314 ("VRA"), the United States has standing to enforce its laws against, *inter alia*, giving false information as to his name, address or period of residence in the voting district for the purpose of establishing the eligibility to register or vote, conspiring for the purpose of encouraging false registration to vote or illegal voting, falsifying or concealing a material fact in any matter within the jurisdiction of an examiner or hearing officer related to an election, or voting more than once. 52 U.S.C. § 10307(c)-(e). Although the VRA channels enforcement of some VRA sections—namely, 52 U.S.C. § 10303-10304—to the U.S. District Court for the District of Columbia, the VRA does not channel actions under § 10307.

26. Individual state courts or U.S. district courts do not—and under the circumstance of contested elections in multiple states, *cannot*—offer an adequate remedy to resolve election disputes within the timeframe set by the Constitution to resolve such disputes and to appoint a President via the electoral college. No court—other than this Court—can redress constitutional injuries spanning multiple States with the sufficient number of states joined as defendants or respondents to make a difference in the Electoral College.

27. This Court is the sole forum in which to exercise the jurisdictional basis for this action.

PARTIES

28. Plaintiff is the United States of America, which is the federal sovereign.

29. Defendants are the Commonwealth of Pennsylvania and the States of Georgia, Michigan, Arizona, Nevada, and Wisconsin, which are sovereign States of the United States.

LEGAL BACKGROUND

30. Under the Supremacy Clause, the "Constitution, and the laws of the United States which shall be made in pursuance thereof ... shall be the supreme law of the land." U.S. CONST. Art. VI, cl. 2.

31. "The individual citizen has no federal constitutional right to vote for electors for the President of the United States unless and until the state legislature chooses a statewide election as the means to implement its power to appoint members of the electoral college." *Bush II*, 531 U.S. at 104 (citing U.S. CONST. art. II, § 1).

32. State legislatures have plenary power to set the process for appointing presidential electors: "Each State shall appoint, in such Manner as the Legislature thereof may direct, a Number of Electors." U.S. CONST. art. II, §1, cl. 2; *see also Bush II*, 531 U.S. at 104 ("[T]he state legislature's power to select the manner for appointing electors is *plenary*." (emphasis added)).

33. At the time of the Founding, most States did not appoint electors through popular statewide elections. In the first presidential election, six of the ten States that appointed electors did so by direct legislative appointment. *McPherson v. Blacker*, 146 U.S. 1, 29-30 (1892).

34. In the second presidential election, nine of the fifteen States that appointed electors did so by direct legislative appointment. *Id.* at 30.

35. In the third presidential election, nine of sixteen States that appointed electors did so by direct legislative appointment. *Id.* at 31. This practice persisted in lesser degrees through the Election of 1860. *Id.* at 32.

36. Though "[h]istory has now favored the voter," *Bush II*, 531 U.S. at 104, "there is no doubt of the right of the legislature to resume the power [of appointing presidential electors] at any time, for *it can neither be taken away nor abdicated.*" *McPherson*, 146 U.S. at 35 (emphasis added); *cf.* 3 U.S.C. § 2 ("Whenever any State has held an election for the purpose of choosing electors, and has failed to make a choice on the day prescribed by law, the electors may be appointed on a subsequent day in such a manner as the legislature of such State may direct.").

37. Given the State legislatures' constitutional primacy in selecting presidential electors, the ability to set rules governing the casting of ballots and counting of votes cannot be usurped by other branches of state government.

38. The Framers of the Constitution decided to select the President through the Electoral College "to afford as little opportunity as possible to tumult and disorder" and to place "every practicable obstacle [to] cabal, intrigue, and corruption," including "foreign powers" that might try to insinuate themselves into our elections. THE FEDERALIST NO. 68, at 410-11 (C. Rossiter, ed. 1961) (Madison, J.).

39. Defendant States' applicable laws are set out under the facts for each Defendant State.

FACTS

40. The use of absentee and mail-in ballots skyrocketed in 2020, not only as a public-health response to the COVID-19 pandemic but also at the urging of mail-in voting's proponents, and most especially executive branch officials in Defendant States. According to the Pew Research Center, in the 2020 general election, a record number of votes— about 65 million were cast via mail compared to 33.5 million mail-in ballots cast in the 2016 general election—an increase of more than 94 percent.

41. In the wake of the contested 2000 election, the bipartisan Jimmy Carter-James Baker commission identified absentee ballots as "the largest source of potential voter fraud." BUILDING CONFIDENCE IN U.S. ELECTIONS: REPORT OF THE COMMISSION ON FEDERAL ELECTION REFORM, at 46 (Sept. 2005).

14

42. Concern over the use of mail-in ballots is not novel to the modern era, Dustin Waters, *Mail-in Ballots Were Part of a Plot to Deny Lincoln Reelection in 1864*, WASH. POST (Aug. 22, 2020),[6] but it remains a *current* concern. *Crawford v. Marion Cty. Election Bd.*, 553 U.S. 181, 194-96 & n.11 (2008); *see also* Texas Office of the Attorney General, *AG Paxton Announces Joint Prosecution of Gregg County Organized Election Fraud in Mail-In Balloting Scheme* (Sept. 24, 2020); Harriet Alexander & Ariel Zilber, *Minneapolis police opens investigation into reports that Ilhan Omar's supporters illegally harvested Democrat ballots in Minnesota*, DAILY MAIL, Sept. 28, 2020.

43. Absentee and mail-in voting are the primary opportunities for unlawful ballots to be cast. As a result of expanded absentee and mail-in voting in Defendant States, combined with Defendant States' unconstitutional modification of statutory protections designed to ensure ballot integrity, Defendant States created a massive opportunity for fraud. In addition, the Defendant States have made it difficult or impossible to separate the constitutionally tainted mail-in ballots from all mail-in ballots.

44. Rather than augment safeguards against illegal voting in anticipation of the millions of additional mail-in ballots flooding their States, Defendant States *all* materially weakened, or did away with, security measures, such as witness or signature verification procedures, required by their respective legislatures. Their legislatures established those commonsense safeguards to prevent—or at least reduce—fraudulent mail-in ballots.

---

[6] https://www.washingtonpost.com/history/2020/08/22/mail-in-voting-civil-war-election-conspiracy-lincoln/

45. Significantly, in Defendant States, Democrat voters voted by mail at two to three times the rate of Republicans. Former Vice President Biden thus greatly benefited from this unconstitutional usurpation of legislative authority, and the weakening of legislatively mandated ballot security measures.

46. The outcome of the Electoral College vote is directly affected by the constitutional violations committed by Defendant States. Those violations proximately caused the appointment of presidential electors for former Vice President Biden. The United States as a sovereign and as *parens patriae* for all its citizens will therefore be injured if Defendant States' unlawfully certify these presidential electors and those electors' votes are recognized.

47. In addition to the unconstitutional acts associated with mail-in and absentee voting, there are grave questions surrounding the vulnerability of electronic voting machines—especially those machines provided by Dominion Voting Systems, Inc. ("Dominion") which were in use in all of the Defendant States (and other states as well) during the 2020 general election.

48. As initially reported on December 13, 2020, the U.S. Government is scrambling to ascertain the extent of broad-based hack into multiple agencies through a third-party software supplied by vendor known as SolarWinds. That software product is used throughout the U.S. Government, and the private sector including, apparently, Dominion.

49. As reported by CNN, what little we know has cybersecurity experts extremely worried.[7] CNN also quoted Theresa Payton, who served as White House Chief Information Officer under President George W. Bush stating: "I woke up in the middle of the night last night just sick to my stomach. . . . On a scale of 1 to 10, I'm at a 9 — and it's not because of what I know; it's because of what we still don't know."

50. Disturbingly, though the Dominion's CEO denied that Dominion uses SolarWinds software, a screenshot captured from Dominion's webpage shows that Dominion does use SolarWinds technology.[8] Further, Dominion apparently later altered that page to remove any reference to SolarWinds, but the SolarWinds website is still in the Dominion page's source code. *Id.*

Commonwealth of Pennsylvania

51. Pennsylvania has 20 electoral votes, with a statewide vote tally currently estimated at 3,363,951 for President Trump and 3,445,548 for former Vice President Biden, a margin of 81,597 votes.

52. On December 14, 2020, the Pennsylvania Republican slate of Presidential Electors, met at the State Capital and cast their votes for President

---

[7] https://www.cnn.com/2020/12/16/tech/solarwinds-orion-hack-explained/index.html

[8] https://www.theepochtimes.com/dominion-voting-systems-ceo-says-company-has-never-used-solarwinds-orion-platform_3619895.html

17

Donald J. Trump and Vice President Michael R. Pence.[9]

53. The number of votes affected by the various constitutional violations exceeds the margin of votes separating the candidates.

54. Pennsylvania's Secretary of State, Kathy Boockvar, without legislative approval, unilaterally abrogated several Pennsylvania statutes requiring signature verification for absentee or mail-in ballots. Pennsylvania's legislature has not ratified these changes, and the legislation did not include a severability clause.

55. On August 7, 2020, the League of Women Voters of Pennsylvania and others filed a complaint against Secretary Boockvar and other local election officials, seeking "a declaratory judgment that Pennsylvania existing signature verification procedures for mail-in voting" were unlawful for a number of reasons. *League of Women Voters of Pennsylvania v. Boockvar*, No. 2:20-cv-03850-PBT, (E.D. Pa. Aug. 7, 2020).

56. The Pennsylvania Department of State quickly settled with the plaintiffs, issuing revised guidance on September 11, 2020, stating in relevant part: "The Pennsylvania Election Code does not authorize the county board of elections to set aside returned absentee or mail-in ballots based solely on signature analysis by the county board of elections."

57. This guidance is contrary to Pennsylvania law. First, Pennsylvania Election Code mandates that, for non-disabled and non-military

---

[9] https://www.foxnews.com/politics/republican-electors-pennsylvania-georgia-vote-for-trump

18

voters, all applications for an absentee or mail-in ballot "shall be signed by the applicant." 25 PA. STAT. §§ 3146.2(d) & 3150.12(c). Second, Pennsylvania's voter signature verification requirements are expressly set forth at 25 PA. STAT. 350(a.3)(1)-(2) and § 3146.8(g)(3)-(7).

58. The Pennsylvania Department of State's guidance unconstitutionally did away with Pennsylvania's statutory signature verification requirements. Approximately 70 percent of the requests for absentee ballots were from Democrats and 25 percent from Republicans. Thus, this unconstitutional abrogation of state election law greatly inured to former Vice President Biden's benefit.

59. In addition, in 2019, Pennsylvania's legislature enacted bipartisan election reforms, 2019 Pa. Legis. Serv. Act 2019-77, that set *inter alia* a deadline of 8:00 p.m. on election day for a county board of elections to receive a mail-in ballot. 25 PA. STAT. §§ 3146.6(c), 3150.16(c). Acting under a generally worded clause that "Elections shall be free and equal," PA. CONST. art. I, § 5, cl. 1, a 4-3 majority of Pennsylvania's Supreme Court in *Pa. Democratic Party v. Boockvar*, 238 A.3d 345 (Pa. 2020), extended that deadline to three days after Election Day and adopted a presumption that even *non-postmarked ballots* were presumptively timely.

60. Pennsylvania's election law also requires that poll-watchers be granted access to the opening, counting, and recording of absentee ballots: "Watchers shall be permitted to be present when the envelopes containing official absentee ballots and mail-in ballots are opened and when such ballots are counted and

recorded." 25 PA. STAT. § 3146.8(b). Local election officials in Philadelphia and Allegheny Counties decided not to follow 25 PA. STAT. § 3146.8(b) for the opening, counting, and recording of absentee and mail-in ballots.

61. Prior to the election, Secretary Boockvar sent an email to local election officials urging them to provide opportunities for various persons—including political parties—to contact voters to "cure" defective mail-in ballots. This process clearly violated several provisions of the state election code.

- Section 3146.8(a) requires: "The county boards of election, upon receipt of official absentee ballots in sealed official absentee ballot envelopes as provided under this article and mail-in ballots as in sealed official mail-in ballot envelopes as provided under Article XIII-D,1 shall safely keep the ballots in sealed or locked containers until they are to be canvassed by the county board of elections."

- Section 3146.8(g)(1)(ii) provides that mail-in ballots shall be canvassed (if they are received by eight o'clock p.m. on election day) in the manner prescribed by this subsection.

- Section 3146.8(g)(1.1) provides that the first look at the ballots shall be "no earlier than seven o'clock a.m. on election day." And the hour for this "pre-canvas" must be publicly announced at least 48 hours in advance. Then the votes are counted on election day.

62. By removing the ballots for examination prior to seven o'clock a.m. on election day, Secretary Boockvar created a system whereby local officials could review ballots without the proper

announcements, observation, and security. This entire scheme, which was only followed in Democrat majority counties, was blatantly illegal in that it permitted the illegal removal of ballots from their locked containers prematurely.

63. Statewide election officials and local election officials in Philadelphia and Allegheny Counties, aware of the historical Democrat advantage in those counties, violated Pennsylvania's election code and adopted the differential standards favoring voters in Philadelphia and Allegheny Counties with the intent to favor former Vice President Biden. *See* Verified Complaint (Doc. No. 1), *Donald J. Trump for President, Inc. v. Boockvar*, 4:20-cv-02078-MWB (M.D. Pa. Nov. 18, 2020) at ¶¶ 3-6, 9, 11, 100-143.

64. Absentee and mail-in ballots in Pennsylvania were thus evaluated under an illegal standard regarding signature verification. It is now impossible to determine which ballots were properly cast and which ballots were not.

65. The changed process allowing the curing of absentee and mail-in ballots in Allegheny and Philadelphia counties is a separate basis resulting in an unknown number of ballots being treated in an unconstitutional manner inconsistent with Pennsylvania statute. *Id.*

66. In addition, a great number of ballots were received after the statutory deadline and yet were counted by virtue of the fact that Pennsylvania did not segregate all ballots received after 8:00 pm on November 3, 2020. Boockvar's claim that only about 10,000 ballots were received after this deadline has no way of being proven since Pennsylvania broke its promise to the Court to segregate ballots and co-

21

mingled perhaps tens, or even hundreds of thousands, of illegal late ballots.

67. On December 4, 2020, fifteen members of the Pennsylvania House of Representatives led by Rep. Francis X. Ryan issued a report to Congressman Scott Perry (the "Ryan Report," App. 139a-144a) stating that "[t]he general election of 2020 in Pennsylvania was fraught with inconsistencies, documented irregularities and improprieties associated with mail-in balloting, pre-canvassing, and canvassing that the reliability of the mail-in votes in the Commonwealth of Pennsylvania is impossible to rely upon."

68. The Ryan Report's findings are startling, including:

- Ballots with NO MAILED date. That total is 9,005.
- Ballots Returned on or BEFORE the Mailed Date. That total is 58,221.
- Ballots Returned one day after Mailed Date. That total is 51,200.

Id. 143a.

69. These nonsensical numbers alone total 118,426 ballots and exceed Mr. Biden's margin of 81,660 votes over President Trump. But these discrepancies pale in comparison to the discrepancies in Pennsylvania's reported data concerning the number of mail-in ballots distributed to the populace—now with no longer subject to legislated mandated signature verification requirements.

70. The Ryan Report also stated as follows:

22

> [I]n a data file received on November 4, 2020, the Commonwealth's PA Open Data sites reported over 3.1 million mail in ballots sent out. The CSV file from the state on November 4 depicts 3.1 million mail in ballots sent out but on November 2, the information was provided that only 2.7 million ballots had been sent out. *This discrepancy of approximately 400,000 ballots from November 2 to November 4 has not been explained.*

Id. at 143a-44a. (Emphasis added).

71. The Ryan Report stated further: "This apparent [400,000 ballot] discrepancy can only be evaluated by reviewing all transaction logs into the SURE system [the Statewide Uniform Registry Electors]."[10]

72. In its opposition brief to Texas's motion to for leave file a bill of complaint, Pennsylvania said nothing about the 118,426 ballots that had no mail date, were nonsensically returned *before* the mailed date, or were improbably returned one day after the mail date discussed above.[11]

73. With respect to the 400,000 discrepancy in mail-in ballots Pennsylvania sent out as reported on November 2, 2020 compared to November 4, 2020 (one day after the election), Pennsylvania asserted

---

[10] Ryan Report at App. a [p.5].

[11] Pennsylvania Opposition To Motion For Leave To File Bill of Complaint and Motion For Preliminary Injunction, Temporary Restraining Order, or Stay ("Pennsylvania Opp. Br.") filed December 10, 2020, Case No. 220155.

that the discrepancy is purportedly due to the fact that "[o]f the 3.1 million ballots sent out, 2.7 million were mail-in ballots and 400,000 were absentee ballots." Pennsylvania offered *no support* for its conclusory assertion. *Id.* at 6. Nor did Pennsylvania rebut the assertion in the Ryan Report that the "discrepancy can only be evaluated by reviewing all transaction logs into the SURE system."

74. These stunning figures illustrate the out-of-control nature of Pennsylvania's mail-in balloting scheme. Democrats submitted mail-in ballots at more than two times the rate of Republicans. This number of constitutionally tainted ballots far exceeds the approximately 81,660 votes separating the candidates.

75. This blatant disregard of statutory law renders all mail-in ballots constitutionally tainted and cannot form the basis for appointing or certifying Pennsylvania's presidential electors to the Electoral College.

76. According to the U.S. Election Assistance Commission's report to Congress *Election Administration and Voting Survey: 2016 Comprehensive Report*, in 2016 Pennsylvania received 266,208 mail-in ballots; 2,534 of them were rejected (.95%). *Id.* at p. 24. However, in 2020, Pennsylvania received more than 10 times the number of mail-in ballots compared to 2016. As explained *supra*, this much larger volume of mail-in ballots was treated in an unconstitutionally modified manner that included: (1) doing away with the Pennsylvania's signature verification requirements; (2) extending that deadline to three days after Election Day and adopting a presumption that even *non-postmarked ballots* were

presumptively timely; and (3) blocking poll watchers in Philadelphia and Allegheny Counties in violation of State law.

77. These non-legislative modifications to Pennsylvania's election rules appear to have generated an outcome-determinative number of unlawful ballots that were cast in Pennsylvania. Regardless of the number of such ballots, the non-legislative changes to the election rules violated the Electors Clause.

State of Georgia

78. Georgia has 16 electoral votes, with a statewide vote tally currently estimated at 2,458,121 for President Trump and 2,472,098 for former Vice President Biden, a margin of approximately 12,670 votes.

79. On December 14, 2020, the Georgia Republican slate of Presidential Electors, including Petitioner Electors, met at the State Capital and cast their votes for President Donald J. Trump and Vice President Michael R. Pence.[12]

80. The number of votes affected by the various constitutional violations far exceeds the margin of votes dividing the candidates.

81. Georgia's Secretary of State, Brad Raffensperger, without legislative approval, unilaterally abrogated Georgia's statutes governing the date a ballot may be opened, and the signature verification process for absentee ballots.

82. O.C.G.A. § 21-2-386(a)(2) prohibits the opening of absentee ballots until after the polls open

---

[12] https://www.foxnews.com/politics/republican-electors-pennsylvania-georgia-vote-for-trump

on Election Day: In April 2020, however, the State Election Board adopted Secretary of State Rule 183-1-14-0.9-.15, Processing Ballots Prior to Election Day. That rule purports to authorize county election officials to begin processing absentee ballots up to *three weeks* before Election Day. Outside parties were then given early and illegal access to purportedly defective ballots to "cure" them in violation of O.C.G.A. §§ 21-2-386(a)(1)(C), 21-2-419(c)(2).

83. Specifically, Georgia law authorizes and requires a single registrar or clerk—after reviewing the outer envelope—to reject an absentee ballot if the voter failed to sign the required oath or to provide the required information, the signature appears invalid, or the required information does not conform with the information on file, or if the voter is otherwise found ineligible to vote. O.C.G.A. § 21-2-386(a)(1)(B)-(C).

84. Georgia law provides absentee voters the chance to "cure a failure to sign the oath, an invalid signature, or missing information" on a ballot's outer envelope by the deadline for verifying provisional ballots (*i.e.*, three days after the election). O.C.G.A. §§ 21-2-386(a)(1)(C), 21-2-419(c)(2). To facilitate cures, Georgia law requires the relevant election official to notify the voter in writing: "The board of registrars or absentee ballot clerk shall promptly notify the elector of such rejection, a copy of which notification shall be retained in the files of the board of registrars or absentee ballot clerk for at least two years." O.C.G.A. § 21-2-386(a)(1)(B).

85. There were 284,817 early ballots corrected and accepted in Georgia out of 4,018,064 early ballots used to vote in Georgia. Former Vice President Biden received nearly twice the number of

mail-in votes as President Trump and thus materially benefited from this unconstitutional change in Georgia's election laws.

86. In addition, on March 6, 2020, in *Democratic Party of Georgia v. Raffensperger*, No. 1:19-cv-5028-WMR (N.D. Ga.), Georgia's Secretary of State entered a Compromise Settlement Agreement and Release with the Democratic Party of Georgia (the "Settlement") to materially change the statutory requirements for reviewing signatures on absentee ballot envelopes to confirm the voter's identity by making it far more difficult to challenge defective signatures beyond the express mandatory procedures set forth at GA. CODE § 21-2-386(a)(1)(B).

87. Among other things, before a ballot could be rejected, the Settlement required a registrar who found a defective signature to now seek a review by two other registrars, and only if a majority of the registrars agreed that the signature was defective could the ballot be rejected but not before all three registrars' names were written on the ballot envelope along with the reason for the rejection. These cumbersome procedures are in direct conflict with Georgia's statutory requirements, as is the Settlement's requirement that notice be provided by telephone (*i.e.*, not in writing) if a telephone number is available. Finally, the Settlement purports to require State election officials to consider issuing guidance and training materials drafted by an expert retained by the Democratic Party of Georgia.

88. Georgia's legislature has not ratified these material changes to statutory law mandated by the Compromise Settlement Agreement and Release, including altered signature verification requirements

27

and early opening of ballots. The relevant legislation that was violated by Compromise Settlement Agreement and Release did not include a severability clause.

89. This unconstitutional change in Georgia law materially benefitted former Vice President Biden. According to the Georgia Secretary of State's office, former Vice President Biden had almost double the number of absentee votes (65.32%) as President Trump (34.68%). *See* Cicchetti Decl. at ¶ 25, App. 7a-8a.

90. The effect of this unconstitutional change in Georgia election law, which made it more likely that ballots without matching signatures would be counted, had a material impact on the outcome of the election.

91. Specifically, there were 1,305,659 absentee mail-in ballots submitted in Georgia in 2020. There were 4,786 absentee ballots rejected in 2020. This is a rejection rate of .37%. In contrast, in 2016, the 2016 rejection rate was 6.42% with 13,677 absentee mail-in ballots being rejected out of 213,033 submitted, which more than *seventeen times greater* than in 2020. *See* Cicchetti Decl. at ¶ 24, App. 7a.

92. If the rejection rate of mailed-in absentee ballots remained the same in 2020 as it was in 2016, there would be 83,517 less tabulated ballots in 2020. The statewide split of absentee ballots was 34.68% for Trump and 65.2% for Biden. Rejecting at the higher 2016 rate with the 2020 split between Trump and Biden would decrease Trump votes by 28,965 and Biden votes by 54,552, which would be a net gain for Trump of 25,587 votes. This would be more than needed to overcome the Biden advantage of 12,670

votes, and Trump would win by 12,917 votes. *Id.* Regardless of the number of ballots affected, however, the non-legislative changes to the election rules violated the Electors Clause.

93. In addition, Georgia uses Dominion's voting machines throughout the State. Less than a month before the election, the United States District Court for the Northern District of Georgia ruled on a motion brought by a citizen advocate group and others seeking a preliminary injunction to stop Georgia from using Dominion's voting systems due to their known vulnerabilities to hacking and other irregularities. *See Curling v. Raffensperger*, 2020 U.S. Dist. LEXIS 188508, No. 1:17-cv-2989-AT (N.D. GA Oct.11, 2020).

94. Though the district court found that it was bound by Eleventh Circuit law to deny plaintiffs' motion, it issued a prophetic warning stating:

> The Court's Order has delved deep into the true risks posed by the new BMD voting system as well as its manner of implementation. These risks are neither hypothetical nor remote under the current circumstances. ***The insularity of the Defendants' and Dominion's stance here in evaluation and management of the security and vulnerability of the BMD system does not benefit the public or citizens' confident exercise of the franchise.*** The stealth vote alteration or operational interference risks posed by malware that can be effectively invisible to detection, whether intentionally seeded or not, are high once implanted, if equipment and software systems are not properly protected, implemented, and audited.

Id. at *176 (Emphasis added).

95. One of those material risks manifested three weeks later as shown by the November 4, 2020 video interview of a Fulton County, Georgia Director

of Elections, Richard Barron. In that interview, Barron stated that the tallied vote of over 93% of ballots were based on a "review panel['s]" determination of the voter's "intent"—not what the voter actually voted. Specifically, he stated that "so far we've scanned 113,130 ballots, we've adjudicated over 106,000. . . . The only ballots that are adjudicated are if we have a ballot with a contest on it in which there's some question as to how the computer reads it so that the vote review panel then determines voter intent."[13]

96. This astounding figure demonstrates the unreliability of Dominion's voting machines. These figures, in and of themselves in this one sample, far exceeds the margin of votes separating the two candidates.

97. Lastly, on December 17, 2020, the Chairman of the Election Law Study Subcommittee of the Georgia Standing Senate Judiciary Committee issued a detailed report discussing a myriad of voting irregularities and potential fraud in the Georgia 2020 general election (the "Report").[14] The Executive Summary states that "[t]he November 3, 2020 General Election (the 'Election') was chaotic and any reported results must be viewed as untrustworthy". After detailing over a dozen issues showing irregularities and potential fraud, the Report concluded:

> The Legislature should carefully consider its obligations under the U.S. Constitution. If a

---

[13] https://www.c-span.org/video/?477819-1/fulton-county-georgia-election-update at beginning at 20 seconds through 1:21.

[14] (App. a -- a)

majority of the General Assembly concurs with the findings of this report, the certification of the Election should be rescinded and the General Assembly should act to determine the proper Electors to be certified to the Electoral College in the 2020 presidential race. Since time is of the essence, the Chairman and Senators who concur with this report recommend that the leadership of the General Assembly and the Governor immediately convene to allow further consideration by the entire General Assembly.

State of Michigan

98. Michigan has 16 electoral votes, with a statewide vote tally currently estimated at 2,650,695 for President Trump and 2,796,702 for former Vice President Biden, a margin of 146,007 votes. In Wayne County, Mr. Biden's margin (322,925 votes) significantly exceeds his statewide lead.

99. On December 14, 2020, the Michigan Republican slate of Presidential Electors *attempted* to meet and cast their votes for President Donald J. Trump and Vice President Michael R. Pence but were denied entry to the State Capital by law enforcement. Their tender of their votes was refused. They instead met on the grounds of the State Capital and cast their votes for President Donald J. Trump and Vice President Michael R. Pence.[15]

100. The number of votes affected by the various constitutional violations exceeds the margin of votes dividing the candidates.

---

[15] https://thepalmierireport.com/michigan-state-police-block-gop-electors-from-entering-capitol/

101. Michigan's Secretary of State, Jocelyn Benson, without legislative approval, unilaterally abrogated Michigan election statutes related to absentee ballot applications and signature verification. Michigan's legislature has not ratified these changes, and its election laws do not include a severability clause.

102. As amended in 2018, the Michigan Constitution provides all registered voters the right to request and vote by an absentee ballot without giving a reason. MICH. CONST. art. 2, § 4.

103. On May 19, 2020, however, Secretary Benson announced that her office would send unsolicited absentee-voter ballot applications by mail to all 7.7 million registered Michigan voters prior to the primary and general elections. Although her office repeatedly encouraged voters to vote absentee because of the COVID-19 pandemic, it did not ensure that Michigan's election systems and procedures were adequate to ensure the accuracy and legality of the historic flood of mail-in votes. In fact, it did the opposite and did away with protections designed to deter voter fraud.

104. Secretary Benson's flooding of Michigan with millions of absentee ballot applications prior to the 2020 general election violated M.C.L. § 168.759(3). That statute limits the procedures for requesting an absentee ballot to three specified ways:

> An application for an absent voter ballot under this section may be made in *any of the following ways*:
>
> (a) By a written request signed by the voter.
>
> (b) On an absent voter ballot application form provided for that purpose by the clerk of the city or township.

32

(c) On a federal postcard application.

M.C.L. § 168.759(3) (emphasis added).

105. The Michigan Legislature thus declined to include the Secretary of State as a means for distributing absentee ballot applications. *Id.* § 168.759(3)(b). Under the statute's plain language, the Legislature explicitly gave *only local clerks* the power to distribute absentee voter ballot applications. *Id.*

106. Because the Legislature declined to explicitly include the Secretary of State as a vehicle for distributing absentee ballots applications, Secretary Benson lacked authority to distribute even a single absentee voter ballot application—much less the *millions* of absentee ballot applications Secretary Benson chose to flood across Michigan.

107. Secretary Benson also violated Michigan law when she launched a program in June 2020 allowing absentee ballots to be requested online, *without* signature verification as expressly required under Michigan law. The Michigan Legislature did not approve or authorize Secretary Benson's unilateral actions.

108. MCL § 168.759(4) states in relevant part: "An applicant for an absent voter ballot shall sign the application. Subject to section 761(2), a clerk or assistant clerk shall not deliver an absent voter ballot to an applicant who does not sign the application."

109. Further, MCL § 168.761(2) states in relevant part: "The qualified voter file must be used to determine the genuineness of a signature on an application for an absent voter ballot", and if "the signatures do not agree sufficiently or [if] the signature is missing" the ballot must be rejected.

110. In 2016 only 587,618 Michigan voters requested absentee ballots. In stark contrast, in 2020, 3.2 million votes were cast by absentee ballot, about 57% of total votes cast – and more than *five times* the number of ballots *even requested* in 2016.

111. Secretary Benson's unconstitutional modifications of Michigan's election rules resulted in the distribution of millions of absentee ballot applications without verifying voter signatures as required by MCL §§ 168.759(4) and 168.761(2). This means that *millions* of absentee ballots were disseminated in violation of Michigan's statutory signature-verification requirements. Democrats in Michigan voted by mail at a ratio of approximately two to one compared to Republican voters. Thus, former Vice President Biden materially benefited from these unconstitutional changes to Michigan's election law.

112. Michigan also requires that poll watchers and inspectors have access to vote counting and canvassing. M.C.L. §§ 168.674-.675.

113. Local election officials in Wayne County made a conscious and express policy decision not to follow M.C.L. §§ 168.674-.675 for the opening, counting, and recording of absentee ballots.

114. Michigan also has strict signature verification requirements for absentee ballots, including that the Elections Department place a written statement or stamp on each ballot envelope where the voter signature is placed, indicating that the voter signature was in fact checked and verified with the signature on file with the State. *See* MCL § 168.765a(6).

115. However, Wayne County made the policy decision to ignore Michigan's statutory signature-verification requirements for absentee ballots. Former Vice President Biden received approximately 587,074, or 68%, of the votes cast there compared to President Trump's receiving approximate 264,149, or 30.59%, of the total vote. Thus, Mr. Biden materially benefited from these unconstitutional changes to Michigan's election law.

116. Numerous poll challengers and an Election Department employee whistleblower have testified that the signature verification requirement was ignored in Wayne County in a case currently pending in the Michigan Supreme Court.[16] For example, Jesse Jacob, a decades-long City of Detroit employee assigned to work in the Elections Department for the 2020 election testified that:

> Absentee ballots that were received in the mail would have the voter's signature on the envelope. While I was at the TCF Center, I was instructed not to look at any of the signatures on the absentee ballots, and I was instructed not to compare the signature on the absentee ballot with the signature on file.[17]

117. In fact, a poll challenger, Lisa Gage, testified that not a single one of the several hundred to a thousand ballot envelopes she observed had a written statement or stamp indicating the voter

---

[16] *Johnson v. Benson*, Petition for Extraordinary Writs & Declaratory Relief filed Nov. 26, 2020 (Mich. Sup. Ct.) at ¶¶ 71, 138-39, App. 25a-51a.

[17] *Id.*, Affidavit of Jessy Jacob, Appendix 14 at ¶15, attached at App. 34a-36a.

35

signature had been verified at the TCF Center in accordance with MCL § 168.765a(6).[18]

118. The TCF was the only facility within Wayne County authorized to count ballots for the City of Detroit.

119. Additional public information confirms the material adverse impact on the integrity of the vote in Wayne County caused by these unconstitutional changes to Michigan's election law. For example, the Wayne County Statement of Votes Report lists 174,384 absentee ballots out of 566,694 absentee ballots tabulated (about 30.8%) as counted without a registration number for precincts in the City of Detroit. *See* Cicchetti Decl. at ¶ 27, App. a. The number of votes not tied to a registered voter by itself exceeds Vice President Biden's margin of margin of 146,007 votes by more than 28,377 votes.

120. The extra ballots cast most likely resulted from the phenomenon of Wayne County election workers running the same ballots through a tabulator multiple times, with Republican poll watchers obstructed or denied access, and election officials ignoring poll watchers' challenges, as documented by numerous declarations. App. 25a-51a.

121. In addition, a member of the Wayne County Board of Canvassers ("Canvassers Board"), William Hartman, determined that 71% of Detroit's Absent Voter Counting Boards ("AVCBs") were unbalanced—*i.e.*, the number of people who checked in did not match the number of ballots cast—without explanation. *Id.* at ¶ 29.

---

[18] Affidavit of Lisa Gage ¶ 17 (App. a).

122. On November 17, 2020, the Canvassers Board deadlocked 2-2 over whether to certify the results of the presidential election based on numerous reports of fraud and unanswered material discrepancies in the county-wide election results. A few hours later, the Republican Board members reversed their decision and voted to certify the results after severe harassment, including threats of violence.

123. The following day, the two Republican members of the Board *rescinded their votes* to certify the vote and signed affidavits alleging they were bullied and misled into approving election results and do not believe the votes should be certified until serious irregularities in Detroit votes are resolved. *See* Cicchetti Decl. at ¶ 29, App. a.

124. Michigan admitted in a filing with this Court that it "is at a loss to explain the[] allegations" showing that Wayne County lists 174,384 absentee ballots that do not tie to a registered voter. *See* State of Michigan's Brief In Opposition To Motions For Leave To File Bill of Complaint and For Injunctive Relief at 15 (filed Dec. 10, 2020), Case No. 220155.

125. Lastly, on November 4, 2020, Michigan election officials in Antrim County admitted that a purported "glitch" in Dominion voting machines caused 6,000 votes for President Trump to be wrongly switched to Democrat Candidate Biden in just one county. Local officials discovered the so-called "glitch" after reportedly questioning Mr. Biden's win in the heavily Republican area and manually checked the vote tabulation.

126. The Dominion voting tabulators used in Antrim County were recently subjected to a forensic

audit.[19] Though Michigan's Secretary of State tried to keep the Allied Report from being released to the public, the court overseeing the audit refused and allowed the Allied Report to made public.[20] The Allied Report concluded that "the vote flip occurred because of machine error built into the voting software designed to create error."[21] In addition, the Allied report revealed that "all server security logs prior to 11:03 pm on November 4, 2020 are missing and that there was other "tampering with data." *See* Allied Report at ¶¶ B.16-17 (App.   a).

127. Further, the Allied Report determined that the Dominion voting system in Antrim County was designed to generate an error rate as high as 81.96% thereby sending ballots for "adjudication" to determine the voter's intent. *See* Allied report at ¶¶ B.2, 8-22 (App.   a--   a).

128. Notably, the extraordinarily high error rate described here is consistent with the same situation that took place in Fulton County, Georgia with an enormous 93% error rate that required "adjudication" of over 106,000 ballots.

129. These non-legislative modifications to Michigan's election statutes resulted in a number of constitutionally tainted votes that far exceeds the margin of voters separating the candidates in

---

[19] Antrim Michigan Forensics Report by Allied Security Operations Group dated December 13, 2020 (the "Allied Report") (App.   a --   a);

[20]   https://themichiganstar.com/2020/12/15/after-examining-antrim-county-voting-machines-asog-concludes-dominion-intentionally-designed-to-create-systemic-fraud/

[21] Allied Report at ¶¶ B.4-9 (App.   a).

Michigan. Regardless of the number of votes that were affected by the unconstitutional modification of Michigan's election rules, the non-legislative changes to the election rules violated the Electors Clause.

State of Wisconsin

130. Wisconsin has 10 electoral votes, with a statewide vote tally currently estimated at 1,610,151 for President Trump and 1,630,716 for former Vice President Biden (*i.e.*, a margin of 20,565 votes). In two counties, Milwaukee and Dane, Mr. Biden's margin (364,298 votes) significantly exceeds his statewide lead.

131. On December 14, 2020, the Wisconsin Republican slate of Presidential Electors met at the State Capital and cast their votes for President Donald J. Trump and Vice President Michael R. Pence.[22]

132. In the 2016 general election some 146,932 mail-in ballots were returned in Wisconsin out of more than 3 million votes cast.[23] In stark contrast, 1,275,019 mail-in ballots, nearly a 900 percent increase over 2016, were returned in the November 3, 2020 election.[24]

133. Wisconsin statutes guard against fraud in absentee ballots: "[V]oting by absentee ballot is a privilege exercised wholly outside the traditional safeguards of the polling place. The legislature finds that the privilege of voting by absentee ballot must be

---

[22] https://wisgop.org/republican-electors-2020/.

[23] Source: U.S. Elections Project, *available at*: http://www.electproject.org/early 2016.

[24] Source: U.S. Elections Project, *available at*: https://electproject.github.io/Early-Vote-2020G/WI.html.

carefully regulated to prevent the potential for fraud or abuse[.]" WISC. STAT. § 6.84(1).

134. In direct contravention of Wisconsin law, leading up to the 2020 general election, the Wisconsin Elections Commission ("WEC") and other local officials unconstitutionally modified Wisconsin election laws—each time taking steps that weakened, or did away with, established security procedures put in place by the Wisconsin legislature to ensure absentee ballot integrity.

135. For example, the WEC undertook a campaign to position hundreds of drop boxes to collect absentee ballots—including the use of unmanned drop boxes.[25]

136. The mayors of Wisconsin's five largest cities—Green Bay, Kenosha, Madison, Milwaukee, and Racine, which all have Democrat majorities— joined in this effort, and together, developed a plan use purportedly "secure drop-boxes to facilitate return of absentee ballots." Wisconsin Safe Voting Plan 2020, at 4 (June 15, 2020).[26]

137. It is alleged in an action recently filed in the United States District Court for the Eastern District of Wisconsin that over five hundred

---

[25] Wisconsin Elections Commission Memoranda, To: All Wisconsin Election Officials, Aug. 19, 2020, *available at*: https://elections.wi.gov/sites/elections.wi.gov/files/2020-08/Drop%20Box%20Final.pdf. at p. 3 of 4.

[26] Wisconsin Safe Voting Plan 2020 Submitted to the Center for Tech & Civic Life, June 15, 2020, by the Mayors of Madison, Milwaukee, Racine, Kenosha and Green Bay *available at*: https://www.techandciviclife.org/wp-content/uploads/2020/07/Approved-Wisconsin-Safe-Voting-Plan-2020.pdf.

unmanned, illegal, absentee ballot drop boxes were used in the Presidential election in Wisconsin.[27]

138. However, the use of *any* drop box, manned or unmanned, is directly prohibited by Wisconsin statute. The Wisconsin legislature specifically described in the Election Code "Alternate absentee ballot site[s]" and detailed the procedure by which the governing body of a municipality may designate a site or sites for the delivery of absentee ballots "other than the office of the municipal clerk or board of election commissioners as the location from which electors of the municipality may request and vote absentee ballots and to which voted absentee ballots shall be returned by electors for any election." Wis. Stat. 6.855(1).

139. Any alternate absentee ballot site "shall be staffed by the municipal clerk or the executive director of the board of election commissioners, or employees of the clerk or the board of election commissioners." Wis. Stat. 6.855(3). Likewise, Wis. Stat. 7.15(2m) provides, "[i]n a municipality in which the governing body has elected to an establish an alternate absentee ballot sit under s. 6.855, the municipal clerk shall operate such site as though it were his or her office for absentee ballot purposes and shall ensure that such site is adequately staffed."

140. Thus, the unmanned absentee ballot drop-off sites are prohibited by the Wisconsin Legislature as they do not comply with Wisconsin law

---

[27] *See* Complaint (Doc. No. 1), *Donald J. Trump, Candidate for President of the United States of America v. The Wisconsin Election Commission*, Case 2:20-cv-01785-BHL (E.D. Wisc. Dec. 2, 2020) (Wisconsin Trump Campaign Complaint") at ¶¶ 188-89.

expressly defining "[a]lternate absentee ballot site[s]". Wis. Stat. 6.855(1), (3).

141. In addition, the use of drop boxes for the collection of absentee ballots, positioned predominantly in Wisconsin's largest cities, is directly contrary to Wisconsin law providing that absentee ballots may only be "mailed by the elector, or delivered *in person* to the municipal clerk issuing the ballot or ballots." Wis. Stat. § 6.87(4)(b)1 (emphasis added).

142. The fact that other methods of delivering absentee ballots, such as through unmanned drop boxes, are *not* permitted is underscored by Wis. Stat. § 6.87(6) which mandates that, "[a]ny ballot not mailed or delivered as provided in this subsection may not be counted." Likewise, Wis. Stat. § 6.84(2) underscores this point, providing that Wis. Stat. § 6.87(6) "shall be construed as mandatory." The provision continues—"Ballots cast in contravention of the procedures specified in those provisions may not be counted. *Ballots counted in contravention of the procedures specified in those provisions may not be included in the certified result of any election.*" Wis. Stat. § 6.84(2) (emphasis added).

143. These were not the only Wisconsin election laws that the WEC violated in the 2020 general election. The WEC and local election officials also took it upon themselves to encourage voters to unlawfully declare themselves "indefinitely confined"—which under Wisconsin law allows the voter to avoid security measures like signature verification and photo ID requirements.

144. Specifically, registering to vote by absentee ballot requires photo identification, except for those who register as "indefinitely confined" or

42

"hospitalized." WISC. STAT. § 6.86(2)(a), (3)(a). Registering for indefinite confinement requires certifying confinement "because of age, physical illness or infirmity or [because the voter] is disabled for an indefinite period." *Id.* § 6.86(2)(a). Should indefinite confinement cease, the voter must notify the county clerk, *id.*, who must remove the voter from indefinite-confinement status. *Id.* § 6.86(2)(b).

145. Wisconsin election procedures for voting absentee based on indefinite confinement enable the voter to avoid the photo ID requirement and signature requirement. *Id.* § 6.86(1)(ag)/(3)(a)(2).

146. On March 25, 2020, in clear violation of Wisconsin law, Dane County Clerk Scott McDonnell and Milwaukee County Clerk George Christensen both issued guidance indicating that all voters should mark themselves as "indefinitely confined" because of the COVID-19 pandemic.

147. Believing this to be an attempt to circumvent Wisconsin's strict voter ID laws, the Republican Party of Wisconsin petitioned the Wisconsin Supreme Court to intervene. On March 31, 2020, the Wisconsin Supreme Court unanimously confirmed that the clerks' "advice was legally incorrect" and potentially dangerous because "voters may be misled to exercise their right to vote in ways that are inconsistent with WISC. STAT. § 6.86(2)."

148. On May 13, 2020, the Administrator of WEC issued a directive to the Wisconsin clerks prohibiting removal of voters from the registry for indefinite-confinement status if the voter is no longer "indefinitely confined."

149. The WEC's directive violated Wisconsin law. Specifically, WISC. STAT. § 6.86(2)(a) specifically

provides that "any [indefinitely confined] elector [who] is no longer indefinitely confined ... shall so notify the municipal clerk." WISC. STAT. § 6.86(2)(b) further provides that the municipal clerk "shall remove the name of any other elector from the list upon request of the elector or upon receipt of reliable information that an elector no longer qualifies for the service."

150. According to statistics kept by the WEC, nearly 216,000 voters said they were indefinitely confined in the 2020 election, nearly a fourfold increase from nearly 57,000 voters in 2016. In Dane and Milwaukee counties, more than 68,000 voters said they were indefinitely confined in 2020, a fourfold increase from the roughly 17,000 indefinitely confined voters in those counties in 2016.

151. On December 16, 2020, the Wisconsin Supreme Court ruled that Wisconsin officials, including Governor Evers, unlawfully told Wisconsin voters to declare themselves "indefinitely confined"—thereby avoiding signature and photo ID requirements. *See Jefferson v. Dane County*, 2020 Wisc. LEXIS 194 (Wis. Dec. 14, 2020). Given the near fourfold increase in the use of this classification from 2016 to 2020, tens of thousands of these ballots could be illegal. The vast majority of the more than 216,000 voters classified as "indefinitely confined" were from heavily democrat areas, thereby materially and illegally, benefited Mr. Biden.

152. Under Wisconsin law, voting by absentee ballot also requires voters to complete a certification, including their address, and have the envelope witnessed by an adult who also must sign and indicate their address on the envelope. *See* WISC. STAT. § 6.87. The sole remedy to cure an "improperly completed

certificate or [ballot] with no certificate" is for "the clerk [to] return the ballot to the elector[.]" *Id.* § 6.87(9). "If a certificate is missing the address of a witness, the ballot *may not be counted.*" *Id.* § 6.87(6d) (emphasis added).

153. However, in a training video issued April 1, 2020, the Administrator of the City of Milwaukee Elections Commission unilaterally declared that a "witness address may be written in red and that is because we were able to locate the witnesses' address for the voter" to add an address missing from the certifications on absentee ballots. The Administrator's instruction violated WISC. STAT. § 6.87(6d). The WEC issued similar guidance on October 19, 2020, in violation of this statute as well.

154. In the Wisconsin Trump Campaign Complaint, it is alleged, supported by the sworn affidavits of poll watchers, that canvas workers carried out this unlawful policy, and acting pursuant to this guidance, in Milwaukee used red-ink pens to alter the certificates on the absentee envelope and then cast and count the absentee ballot. These acts violated WISC. STAT. § 6.87(6d) ("If a certificate is missing the address of a witness, the ballot may not be counted"). *See also* WISC. STAT. § 6.87(9) ("If a municipal clerk receives an absentee ballot with an improperly completed certificate or with no certificate, the clerk may return the ballot to the elector . . . whenever time permits the elector to correct the defect and return the ballot within the period authorized.").

155. Wisconsin's legislature has not ratified these changes, and its election laws do not include a severability clause.

156. In addition, Ethan J. Pease, a box truck delivery driver subcontracted to the U.S. Postal Service ("USPS") to deliver truckloads of mail-in ballots to the sorting center in Madison, WI, testified that USPS employees were backdating ballots received after November 3, 2020. Decl. of Ethan J. Pease at ¶¶ 3-13. Further, Pease testified how a senior USPS employee told him on November 4, 2020 that "[a]n order came down from the Wisconsin/Illinois Chapter of the Postal Service that 100,000 ballots were missing" and how the USPS dispatched employees to "find[] . . . the ballots." *Id.* ¶¶ 8-10. One hundred thousand ballots supposedly "found" after election day would far exceed former Vice President Biden margin of 20,565 votes over President Trump.

State of Arizona

157. Arizona has 11 electoral votes, with a state-wide vote tally currently estimated at 1,661,677 for President Trump and 1,672,054 for former Vice President Biden, a margin of 10,377 votes. In Arizona's most populous county, Maricopa County, Mr. Biden's margin (45,109 votes) significantly exceeds his statewide lead.

158. On December 14, 2020, the Arizona Republican slate of Presidential Electors met at the State Capital and cast their votes for President Donald J. Trump and Vice President Michael R. Pence.[28]

---

[28] https://arizonadailyindependent.com/2020/12/14/az-democrat-electors-vote-biden-republicans-join-pennsylvania-georgia-nevada-in-casting-electoral-college-votes-for-trump/

46

159. Since 1990, Arizona law has required that residents wishing to participate in an election submit their voter registration materials no later than 29 days prior to election day in order to vote in that election. Ariz. Rev. Stat. § 16-120(A). For 2020, that deadline was October 5.

160. In *Mi Familia Vota v. Hobbs*, No. CV-20-01903-PHX-SPL, 2020 U.S. Dist. LEXIS 184397 (D. Ariz. Oct. 5, 2020), however, a federal district court violated the Constitution and enjoined that law, extending the registration deadline to October 23, 2020. The Ninth Circuit stayed that order on October 13, 2020 with a two-day grace period, *Mi Familia Vota v. Hobbs*, 977 F.3d 948, 955 (9th Cir. 2020).

161. However, the Ninth Circuit did not apply the stay retroactively because neither the Arizona Secretary of State nor the Arizona Attorney General requested retroactive relief. *Id.* at 954-55. As a net result, the deadline was unconstitutionally extended from the statutory deadline of October 5 to October 15, 2021, thereby allowing potentially thousands of illegal votes to be injected into the state.

162. In addition, on December 15, 2020, the Arizona state Senate served two subpoenas on the Maricopa County Board of Supervisors (the "Maricopa Board") to audit scanned ballots, voting machines, and software due to the significant number of voting irregularities. Indeed, the Arizona Senate Judiciary Chairman stated in a public hearing earlier that day that "[t]here is evidence of tampering, there is evidence of fraud" with vote in Maricopa County. The Board then voted to refuse to comply with those subpoenas necessitating a lawsuit to enforce the

subpoenas filed on December 21, 2020. That litigation is currently ongoing.

State of Nevada

163. Nevada has 6 electoral votes, with a statewide vote tally currently estimated at 669,890 for President Trump and 703,486 for former Vice President Biden, a margin of 33,596 votes. Nevada voters sent in 579,533 mail-in ballots. In Clark County, Mr. Biden's margin (90,922 votes) significantly exceeds his statewide lead.

164. On December 14, 2020 the Republican slate of Presidential Electors met at the State Capital and cast their votes for President Donald J. Trump and Vice President Michael R. Pence.[29]

165. In response to the COVID-19 pandemic, the Nevada Legislature enacted—and the Governor signed into law—Assembly Bill 4, 2020 Nev. Ch. 3, to address voting by mail and to require, for the first time in Nevada's history, the applicable county or city clerk to mail ballots to all registered voters in the state.

166. Under Section 23 of Assembly Bill 4, the applicable city or county clerk's office is required to review the signature on ballots, without permitting a computer system to do so: "The *clerk or employee shall check* the signature used for the mail ballot against all signatures of the voter available in the records of the clerk." *Id.* § 23(1)(a) (codified at NEV. REV. STAT. § 293.8874(1)(a)) (emphasis add). Moreover, the system requires that two or more employees be included: "If at least two employees in the office of the clerk believe there is a reasonable question of fact as to whether the

---

[29] https://nevadagop.org/42221-2/

signature used for the mail ballot matches the signature of the voter, the clerk shall contact the voter and ask the voter to confirm whether the signature used for the mail ballot belongs to the voter." *Id.* § 23(1)(b) (codified at NEV. REV. STAT. § 293.8874(1)(b)). A signature that differs from on-file signatures in multiple respects is inadequate: "There is a reasonable question of fact as to whether the signature used for the mail ballot matches the signature of the voter if the signature used for the mail ballot differs in multiple, significant and obvious respects from the signatures of the voter available in the records of the clerk." *Id.* § 23(2)(a) (codified at NEV. REV. STAT. § 293.8874(2)(a)). Finally, under Nevada law, "each voter has the right ... [t]o have a uniform, statewide standard for counting and recounting all votes accurately." NEV. REV. STAT. § 293.2546(10).

167. Nevada law does not allow computer systems to substitute for review by clerks' employees.

168. However, county election officials in Clark County ignored this requirement of Nevada law. Clark County, Nevada, processed all its mail-in ballots through a ballot sorting machine known as the Agilis Ballot Sorting System ("Agilis"). The Agilis system purported to match voters' ballot envelope signatures to exemplars maintained by the Clark County Registrar of Voters.

169. Anecdotal evidence suggests that the Agilis system was prone to false positives (*i.e.*, accepting as valid an invalid signature). Victor Joecks, *Clark County Election Officials Accepted My Signature—on 8 Ballot Envelopes*, LAS VEGAS REV.-J. (Nov. 12, 2020) (Agilis system accepted 8 of 9 false signatures).

49

170. Even after adjusting the Agilis system's tolerances outside the settings that the manufacturer recommends, the Agilis system nonetheless rejected approximately 70% of the approximately 453,248 mail-in ballots.

171. More than 450,000 mail-in ballots from Clark County either were processed under weakened signature-verification criteria in violation of the statutory criteria for validating mail-in ballots. The number of contested votes exceeds the margin of votes dividing the parties.

172. With respect to approximately 130,000 ballots that the Agilis system approved, Clark County did not subject those signatures to review by two or more employees, as Assembly Bill 4 requires. To count those 130,000 ballots without review not only violated the election law adopted by the legislature but also subjected those votes to a different standard of review than other voters statewide.

173. With respect to approximately 323,000 ballots that the Agilis system rejected, Clark County decided to count ballots if a signature matched at least one letter between the ballot envelope signature and the maintained exemplar signature. This guidance does not match the statutory standard "differ[ing] in multiple, significant and obvious respects from the signatures of the voter available in the records of the clerk."

174. Out of the nearly 580,000 mail-in ballots, registered Democrats returned almost twice as many mail-in ballots as registered Republicans. Thus, this violation of Nevada law appeared to materially benefited former Vice President Biden's vote tally. Regardless of the number of votes that were affected

by the unconstitutional modification of Nevada's election rules, the non-legislative changes to the election rules violated the Electors Clause.

COUNT I: ELECTORS CLAUSE

175. The United States repeats and re-alleges the allegations above, as if fully set forth herein.

176. The Electors Clause of Article II, Section 1, Clause 2, of the Constitution makes clear that only the legislatures of the States are permitted to determine the rules for appointing presidential electors. The pertinent rules here are the state election statutes, specifically those relevant to the presidential election.

177. Non-legislative actors lack authority to amend or nullify election statutes. *Bush II*, 531 U.S. at 104 (quoted *supra*).

178. Under *Heckler v. Chaney*, 470 U.S. 821, 833 n.4 (1985), conscious and express executive policies—even if unwritten—to nullify statutes or to abdicate statutory responsibilities are reviewable to the same extent as if the policies had been written or adopted. Thus, conscious and express actions by State or local election officials to nullify or ignore requirements of election statutes violate the Electors Clause to the same extent as formal modifications by judicial officers or State executive officers.

179. The actions set out in Paragraphs 41-128 constitute non-legislative changes to State election law by executive-branch State election officials, or by judicial officials, in Defendant States Pennsylvania, Georgia, Michigan, Wisconsin, Arizona, and Nevada in violation of the Electors Clause.

51

180. Electors appointed to Electoral College in violation of the Electors Clause cannot cast constitutionally valid votes for the office of President.

COUNT II: EQUAL PROTECTION

181. The United States repeats and re-alleges the allegations above, as if fully set forth herein.

182. The Equal Protection Clause prohibits the use of differential standards in the treatment and tabulation of ballots within a State. *Bush II*, 531 U.S. at 107.

183. The one-person, one-vote principle requires counting valid votes and not counting invalid votes. *Reynolds*, 377 U.S. at 554-55; *Bush II*, 531 U.S. at 103 ("the votes eligible for inclusion in the certification are the votes meeting the properly established legal requirements").

184. The actions set out in Paragraphs ___ (Georgia), ___ (Michigan), ___ (Pennsylvania), ___ (Wisconsin), ___ (Arizona), and ___ (Nevada) created differential voting standards in Defendant States Pennsylvania, Georgia, Michigan, Wisconsin, [Arizona (maybe not)], and Nevada in violation of the Equal Protection Clause.

185. The actions set out in Paragraphs ___ (Georgia), ___ (Michigan), ___ (Pennsylvania), ___ (Wisconsin), ___ (Arizona). And ___ (Nevada) violated the one-person, one-vote principle in Defendant States Pennsylvania, Georgia, Michigan, Wisconsin, Arizona, and Nevada.

186. By the shared enterprise of the entire nation electing the President and Vice President, equal protection violations in one State can and do adversely affect and diminish the weight of votes cast in other States that lawfully abide by the election

structure set forth in the Constitution. The United States is therefore harmed by this unconstitutional conduct in violation of the Equal Protection or Due Process Clauses.

COUNT III: DUE PROCESS

187. The United States repeats and re-alleges the allegations above, as if fully set forth herein.

188. When election practices reach "the point of patent and fundamental unfairness," the integrity of the election itself violates substantive due process. *Griffin v. Burns*, 570 F.2d 1065, 1077 (1st Cir. 1978); *Duncan v. Poythress*, 657 F.2d 691, 702 (5th Cir. 1981); *Florida State Conference of N.A.A.C.P. v. Browning*, 522 F.3d 1153, 1183-84 (11th Cir. 2008); *Roe v. State of Ala. By & Through Evans*, 43 F.3d 574, 580-82 (11th Cir. 1995); *Roe v. State of Ala.*, 68 F.3d 404, 407 (11th Cir. 1995); *Marks v. Stinson*, 19 F. 3d 873, 878 (3rd Cir. 1994).

189. Under this Court's precedents on procedural due process, not only intentional failure to follow election law as enacted by a State's legislature but also random and unauthorized acts by state election officials and their designees in local government can violate the Due Process Clause. *Parratt v. Taylor*, 451 U.S. 527, 537-41 (1981), *overruled in part on other grounds by Daniels v. Williams*, 474 U.S. 327, 330-31 (1986); *Hudson v. Palmer*, 468 U.S. 517, 532 (1984). The difference between intentional acts and random and unauthorized acts is the degree of pre-deprivation review.

190. Defendant States acted unconstitutionally to lower their election standards—including to allow invalid ballots to be counted and valid ballots to not be counted—with the express

intent to favor their candidate for President and to alter the outcome of the 2020 election. In many instances these actions occurred in areas having a history of election fraud.

191. The actions set out in Paragraphs (Georgia), (Michigan), (Pennsylvania), (Wisconsin), (Arizona), and (Nevada) constitute intentional violations of State election law by State election officials and their designees in Defendant States Pennsylvania, Georgia, Michigan, Wisconsin, and Arizona, and Nevada in violation of the Due Process Clause.

PRAYER FOR RELIEF

WHEREFORE, the United States respectfully request that this Court issue the following relief:

A. Declare that Defendant States Pennsylvania, Georgia, Michigan, Wisconsin, Arizona, and Nevada administered the 2020 presidential election in violation of the Electors Clause and the Fourteenth Amendment of the U.S. Constitution.

B. Declare that the electoral college votes cast by such presidential electors appointed in Defendant States Pennsylvania, Georgia, Michigan, Wisconsin, Arizona, and Nevada are in violation of the Electors Clause and the Fourteenth Amendment of the U.S. Constitution and cannot be counted.

C. Enjoin Defendant States' use of the 2020 election results for the Office of President to appoint presidential electors to the Electoral College.

D. Enjoin Defendant States' use of the 2020 election results for the Office of President to appoint presidential electors to the Electoral College and authorize, pursuant to the Court's remedial authority, the Defendant States to conduct a special election to appoint presidential electors.

  E. Enjoin Defendant States' use of the 2020 election results for the Office of President to appoint presidential electors to the Electoral College and authorize, pursuant to the Court's remedial authority, the Defendant States to conduct an audit of their election results, supervised by a Court-appointed special master, in a manner to be determined separately.

  F. Award costs to the United States.

  G. Grant such other relief as the Court deems just and proper.

Respectfully submitted,

December , 2020

Key Document M

Introduction by Thomas Fensch

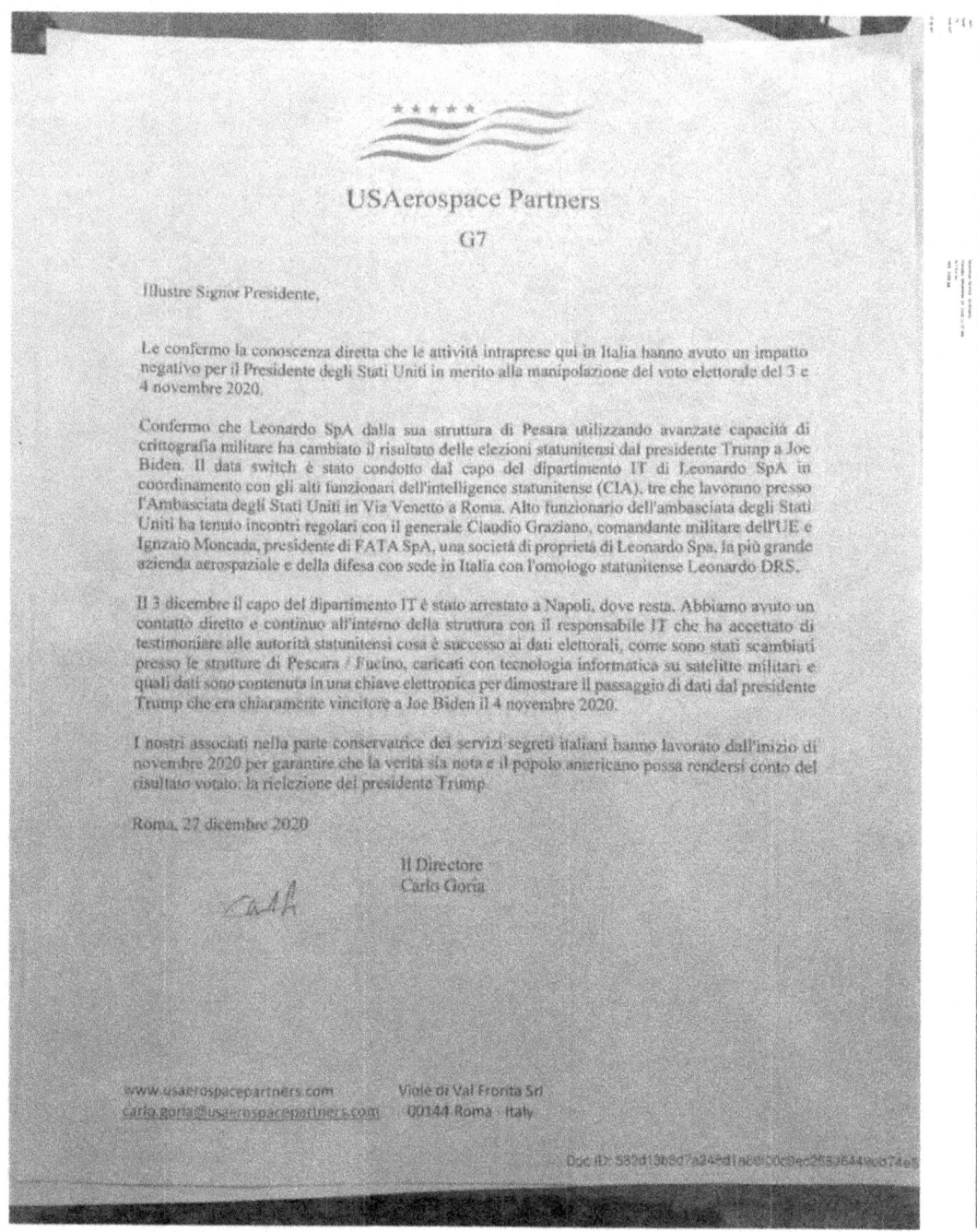

USAerospace Partners
G7

Illustre Signor Presidente,

Le confermo la conoscenza diretta che le attività intraprese qui in Italia hanno avuto un impatto negativo per il Presidente degli Stati Uniti in merito alla manipolazione del voto elettorale del 3 e 4 novembre 2020.

Confermo che Leonardo SpA dalla sua struttura di Pescara utilizzando avanzate capacità di crittografia militare ha cambiato il risultato delle elezioni statunitensi dal presidente Trump a Joe Biden. Il data switch è stato condotto dal capo del dipartimento IT di Leonardo SpA in coordinamento con gli alti funzionari dell'intelligence statunitense (CIA), tre che lavorano presso l'Ambasciata degli Stati Uniti in Via Veneto a Roma. Alto funzionario dell'ambasciata degli Stati Uniti ha tenuto incontri regolari con il generale Claudio Graziano, comandante militare dell'UE e Ignazio Moncada, presidente di FATA SpA, una società di proprietà di Leonardo Spa, la più grande azienda aerospaziale e della difesa con sede in Italia con l'omologo statunitense Leonardo DRS.

Il 3 dicembre il capo del dipartimento IT è stato arrestato a Napoli, dove resta. Abbiamo avuto un contatto diretto e continuo all'interno della struttura con il responsabile IT che ha accettato di testimoniare alle autorità statunitensi cosa è successo ai dati elettorali, come sono stati scambiati presso le strutture di Pescara / Fucino, caricati con tecnologia informatica su satelliti militari e quali dati sono contenuti in una chiave elettronica per dimostrare il passaggio di dati dal presidente Trump che era chiaramente vincitore a Joe Biden il 4 novembre 2020.

I nostri associati nella parte conservatrice dei servizi segreti italiani hanno lavorato dall'inizio di novembre 2020 per garantire che la verità sia nota e il popolo americano possa rendersi conto del risultato votato: la rielezione del presidente Trump.

Roma, 27 dicembre 2020

Il Directore
Carlo Goria

www.usaerospacepartners.com
carla.goria@usaerospacepartners.com

Viale di Val Fronta Srl
00144 Roma - Italy

Key Document N

Introduction by Thomas Fensch

Mastriano, Doug

From:	Mastriano, Doug
Sent:	Tuesday, December 29, 2020 11:28 AM
To:	Richard.Donoghue2@usdoj.gov
Subject:	Sen Mastriano (PA) letter on election irregularities in Pennsylvania
Attachments:	donoghue elections investigate.pdf
Importance:	High

Dear AG Donoghue,

As part of my constitutional responsibilities, I held an election hearing on November 25 pertaining to the recent General Election. I am increasingly concerned by broad and extensive irregularities on multiple levels in the Commonwealth that both undermined and undercut the outcome of the presidential election.

Please do not hesitate to reach out to me with any questions.

Sincerely,
Sen Doug Mastriano
(b) (6)

33RD SENATORIAL DISTRICT

☐ SENATE BOX 203033
HARRISBURG, PA 17120-3033
PHONE: 717-787-4651
FAX: 717-772-2753

☐ 37 SOUTH MAIN STREET, SUITE 200
CHAMBERSBURG, PA 17201
PHONE: 717-264-6100
FAX: 717-264-3652

☐ 16-A DEATRICK DRIVE
GETTYSBURG, PA 17325
PHONE: 717-334-4169
FAX: 717-334-5911

☐ 118 CARLISLE STREET, SUITE 309
HANOVER, PA 17331
PHONE: 717-632-1153
FAX: 717-632-1183

DOUG MASTRIANO
SENATOR

COMMITTEES

INTERGOVERNMENTAL OPERATIONS
CHAIR

AGRICULTURE & RURAL AFFAIRS
VICE CHAIR

GAME & FISHERIES

STATE GOVERNMENT

TRANSPORTATION

VETERANS AFFAIRS & EMERGENCY
PREPAREDNESS

SENATORMASTRIANO.COM
FACEBOOK.COM/SENATORDOUGMASTRIANO/
TWITTER.COM/SENMASTRIANO
INSTAGRAM.COM/SENATORMASTRIANO/

December 28, 2020

Acting Deputy Attorney General Richard Donoghue
U.S. Department of Justice
950 Pennsylvania Avenue, NW
Washington, DC 20530-0001

RE: General Election Irregularities in Pennsylvania during the November 2020 cycle

Dear Honorable Donoghue:

Election fraud is real and prevalent in Pennsylvania. Yet, despite evidence, our Governor and Secretary of State inexplicably refuse to investigate. Every legal vote must count. Our Republic cannot long endure without free and fair elections where each person has one legal vote. However, allegations of fraudulent activity, as well as violations of election law in 2020 have placed the nation's eyes upon this Commonwealth.

Several of the key findings are delineated below:

1. Senate Majority Policy Committee November hearing review on statistical anomalies, such as hundreds of thousands of votes being dumped into a processing facility, with 570,000 Vice President Biden, and only 3,200 for President Trump (https://policy.pasenategop.com/112520/).

    Testimony provided at a Senate hearing from witnesses in Philadelphia, Northampton, Luzerne, Montgomery, Allegheny and Delaware counties detailed instances of:

    (a) Interference with poll watchers' ability to perform functions as provided for in the state election code, specifically regarding the submission, review and canvasing of mail-in ballots;

    (b) Delayed opening or closing of polling locations on Election Day;

    (c) Improper forfeiture and spoiling of mail-in ballots;

    (d) Illegal ballot harvesting;

    (e) Improper "curing" of insufficiently completed mail-in ballots;

Page 2 of 5
AG Donoghue

    (f) Poll worker intimidation and harassment;

    (g) Voter intimidation;

    (h) Improper chain of custody of ballots and election materials;

    (i) Submission of fraudulent ballots by an individual other than the named voter.

2. There is a massive **VOTER DEFICIT** in Pennsylvania. 205,122 more votes were counted than total number of voters who voted: A comparison of official county election results to the total number of voters who cast ballots November 3, 2020…as recorded by the Department of State…shows the difference of 205,122 more votes cast than voters actually voting. (Rep Frank Ryan, http://www.repfrankryan.com/News/18754/Latest-News/PA-Lawmakers-Numbers-Don%E2%80%99t-Add-Up,-Certification-of-Presidential-Results-Premature-and-In-Error).

3. *Unidentified* Voters: When anyone registers to vote online or by paper, two options are provided for gender: Male or Female. If left blank; gender defaults to "No" leaving three types of voters: Male, Female and "No." However, there are four genders in state voter rolls: Male, Female, "No" and *Unidentified*. It has been estimated that there are 121,000 "non-female/male voters" on state voter rolls, and 90,000 voted in 2020. Initial assessments have concluded *that at least 1/3 of these "U" voters are fraudulent* (Unidentified "U" Voters, Kathy Barnette for Congress); (Unidentified "U" Voters, Kathy Barnette for Congress);

4. The mandate by Governor Wolf last year, requiring new voting machines for 2020 raised concerns from county officials and state lawmakers. As a result, 14 counties are using Dominion voting machines. The counties using Dominion voting equipment (1.3 million voters in Pennsylvania): York, Erie, Montgomery, Bedford, Armstrong, Carbon, Crawford, Clarion, Fayette, Luzerne, Fulton, Jefferson, Pike and Warren." (*"As Pennsylvania Counties Ring in the New year with New Voting Machines, Pressure from Election Security Advocates Remains,"* The PLS Reporter, 01/06/2020; https://www.pennlive.com/politics/2018/12/county-commissioners-question-the-funding-the-timing-the-need-for-replacing-voting-machines.html; *Questions Abound Over New Voting Machines, Citizens' Voice, 03/22/2019*; https://whyy.org/articles/despite-gop-objections-wolf-moves-to-upgrade-voting-machines-unilaterally/; *As Wolf Administration Pushes to Replace All Voting Machines by 2020, Lawmakers and County Officials Question Rush and Expense, PA Watchdog, 03/29/2019*).

5. Statistical experts examined Pennsylvania voting records and reached conclusions indicating there are "major statistical aberrations" in state voting records that are "unlikely to occur in a normal setting;" eleven counties (Montgomery, Allegheny, Chester, Bucks, Delaware, Lancaster, Cumberland, Northampton, Lehigh, Dauphin, York) showed "distinctive signs of voting abnormalities" for Vice President Biden. These analyses "provide scientific evidence that the reported results are highly unlikely to be an accurate reflection of how Pennsylvania citizens voted." (*Pennsylvania 2020 Voting Analysis Report, 11/16/2020*).

6. Gettysburg Senate Hearing - On November 25, Senator Doug Mastriano, together with Senator David Argall, hosted the Senate Majority Policy Committee hearing in Gettysburg where hours of testimony were presented, reviewed, and vetted regarding voting fraud and violations of voting law in Pennsylvania. The hearing demonstrated that there is rampant election fraud in Pennsylvania that must be investigated, remedied and rectified. The purpose of the hearing was to find out what happened in

Page 3 of 5
AG Donoghue

Pennsylvania in the aftermath of hearing allegations from thousands of people from across the Commonwealth sharing stories of violations of election law and other infringements of voting law related to the November 03, 2020 general election. We heard eyewitness testimony from citizens who experienced their rights being violated. Additionally, during the hearing, expert witnesses testified to statistical anomalies, where massive quantities of ballots arrived without a chain of custody. **In one such spike, close to 600k votes were dumped in a processing facility with 570k of these votes going for Biden, and a paltry 3,200 for President Trump**. Another witness testified that an election worker was plugging flash drives into voting machines in a heavily democrat area, for no stated purpose.

Other irregularities included in the testimony presented at the hearing included:

(a) Mail-in ballots were not inspected by Republican representatives in portions of Philadelphia and Allegheny County;

(b) Montgomery County was never provided with guidelines from State Department Secretary about "curing" defective ballots;

(c) Timeline spikes depict more ballots being processed during specific periods than voting machines are capable of tabulating;

(d) The Philadelphia Board of Elections processed hundreds of thousands of mail-in ballots with zero civilian oversight.

(e) Ballots were separated from envelopes in numerous precincts; a recount is useless because the votes cannot be verified;

(f) Observers were corralled behind fencing in Philadelphia, at least 10 feet away from processors; similarly, in Allegheny County, observers were placed at least 15 feet away;

(g) Mail-in ballots were already opened in portions of Allegheny County; no one observed the opening of these ballots;

(h) Illegal "pop-up" election sites developed, where voters would apply, receive a ballot and vote;

(i) Forensic evidence in Delaware County has disappeared;

(j) A poll watcher with appropriate certificates and clearances was denied access;

(k) There was no meaningful observation of ballots in Montgomery County, and no signature verification, as well;

(l) A senior citizen voted for President Trump, but it was not displayed on receipt;

(m) Election workers illegally pre-canvased ballots in Northampton County; no meaningful canvas observation was permitted;

Page 4 of 5
AG Donoghue

(n) several voters from across the state went to vote in person but when they arrived, they were told "they already voted" and were turned away and could not actually vote or were able to fill out a provisional ballot but was it really counted?

Despite the mounting evidence, our Governor and Secretary of State decline to investigate these serious allegations.

The United States of America has spent millions of dollars and put her men and women in harm's way to oversee safer, more reliable and freer elections in Afghanistan, Iraq, Kosovo and Bosnia. Why is the very state where the light of liberty was lit in 1776 is unable or unwilling to have elections as free and safe as war-torn Afghanistan? Something is seriously wrong in this Commonwealth and unless this is corrected, our republic cannot long endure.

The odyssey of PA finding itself in this position began in early 2020. Using the COVID-19 pandemic as a pretense, the Wolf Administration, together with the Pennsylvania Supreme Court, threw voting law into disarray.

The General Assembly (State House and State Senate) are constitutionally responsible for writing election law, not Gov Wolf, Secretary of Secretary Boockvar or the PA Supreme Court. These altered the original meaning of key provisions of Act 77. The state Supreme Court and Secretary Boockvar fundamentally altered and unconstitutionally rewrote the original meaning of key provisions of Act 77.

Voting law, as passed by the General Assembly in 2019, was clear and specific:

- All mail-in ballots must be received by 8 p.m. on Election Day;

- Officials at polling locations must authenticate the signatures of voters;

- County Boards of Elections can conduct pre-canvasing of absentee and mail-in ballots after 8 a.m. on Election Day;

- Defective absentee and mail-in ballots shall not be counted; and

- "Watchers" selected by candidates and political parties are permitted to observe the process of canvasing absentee and mail-in ballots.

The corruption of our election began with Governor Wolf during the COVID crisis. Wolf urged mail in voting upon people with a campaign to perpetuate the dangers of COVID. Likewise, he inferred that polling stations would be closed or undermanned due to the risk of the virus.

But the coup de main was seven weeks before Election Day, where the PA Supreme Court unilaterally and in direct contravention of the wording of election law extended the deadline for mailed ballots to be received from Election Day, to three days later. Similarly, the court declared that ballots mailed without a postmark must be counted. Additionally, the court mandated that mail-in ballots lacking a verified signature be accepted.

Page 5 of 5
AG Donoghue

On the eve of Election Day, the State Department encouraged some counties — but not all — to notify party and candidate representatives of mail-in voters, whose ballots contained disqualifying defects, thereby enabling voters to cure said defects. This was unprecedented as it had never happened before in our Commonwealth. Election law is very specific to the way defects of mail-in ballots are to be treated, and it provides no authority for county officials to contact campaigns, or other political operatives, to affect the cure of such defects.

Actions taken by the PA State Supreme Court and Secretary Boockvar in the 2020 general election were so fraught with inconsistencies, improprieties and irregularities that the results for the office of President of the United States cannot be determined in our state.

This election is an embarrassment to our nation. John Adams rightly said that, "Facts are stubborn things," and armed with this, as Jesus stated, "We shall know the truth and the truth shall set us free." What happened on November 3, 2020 must be immediately addressed using facts and the testimony of the good people of our state.

Sincerely,

Senator Doug Mastriano
33rd Senate District

DM/kms

cc: Hon. United States Attorney William McSwain
U.S. Attorney's Office
504 W. Hamilton St., #3701
Allentown, PA 18101

INTRODUCTION BY THOMAS FENSCH

Key Document O

kurt olsen

From: kurt olsen
Sent: Tuesday, December 29, 2020 12:45 PM
To: john.moran3@usdoj.gov
Subject: Meeting with AG Rosen
Attachments: US-v-States-Compl 2020-12-29 (final draft).docx

Dear John,

Thank you for calling me on behalf of AG Rosen. Attached is a draft complaint to be brought by the United States modeled after the Texas action. As I said on our call, the President of the United States has seen this complaint, and he directed me last night to brief AG Rosen in person today to discuss bringing this action. I have been instructed to report back to the President this afternoon after this meeting. I can be at Main Justice (or anywhere else in the DC Metropolitan area) with an hour's notice. I will call you at 1:15 pm today to follow up on when and where I can meet AG Rosen. Another lawyer may accompany me. Please acknowledge receipt of this email. Thank you.

Sincerely,

Kurt B. Olsen

INTRODUCTION BY THOMAS FENSCH

Key Document P

Mtg w/: Rog S, WH Counsel (PC + PP), DAAG RD, SE   12/29/20

Mark Martin } P trusts their view — they say
John Eastman }
            └ Could call him

[Non-Responsive]

[Non-Responsive]

3) Pd — election issue — admitted that we are badly at the
       claim that certification > # of votes cast.

4) Orig. J. Conf — U.S. does not have standing. DOJ
       should talk to the Orleans (attys who
       filed similar case)

Arturo D'Elio — RFD to check his background w/ FBI +
    - La = Leonardo SpA — Pesara Facility
    - purportedly under protection of an agency in Italy
    - Sent letter on his co's stationary
    - Claims involvement in vote changing in US 2020
    - claims in coordination w/ CIA officers in Embassy
       - Via Veneto — US Embassy, Rome
    - US Aerospace Partners — two towards US soil ?

S Damons
mtg on 12/29/20
time

INTRODUCTION BY THOMAS FENSCH

Key Document Q

Meadows, Mark R. EOP/WHO

From:	Meadows, Mark R. EOP/WHO
Sent:	Wednesday, December 30, 2020 9:31 AM
To:	Jeff Rosen
Subject:	Fwd: [EXTERNAL] Fwd: December 4, 2020 - Petition and Press Statement - R Smith.docx
Attachments:	December 4, 2020 - Press Statement - R Smith.docx; VERIFIED PETITION TO CONTEST GEORGIA ELECTION.pdf

Can you have your team look into these allegations of wrongdoing. Only the alleged fraudulent activity. Thanks Mark

Sent from my iPhone

Begin forwarded message:

> **From:** Mark Meadows <(b) (6)>
> **Date:** December 30, 2020 at 9:28:38 AM EST
> **To:** "Meadows, Mark R. EOP/WHO" <(b) (6)>
> **Subject: [EXTERNAL] Fwd: December 4, 2020 - Petition and Press Statement - R Smith.docx**

Sent from my iPhone

Begin forwarded message:

> **From:** "Mitchell, Cleta" <CMitchell@foley.com>
> **Date:** December 30, 2020 at 9:07:45 AM EST
> **To:** Mark Meadows <(b) (6)>
> **Subject: December 4, 2020 - Petition and Press Statement - R Smith.docx**

This is the petition filed in GA state court and the press release issued about it.

I presume the DOJ would want all the exhibits - that's 1800 pages total. I need to get someone to forward that to a drop box.

Plus I don't know what is happening re investigating the video issues in Fulton County. And the equipment. We didn't include the equipment in our lawsuit but there are certainly many issues and questions that some resources need to be devoted to reviewing. We had no way to conduct proper due diligence to include the equipment / software.

INTRODUCTION BY THOMAS FENSCH

Cleta Mitchell, Esq.
Foley & Lardner, LLP
cmitchell@foley.com
(b) (6) (cell)
202.295.4081 (office)
Sent from my iPhone

The information contained in this message, including but not limited to any attachments, may be confidential or protected by the attorney-client or work-product privileges. It is not intended for transmission to, or receipt by, any unauthorized persons. If you have received this message in error, please (i) do not read it, (ii) reply to the sender that you received the message in error, and (iii) erase or destroy the message and any attachments or copies. Any disclosure, copying, distribution or reliance on the contents of this message or its attachments is strictly prohibited, and may be unlawful. Unintended transmission does not constitute waiver of the attorney-client privilege or any other privilege. Legal advice contained in the preceding message is solely for the benefit of the Foley & Lardner LLP client(s) represented by the Firm in the particular matter that is the subject of this message, and may not be relied upon by any other party. Unless expressly stated otherwise, nothing contained in this message should be construed as a digital or electronic signature, nor is it intended to reflect an intention to make an agreement by electronic means.

FOR IMMEDIATE RELEASE

December 4, 2020

TRUMP CAMPAIGN FILES ELECTION CONTEST IN GEORGIA

Election Contest Lawsuit Documents Tens Thousands of Illegal Votes Included in the GA Presidential Vote Totals Rendering November 3, 2020 Election Results Null and Void; Suit Asks Court to Vacate and Enjoin the Certification of the Election

ATLANTA, GA - The Trump Campaign filed an election contest today in Georgia state court seeking to invalidate the state's November 3, 2020 presidential election results. Joining President Trump and the Trump campaign in the lawsuit is David Shafer, Chairman of the Georgia Republican Party, who is also a Trump presidential elector.

"What was filed today clearly documents that there are literally tens of thousands of illegal votes that were cast, counted, and included in the tabulations the Secretary of State is preparing to certify," said Ray S. Smith III, lead counsel for the Trump Campaign. "The massive irregularities, mistakes, and potential fraud violate the Georgia Election Code, making it impossible to know with certainty the actual outcome of the presidential race in Georgia."

Attached to the complaint are sworn affidavits from dozens of Georgia residents swearing under penalty of perjury to what they witnessed during the election: failure to process and secure the ballots, failure to verify the signatures on absentee ballots, the appearance of mysterious "pristine" absentee ballots not received in official absentee ballot envelopes that were voted almost solely for Joe Biden, failure to allow poll watchers meaningful access to observe the election, among other violations of law.

Data experts also provided sworn testimony in the lawsuit identifying thousands of illegal votes: 2,560 felons; 66,247 underage voters, 2,423 votes from people not registered; 1,043 individuals registered at post office boxes; 4,926 individuals who voted in Georgia after registering in another state; 395 individuals who voted in two states; 15,700 votes from people who moved out of state before the election; 40,279 votes of people who moved without re-registering in their new county; and another 30,000 to 40,000 absentee ballots lacking proper signature matching and verification.   MORE

2-2-2

"The Secretary of State has orchestrated the worst excuse for an election in Georgia history," added Smith. "We are asking the Court to vacate the certification of the presidential election and to order a new statewide election for president. Alternatively, we are asking the Court to enjoin the certification and allow the Georgia legislature to reclaim its duty under the U.S. Constitution to appoint the presidential electors for the state," Smith concluded.

###

For additional information contact:

IN THE SUPERIOR COURT OF FULTON COUNTY
STATE OF GEORGIA

DONALD J. TRUMP, in his capacity as a Candidate for President, DONALD J. TRUMP FOR PRESIDENT, INC., and DAVID J. SHAFER, in his capacity as a Registered Voter and Presidential Elector pledged to Donald Trump for President,

    Petitioners,

v.

BRAD RAFFENSPERGER, in his official capacity as Secretary of State of Georgia, REBECCA N. SULLIVAN, in her official capacity as Vice Chair of the Georgia State Election Board, DAVID J. WORLEY, in his official capacity as a Member of the Georgia State Election Board, MATTHEW MASHBURN, in his official capacity as a Member of the Georgia State Election Board, ANH LE, in her official capacity as a Member of the Georgia State Election Board, RICHARD L. BARRON, in his official capacity as Director of Registration and Elections for Fulton County, JANINE EVELER, in her official capacity as Director of Registration and Elections for Cobb County, ERICA HAMILTON, in her official capacity as Director of Voter Registration and Elections for DeKalb County, KRISTI ROYSTON, in her official capacity as Elections Supervisor for Gwinnett County, RUSSELL BRIDGES, in his official capacity as Elections Supervisor for Chatham County, ANNE DOVER, in her official capacity as Acting Director of Elections and Voter Registration for Cherokee County, SHAUNA DOZIER, in her official capacity as Elections Director for Clayton County, MANDI SMITH, in her official capacity as Director of Voter Registration and Elections for Forsyth

CIVIL ACTION FILE NO.

_____

County, **AMEIKA PITTS**, in her official capacity as Director of the Board of Elections & Registration for Henry County, **LYNN BAILEY**, in her official capacity as Executive Director of Elections for Richmond County, **DEBRA PRESSWOOD**, in her official capacity as Registration and Election Supervisor for Houston County, **VANESSA WADDELL**, in her capacity as Chief Clerk of Elections for Floyd County, **JULIANNE ROBERTS**, in her official capacity as Supervisor of Elections and Voter Registration for Pickens County, **JOSEPH KIRK**, in his official capacity as Elections Supervisor for Bartow County, and **GERALD MCCOWN**, in his official capacity as Elections Supervisor for Hancock County,

Respondents.

VERIFIED PETITION TO CONTEST GEORGIA'S PRESIDENTIAL ELECTION RESULTS FOR VIOLATIONS OF THE CONSTITUTION AND LAWS OF THE STATE OF GEORGIA, AND REQUEST FOR EMERGENCY DECLARATORY AND INJUNCTIVE RELIEF

COME NOW Donald J. Trump, in his capacity as a Candidate for President, Donald J. Trump for President, Inc., and David J. Shafer, in his capacity as a Georgia Registered Voter and Presidential Elector pledged to Donald Trump for President (collectively "Petitioners"), Petitioners in the above-styled civil action, by and through their undersigned counsel of record, and file this, their Verified Petition to Contest Georgia's Presidential Election Results for Violations of the Constitution and Laws of the State of Georgia, and Request for Emergency Declaratory and Injunctive Relief (the "Petition"), respectfully showing this honorable Court as follows:

INTRODUCTION

1.

The United States Constitution sets forth the authority to regulate federal elections: "The Times, Places and Manner of holding Elections for Senators and Representatives shall be prescribed in each State by the Legislature thereof; but the Congress may at any time by Law make or alter such Regulations, except as to the Places of choosing Senators." U.S. Const. art. I, § 4.

2.

With respect to the appointment of presidential electors, the Constitution further provides, "[e]ach State shall appoint, in such Manner as the Legislature thereof may direct, a Number of Electors, equal to the whole Number of Senators and Representatives to which the State may be entitled in Congress." U.S. Const. art. II, § 1.

3.

In Georgia, the General Assembly is the "legislature." *See* Ga. Const. art. III, § 1, para. I.

4.

Pursuant to the legislative power vested in the Georgia General Assembly (the "Legislature"), the Legislature enacted the Georgia Election Code governing the conduct of elections in the State of Georgia. *See* O.C.G.A. §§ 21-2-1 et seq. (the "Election Code").

5.

Thus, through the Election Code, the Legislature promulgated a statutory framework for choosing the presidential electors, as directed by the Constitution.

Introduction by Thomas Fensch

6.

In this case, Petitioners present to this Court substantial evidence that the November 3, 2020, Presidential Election in Georgia (the "Contested Election") was not conducted in accordance with the Election Code and that the named Respondents deviated significantly and substantially from the Election Code.

7.

Due to significant systemic misconduct, fraud, and other irregularities occurring during the election process, many thousands of illegal votes were cast, counted, and included in the tabulations from the Contested Election for the Office of the President of the United States, thereby creating substantial doubt regarding the results of that election.

8.

Petitioners demonstrate that the Respondents' repeated violations of the Election Code constituted an abandonment of the Legislature's duly enacted framework for conducting the election and for choosing presidential electors, contrary to Georgia law and the United States Constitution.

9.

Petitioners bring this contest pursuant to O.C.G.A. §21-2-522.

10.

"Honest and fair elections must be held in the selection of the officers for the government of this republic, at all levels, or it will surely fall. If [this Court] place[s] its stamp of approval upon an election held in the manner this one [was] held, it is only a matter of a short time until unscrupulous men, taking advantage of the situation, will steal the offices from the people and set up an intolerable, vicious, corrupt dictatorship." *Bush v. Johnson*, 111 Ga. App. 702, 705, 143 S.E.2d 21, 23 (1965).

11.

The Georgia Supreme Court has made clear that it is not incumbent upon Petitioners to show how voters casting irregular ballots would have voted had their ballots been regular. Petitioners "only [have] to show that there were enough irregular ballots to place in doubt the result." *Mead v. Sheffield*, 278 Ga. 268, 271, 601 S.E.2d 99, 101 (2004) (citing *Howell v. Fears*, 275 Ga. 627, 628, 571 S.E.2d 392, 393 (2002)).

12.

To allow Georgia's presidential election results to stand uncontested, and its presidential electors chosen based upon election results that are erroneous, unknowable, not in accordance with the Election Code and unable to be replicated with certainty, constitutes a fraud upon Petitioners and the Citizens of Georgia, an outcome that is unlawful and must not be permitted.

THE PARTIES

13.

President Donald J. Trump ("President Trump") is President of the United States of America and a natural person. He is the Republican candidate for reelection to the Presidency of the United States of America in the November 3, 2020, General Election conducted in the State of Georgia.

14.

Donald J. Trump for President, Inc. is a federal candidate committee registered with, reporting to, and governed by the regulations of the Federal Election Commission, established pursuant to 52 U.S.C. §§ 30101 et seq. as the principal authorized committee of President Trump, candidate for President, which also serves as the authorized committee for the election of the Vice Presidential candidate on the same ticket as President Trump (the "Committee"). The agent designated by the Committee in the State of Georgia is Robert Sinners, Director of Election Day Operations for the State of Georgia for President Trump (collectively the "Trump Campaign"). The Trump Campaign serves as the primary organization supporting the election of presidential electors pledged to President Trump and Vice President Pence.

15.

David J. Shafer ("Elector Shafer") is a resident of the State of Georgia and an aggrieved elector who was entitled to vote, and did vote, for President Trump in the November 3, 2020, General Election. Elector Shafer is an elector pledged to vote for President Trump at the Meeting of Electors pursuant to United States Constitution and the laws of the State of Georgia.

16.

Petitioners are "Contestants" as defined by O.C.G.A. § 21-2-520(1) who are entitled to bring an election contest under O.C.G.A. § 21-2-521 (the "Election Contest").

17.

Respondent Brad Raffensperger is named in his official capacity as the Secretary of State of Georgia.[1] Secretary Raffensperger serves as the Chairperson of Georgia's State Election Board, which promulgates and enforces rules and regulations to (i) obtain uniformity in the practices and proceedings of election officials as well as legality and purity in all primaries and general elections, and (ii) be conducive to the fair, legal, and orderly conduct of primaries and general elections. *See* O.C.G.A. §§ 21-2-30(d), 21-2-31, 21-2-33.1. Secretary Raffensperger, as Georgia's chief elections officer, is also responsible for the administration of the Election Code. *Id.*

18.

Respondents Rebecca N. Sullivan, David J. Worley, Matthew Mashburn, and Anh Le in their official capacities as members of the Georgia State Election Board (the "State Election Board"), are members of the State Election Board in Georgia, responsible for "formulat[ing], adopt[ing], and promulgat[ing] such rules and regulations, consistent with law, as will be conducive to the fair, legal, and orderly conduct of primaries and elections." O.C.G.A. § 21-2-31(2). Further, the State Election Board "promulgate[s] rules and regulations to define uniform and nondiscriminatory standards concerning what constitutes a vote and what will be counted as a vote for each category of voting system" in Georgia. O.C.G.A. § 21-2-31(7).

---

[1] Secretary Raffensperger is a state official subject to suit in his official capacity because his office "imbues him with the responsibility to enforce the [election laws]." *Grizzle v. Kemp*, 634 F.3d 1314, 1319 (11th Cir. 2011).

19.

Respondent Richard L. Barron is named in his official capacity as Director of Registration and Elections for Fulton County, Georgia, and conducted the Contested Election within that county.

20.

Respondent Janine Eveler is named in her official capacity as Director of Registration and Elections for Cobb County, Georgia, and conducted the Contested Election within that county.

21.

Respondent Erica Hamilton is named in her official capacity as Director of Voter Registration and Elections for DeKalb County, Georgia, and conducted the Contested Election within that county.

22.

Respondent Kristi Royston is named in her official capacity as Elections Supervisor for Gwinnett County, Georgia, and conducted the Contested Election within that county.

23.

Respondent Russell Bridges is named in his official capacity as Elections Supervisor for Chatham County, Georgia, and conducted the Contested Election within that county.

24.

Respondent Anne Dover is named in her official capacity as Acting Director of Elections and Voter Registration for Cherokee County, Georgia, and conducted the Contested Election within that county.

25.

Respondent Shauna Dozier is named in her official capacity as Elections Director for Clayton County, Georgia, and conducted the Contested Election within that county.

26.

Respondent Mandi Smith is named in her official capacity as Director of Voter Registration and Elections for Forsyth County, Georgia, and conducted the Contested Election within that county.

27.

Respondent Ameika Pitts is named in her official capacity as Director of the Board of Elections & Registration for Henry County, Georgia, and conducted the Contested Election within that county.

28.

Respondent Lynn Bailey is named in her official capacity as Executive Director of Elections for Richmond County, Georgia, and conducted the Contested Election within that county.

29.

Respondent Debra Presswood is named in her official capacity as Registration and Election Supervisor for Houston County, Georgia, and conducted the Contested Election within that county.

30.

Respondent Vanessa Waddell is named in her official capacity as Chief Clerk of Elections for Floyd County, Georgia, and conducted the Contested Election within that county.

31.

Respondent Julianne Roberts is named in her official capacity as Supervisor of Elections and Voter Registration for Pickens County, Georgia, and conducted the Contested Election within that county.

32.

Respondent Joseph Kirk is named in his official capacity as Elections Supervisor for Bartow County, Georgia, and conducted the Contested Election within that county.

33.

Respondent Gerald McCown is named in his official capacity as Elections Supervisor for Hancock County, Georgia, and conducted the Contested Election within that county.

34.

All references to Respondents made herein include named Respondent and those election workers deputized by Respondents to act on their behalf during the Contested Election.

JURISDICTION AND VENUE

35.

Jurisdiction is proper in this Court pursuant to O.C.G.A. § 21-2-523(a) as the Superior Court of the county where Secretary Raffensperger, the State Board of Elections, and Respondent Richard L. Barron are located. *See also Ga. Dep't of Human Servs. v. Dougherty Cty.*, 330 Ga. App. 581, 582, 768 S.E.2d 771, 772 (2015).

36.

Venue is proper before this Court.

FACTUAL BACKGROUND

The Georgia Election Code and Election Contest Provisions

37.

The Election Code sets forth the manner in which the Citizens of Georgia are allowed to participate in the Legislature's duty of choosing presidential electors by specifying, *inter alia*, which persons are eligible to register to vote in Georgia, the circumstances and actions by which a voter cancels his or her voter registration, the procedures for voting in person and by absentee ballot, the manner in which elections are to be conducted, and the specific protocols and procedures for recounts, audits, and recanvasses. *See* O.C.G.A. §§ 21-2-1 et seq.

38.

The Election Code in O.C.G.A. § 21-2-522 provides the means for a candidate in a federal election to contest the results of said election based on:

1. Misconduct, fraud, or irregularity by any primary or election official or officials sufficient to change or place in doubt the result;
2. When the defendant is ineligible for the nomination or office in dispute;
3. When illegal votes have been received or legal votes rejected at the polls sufficient to change or place in doubt the result;
4. For any error in counting the votes or declaring the result of the primary or election, if such error would change the results; or
5. For any other cause which shows that another was the person legally nominated, elected, or eligible to compete in a run-off primary or election.[2]

39.

The results of an election may be set aside when a candidate has "clearly established a violation of *election procedures* and has demonstrated that the violation has placed the result of the election in doubt." *Martin v. Fulton Cty. Bd. of Registration & Elections*, 307 Ga. 193-94, 835 S.E.2d 245, 248 (2019) (quoting *Hunt v. Crawford*, 270 GA 7, 10, 507 S.E.2d 723 (1998) (emphasis added).

40.

The Election Code "allows elections to be contested through litigation, both as a check on the integrity of the election process and as a means of ensuring the fundamental right of citizens to vote and to have their votes counted securely." *Martin*, 307 Ga. at 194.

41.

The Georgia Supreme Court has made clear that "it [is] not incumbent upon [Petitioners] to show ***how . . . voters would have voted*** if their . . . ballots had been regular. [Petitioners] only ha[ve] to show that there were enough irregular ballots to place in doubt the result." *Mead* at 268 (emphasis added).

---

[2] Petitioners do not contest pursuant O.C.G.A. § 21 2 522 Ground (2).

The Contested Election

42.

On November 3, 2020, the Contested Election for electors for President of the United States took place in the State of Georgia.

43.

President Trump, former Vice President Joseph R. Biden (Mr. Biden), and Jo Jorgensen were the only candidates on the ballot for President in the Contested Election.

44.

The original results reported by Secretary Raffensperger for the Contested Election (the "Original Result") consisted of a purported total of 4,995,323 votes cast, with Mr. Biden "ahead" by a margin of 12,780 votes.

45.

The results of the subsequent Risk Limiting Audit conducted by the Secretary of State (the "Risk Limiting Audit") included a total of 5,000,585 votes cast, with Mr. Biden "ahead" by a margin of 12,284 votes.

46.

On November 20, 2020, the Contested Election was declared and certified for Mr. Biden by a margin of only 12,670 votes (the "Certified Result").[3]

---

[3] The first certified number of votes.

47.

On November 21, 2020, President Trump and the Trump Campaign notified Secretary Raffensperger of President Trump's request to invoke the statutory recount authorized by O.C.G.A. § 21-2-495(c) for elections in which the margin is less than one-half of one percent (the "Statutory Recount"). A true and correct copy of President Trump's request for the Statutory Recount is attached hereto and incorporated by reference as **Exhibit 1**.

48.

The Statutory Recount is ongoing as of the time of the filing of this Petition.

49.

On multiple occasions Secretary Raffensperger announced he does not anticipate the Statutory Recount to yield a substantial change in the results of the Contested Election.

50.

On December 1, 2020, Robert Gabriel Sterling, Statewide Voting System Implementation Manager for the Secretary of State, gave a press conference to discuss the status of the ongoing Statutory Recount.

51.

During his press conference, Mr. Sterling stated that at least two counties needed to recertify their vote counts as the totals reached during the Statutory Recount differed from the Certified Results.

52.

As of the date of this Petition, not all of Georgia's 159 counties have certified their results from the Statutory Recount.

53.

Consequently, as of the date of this Petition, Secretary Raffensperger has yet to certify the results from the Statutory Recount.

54.

The presidential electors of the States are scheduled to meet on December 14, 2020. Therefore, this matter is ripe, and time is of the essence.

55.

An actual controversy exists.

56.

Because the outcome of the Contested Election is in doubt, Petitioners jointly and severally hereby contest Georgia's November 3, 2020, election results for President of the United States pursuant to O.C.G.A. §§ 21-2-521 and 21-2-522 et seq.

57.

Petitioners assert that the laws of the State of Georgia governing the conduct of the Contested Election were disregarded, abandoned, ignored, altered, and otherwise violated by Respondents, jointly and severally, allowing a sufficient number of illegal votes to be included in the vote tabulations, such that the results of the Contested Election are invalid, and the declaration of the presidential election in favor of Mr. Biden must be enjoined, vacated, and nullified.

THERE WERE SYSTEMIC IRREGULARITIES AND VIOLATIONS OF THE GEORGIA ELECTION CODE IN THE CONTESTED ELECTION

Requirements to Legally Vote in Georgia

58.

The Election Code sets forth the requirements for voting in Georgia, including the requirements that a voter must be: (1) "Registered as an elector in the manner prescribed by law; (2) A citizen of this state and of the United States; (3) At least 18 years of age on or before the date of the...election in which such person seeks to vote; (4) A resident of this state and of the county or municipality in which he or she seeks to vote; and (5) "Possessed of all other qualifications prescribed by law." O.C.G.A. § 21-2-216(a). "No person shall remain an elector longer than such person shall retain the qualifications under which such person registered." O.C.G.A. § 21-2-216(f).

59.

In violation of O.C.G.A. § 21-2-216, Respondents, jointly and severally, allowed thousands of unqualified persons to register to vote and to cast their vote in the Contested Election. These illegal votes were counted in violation of Georgia law. **Exhibits 2, 3, 4, and 10** attached hereto and incorporated by reference.

60.

O.C.G.A. § 21-2-216(b) provides that "[n]o person who has been convicted of a felony involving moral turpitude may register, remain registered, or vote except upon completion of the sentence."

61.

In violation of O.C.G.A. § 21-2-216(b), Respondents, jointly and severally, allowed as many as 2,560 felons with an uncompleted sentence to register to vote and to cast their vote in the Contested Election. **Exhibit 3** attached hereto and incorporated by reference.

62.

In violation of Georgia law, Respondents, jointly and severally, counted these illegal votes in the Contested Election.

63.

"Any person who possesses the qualifications of an elector except that concerning age shall be permitted to register to vote if such person will acquire such qualification within six months after the day of registration." O.C.G.A. § 21-2-216(c).

64.

In violation of O.C.G.A. § 21-2-216(c), Respondents, jointly and severally, allowed at least 66,247 underage and therefore ineligible people to illegally register to vote, and subsequently illegally vote. *See* **Exhibit 3**.

65.

In violation of Georgia law, Respondents, jointly and severally, counted these illegal votes in the Contested Election.

66.

In order to vote in Georgia, a person must register to vote.

67.

Respondents, jointly and severally, allowed at least 2,423 individuals to vote who were not listed in the State's records as having been registered to vote. *See* **Exhibit 3**.

68.

Respondents then, jointly and severally, improperly counted these illegal votes in the Contested Election.

69.

Because determining a voter's residency is necessary to confirm he or she is a qualified voter in this state and in the county in which he or she seeks to vote, the Election Code provides rules for determining a voter's residency and when a voter's residency is deemed abandoned. *See* O.C.G.A. § 21-2-217.

70.

"The residence of any person shall be held to be in that place in which such person's habitation is fixed." O.C.G.A. § 21-2-217(a)(1).

71.

Additionally, "[t]he specific address in the county...in which a person has declared a homestead exemption...shall be deemed the person's residence address." O.C.G.A. § 21-2-217(a)(14).

72.

A voter loses his or her Georgia and/or specific county residence if he or she: (1) "register[s] to vote or perform[s] other acts indicating a desire to change such person's citizenship and residence;" (2) "removes to another state with the intention of making it such person's residence;" (3) "removes to another county or municipality in this state with the intention of making it such person's residence;" or (4) "goes into another state and while there exercises the right of a citizen by voting." O.C.G.A. § 21-2-217(a); *see also* O.C.G.A. § 21-2-218(f) ("No person shall vote in any county or municipality other than the county or municipality of such person's residence except ["an elector who moves from one county...to another after the fifth Monday prior to a[n]...election"] O.C.G.A.§ 21-2-218(e).)

73.

In violation of O.C.G.A. § 21-2-217, Respondents, jointly and severally, allowed at least 4,926 individuals to vote in Georgia who had registered to vote in another state after their Georgia voter registration date. *See* **Exhibit 2**.

74.

It is illegal to vote in the November 3, 2020, general election for president in two different states.

75.

It is long established that "one man" or "one person" has only one vote.

76.

In violation of O.C.G.A. § 21-2-217, Respondents, jointly and severally, allowed at least 395 individuals to vote in Georgia who also cast ballots in another state (the "Double Voters"). *See* **Exhibit 2**.

77.

The number of Double Voters is likely higher than 395, yet Respondents have the exclusive capability and access to data to determine the true number of Double Voters.

78.

Respondents, jointly and severally, improperly counted these illegal votes in the Contested Election.

79.

Despite having the exclusive ability to determine the true number of Double Voters in Contested Election, to date Respondents, jointly and severally, have failed to properly analyze and remove the Double Voters from the election totals.

80.

To date, and despite multiple requests, Respondents, jointly and severally, have failed to provide identifying information or coordinate with the other 49 states and U.S. Territories to adequately determine the number of Double Voters.

81.

Respondents, jointly and severally, improperly counted these illegal votes in the Contested Election.

82.

In violation of O.C.G.A. § 21-2-217, Respondents, jointly and severally, allowed at least 15,700 individuals to vote in Georgia who had filed a national change of address with the United States Postal Service prior to November 3, 2020. *See* **Exhibit 2**.

83.

Respondents, jointly and severally, improperly counted these illegal votes in the Contested Election.

84.

If a Georgia voter "who is registered to vote in another county…in this state…moves such person's residence from that county…to another county…in this state," that voter "shall, at the time of making application to register to vote in that county…provide such information as specified by the Secretary of State in order to notify such person's former voting jurisdiction of the person's application to register to vote in the new place of residence and to cancel such person's registration in the former place of residence." O.C.G.A. § 21-2-218(b); *see also The Democratic Party of Georgia, Inc. v. Crittenden*, Civil Action File No. 1:18-CV-05181-SCJ, Doc. 33, Supplemental Declaration of Chris Harvey, Elections Director of the Office of the Secretary of State, ¶ 11 (N.D. Ga. Nov. 13, 2018) ("If the state allowed out of county voting, there would be no practical way of knowing if a voter voted in more than one county.").

85.

In violation of O.C.G.A. § 21-2-218(b), Respondents, jointly and severally, allowed at least 40,279 individuals to vote who had moved across county lines at least 30 days prior to Election Day and who had failed to properly re-register to vote in their new county after moving. **Exhibit 4** attached hereto and incorporated by reference.

86.

Respondents, jointly and severally, improperly counted these illegal votes in the Contested Election.

87.

In violation of O.C.G.A. § 21-2-217, Respondents, jointly and severally, allowed at least 1,043 individuals to cast ballots who had illegally registered to vote using a postal office box as their habitation. *See* **Exhibit 2**.

88.

Respondents then, jointly and severally improperly counted these illegal votes in the Contested Election.

89.

A postal office box is not a residential address.

90.

One cannot reside within a postal office box.

91.

It is a violation of Georgia law to list a postal office box as one's voter place of habitation. *See* O.C.G.A. § 21-2-217(a)(1).

92.

A person desiring "to vote at any…general election" must apply to register to vote "by the close of business on the fifth Monday…prior to the date of such…general election." O.C.G.A. § 21-2-224(a).

93.

The application for registration is "deemed to have been made as of the date of the postmark affixed to such application," or if received by the Secretary of State through the United States Postal Service, by "the close of business on the fourth Friday prior to a . . . general election." O.C.G.A. § 21-2-224(c).

94.

In violation of O.C.G.A. § 21-2-224, Respondents, jointly and severally, allowed at least 98 individuals to vote who the state records as having registered after the last day permitted under law. *See* **Exhibit 3**.

95.

Respondents, jointly and severally, improperly counted these illegal votes in the Contested Election.

96.

"Each elector who makes timely application for registration, is found eligible by the board of registrars and placed on the official list of electors, and is not subsequently found to be disqualified to vote shall be entitled to vote in any…election." O.C.G.A. § 21-2-224(d).

97.

Secretary Raffensperger is required to maintain and update a list of registered voters within this state.

98.

On the 10th day of each month, each county is to provide to the Secretary of State a list of convicted felons, deceased persons, persons found to be non-citizens during a jury selection process, and those declared mentally incompetent. *See* O.C.G.A. § 21-2-231(a)-(b), (d).

99.

In turn, any person on the Secretary of State's list of registered voters is to be removed from the registration list if the voter dies, is convicted of a felony, is declared mentally incompetent, confirms in writing a change of address outside of the county, requests his or her name be removed from the registration list, or does not vote or update his or her voter's registration through two general elections. *See* O.C.G.A. §§ 21-2-231, 21-2-232, 21-2-235.

100.

Respondents, jointly and severally, did not update the voter registration list(s).

101.

In violation of O.C.G.A. § 21-2-231(a)-(b) and (d), Respondents, jointly and severally, allowed as many as 10,315 or more individuals to vote who were deceased by the time of Election Day. *See* **Exhibit 3**.

102.

Respondents, jointly and severally, improperly counted these illegal votes in the Contested Election.

103.

Of these individuals, 8,718 are recorded as having perished prior to the date the State records as having accepted their vote. *See* **Exhibit 3**.

104.

Respondents, jointly and severally, improperly counted these illegal votes in the Contested Election.

105.

For example, Affiant Lisa Holst received three absentee mail-in ballots for her late father-in-law, Walter T. Holst, who died on May 13, 2010. **Exhibit 5** attached hereto and incorporated by reference.

106.

Voter history shows that an absentee ballot was returned for Mr. Holst on October 28, 2020.

107.

Someone deceased for 10 years should not have received three absentee ballots.

108.

Someone deceased for 10 years should not have received any absentee ballot.

109.

Someone deceased for 10 years should not have had any absentee ballot counted.

110.

Another Affiant, Sandy Rumph, has stated that her father-in-law, who died on September 9, 2019, had his voter registration change from "deceased" to "active" 8 days *after* he passed away. **Exhibit 6** attached hereto and incorporated by reference.

111.

With his registration status change, his address was also changed online from his real address in Douglasville to an unfamiliar address in DeKalb County. *Id.*

112.

Respondents jointly and severally failed to maintain and update voter registration lists which allowed voter registration information to be changed after the death of an elector.

113.

Respondents jointly and severally failed to maintain and update voter registration lists which allowed absentee ballots to be used fraudulently.

RESPONDENTS COMMITTED SUBSTANTIAL VIOLATIONS OF GEORGIA LAW WITH RESPECT TO ABSENTEE BALLOTS

114.

The Legislature has established procedures for absentee voting in the state.

115.

Pursuant to O.G.C.A. 21-2-381, absentee ballots must be requested by the voter, or the voter's designee, before they can be sent out.

116.

In violation of O.C.G.A. § 21-2-381, Respondent Raffensperger sent unsolicited absentee ballot applications before the 2020 primary election to all persons on the list of qualified electors, whether or not an application had been requested by the voter.

117.

The unlawfully sent applications allowed the recipient to check a box to request an absentee ballot for the Contested Election in advance of the period for which an absentee ballot could be requested.

118.

Individuals wishing to vote absentee may apply for a mail-in ballot "**not more than 180 days prior to the date of the primary or election.**" O.C.G.A. § 21-2-381(a)(1)(A) (emphasis added).

119.

In violation of O.C.G.A. § 21-2-381(a)(1)(A), Respondents, jointly and severally, allowed at least 305,701 individuals to vote who, according to State records, applied for an absentee ballot more than 180 days prior to the Contested Election. *See* **Exhibit 3**.

120.

Respondents then, jointly and severally, improperly counted these illegal votes in the Contested Election. *Id.*

121.

Pursuant to O.C.G.A. § 21-2-381(b) an absentee voter must have requested an absentee ballot before such ballot is capable of being received by the voter.

122.

If such applicant is eligible under the provisions of the Election Code, an absentee ballot is to be mailed to the voter.

123.

In violation of O.C.G.A. § 21-2-385, Respondents, jointly and severally, allowed at least 92 individuals to vote whose absentee ballots, according to State records, were returned and accepted prior to that individual requesting an absentee ballot. *See* **Exhibit 3**.

124.

Respondents then, jointly and severally, improperly counted these illegal votes in the Contested Election. *Id.*

125.

Absentee ballots may only be mailed after determining the applicant is registered and eligible to vote in the election. O.C.G.A. § 21-2-381(b)(1).

126.

In violation of O.C.G.A. § 21-2-381(b)(1), Respondents, jointly and severally, allowed state election officials to mail at least 13 absentee ballots to individuals who were not yet registered to vote according to the state's records. *See* **Exhibit 3**.

127.

Respondents then, jointly and severally, improperly counted these illegal votes in the Contested Election. *Id.*

128.

Pursuant to O.C.G.A. § 21-2-384(a)(2) absentee ballots may not be mailed more than 49 days prior to an election.

129.

Respondents, jointly and severally, mailed at least 2,664 absentee ballots to individuals prior to the earliest date permitted by law. *See* **Exhibit 3**.

130.

Respondents then, jointly and severally, improperly counted these illegal votes in the Contested Election. *Id.*

131.

According to State records, Respondents jointly and severally allowed at least 50 individuals to vote whose absentee ballots were returned and accepted prior to the earliest date that absentee ballots were permitted by law to be sent out. *See* **Exhibit 3**.

132.

Respondents then, jointly and severally improperly counted these illegal votes in the Contested Election. *Id.*

133.

An absentee voter's application for an absentee ballot must have been accepted by the election registrar or absentee ballot clerk in order for that individual's absentee ballot vote to be counted. O.C.G.A. § 21-2-385.

134.

In violation of O.C.G.A. § 21-2-385, Respondents, jointly and severally, allowed at least 2 individuals to vote whose absentee ballot applications had been rejected, according to state records. *See* **Exhibit 3**.

135.

Respondents, jointly and severally, improperly counted these illegal votes in the Contested Election. *Id.*

136.

It is not possible for an absentee voter to have applied by mail, been issued by mail, and returned by mail an absentee ballot, and for that ballot to have accepted by election officials, all on the same day.

137.

In violation of O.C.G.A. § 21-2-384, Respondents, jointly and severally, allowed at least 217 individuals to vote whose absentee ballots, according to state records, were applied for, issued, and received all on the same day. *See* **Exhibit 3**.

138.

Respondents then, jointly and severally, improperly counted these illegal votes in the Contested Election. *Id.*

RESPONDENTS FAILED TO COMPLY WITH GEORGIA LAW PROVISIONS FOR MATCHING SIGNATURES AND CONFIRMING VOTER IDENTITY FOR ELECTORS SEEKING TO VOTE ABSENTEE

139.

O.C.G.A. §21-2-381(b) mandates the procedures to be followed by election officials upon receipt of an absentee ballot application:

> "Upon receipt of a timely application for an absentee ballot, a registrar or absentee ballot clerk...shall determine...if the applicant is eligible to vote in the...election involved. In order to be found eligible to vote an absentee ballot by mail, the registrar or absentee ballot clerk **shall compare the identifying information on the application with the information on file in the registrar's office and, if the application is signed by the elector, compare the signature or mark of the elector on the application with the signature or mark of the elector on the elector's voter registration card.** In order to be found eligible to vote an absentee ballot in person...**shall show one of the forms of identification listed in Code Section 21-2-417** and the registrar or absentee ballot clerk **shall compare the**

identifying information on the application with the information on file in the registrar's office." O.C.G.A. § 21-2-381(b) (emphasis added).

140.

O.C.G.A. § 21-2-386(a)(1)(B) mandates the procedures to be followed by election officials upon receipt of an absentee ballot:

> Upon receipt of each [absentee] ballot, a registrar or clerk shall write the day and hour of the receipt of the ballot on its envelope. The registrar or clerk **shall then compare the identifying information on the oath with the information on file in his or her office, shall compare the signature or make on the oath with the signature or mark on the absentee elector's voter card or the most recent update to such absentee elector's voter registration card and application for absentee ballot or a facsimile of said signature or maker taken from said card or application**, and shall, if the information and signature appear to be valid and other identifying information appears to be correct, so certify by signing or initialing his or her name below the voter's oath. Each elector's name so certified shall be listed by the registrar or clerk on the numbered list of absentee voters prepared for his or her precinct. O.C.G.A. § 21-2-386(a)(1)(B) (emphasis added).

141.

O.C.G.A. § 21-2-386(a)(1)(C) mandates the procedures to be followed by election officials with respect to defective absentee ballots:

> **If the elector has failed to sign the oath, or if the signature does not appear to be valid, or if the elector has failed to furnish required information or information so furnished does not conform with that on file in the registrar's or clerk's office**, or if the elector is otherwise found disqualified to vote, the registrar or clerk *shall* write across the face of the envelope "Rejected," giving the reason therefor. The board of registrars or absentee ballot clerk *shall* promptly **notify the elector of such rejection**, a copy of which notification *shall* be retained in the files of the board of registrars or absentee ballot clerk for at least one year. O.C.G.A. § 21-2-386(a)(1)(C) (emphasis added).

RESPONDENT RAFFENSPERGER DISREGARDED THE ELECTION CODE BY FIAT AND INSTRUCTED THE RESPONDENT COUNTIES TO DO LIKEWISE

142.

On March 6, 2020, Respondents Raffensperger and the State Election Board entered into a "Compromise and Settlement Agreement and Release" (the "Consent Decree") in litigation filed by the Democratic Party of Georgia, Inc., the Democrat Senatorial Campaign Committee, and the Democratic Congressional Campaign Committee (collectively the "Democrat Party Agencies").[4] A true and correct copy of the Consent Decree is attached hereto and incorporated by reference as **Exhibit 7**.

143.

The litigation was one of more than one hundred lawsuits nationwide filed by Democrats and partisan affiliates of the Democratic Party to seeking to rewrite the duly enacted election laws of the states. **Exhibit 8** attached hereto and incorporated by reference.

144.

Without legislative authority, Respondents unlawfully adopted standards to be followed by the clerks and registrars in processing absentee ballots inconsistent with the election code.

145.

The Consent Decree exceeded Respondents' authority under the Georgia Constitution. *See* Ga. Const. art. III, §1; **Exhibit 15** attached hereto and incorporated by reference; *see also* O.C.G.A. § 21-2-31 (providing that the State Election Board shall "formulate, adopt, and promulgate such

---

[4] *See Democratic Party of Georgia, Inc., et al. v. Raffensperger, et al.*, Civil Action File No. 1:19 cv 05028 WMR, Doc. 56 1, Joint Notice of Settlement as to State Defendants, Att. A, Compromise Settlement Agreement and Release (N.D. Ga. Mar. 6, 2020).

rules and regulations, *consistent with the law*, as will be conducive to the fair, legal, and orderly conduct of primaries and elections" (emphasis added)).

146.

The Consent Decree changed the plain language of the statute for receiving and processing absentee ballot applications and ballots.

147.

The Consent Decree increased the burden on election officials to conduct the mandatory signature verification process by adding additional, cumbersome steps.

148.

For example, the Consent Decree tripled the number of personnel required for an absentee ballot application or ballot to be rejected for signature mismatch.

149.

The unlawful Consent Decree further violated the Election Code by purporting to allow election officials to match signatures on absentee ballot envelopes against the application, rather than the voter file as required by O.C.G.A. §§ 21-2-381, 21-2-385.

RESPONDENTS DID NOT CONDUCT MEANINGFUL VERIFICATION OF ABSENTEE BALLOT APPLICANT AND VOTER IDENTITIES

150.

Notwithstanding the unlawful changes made by the Consent Decree, the mandatory signature verification and voter identification requirements were not altogether eliminated.

151.

Despite the legal requirement for signature matching and voter identity verification, Respondents failed to ensure that such obligations were followed by election officials. **Exhibit 9** attached hereto and incorporated by reference.

152.

According to state records, an unprecedented 1,768,972 absentee ballots were mailed out in the Contested Election. **Exhibit 10** attached hereto and incorporated by reference.

153.

Of the total number of absentee ballots mailed out in the Contested Election, 1,317,000 were returned (i.e., either accepted, spoiled, or rejected). *Id.*

154.

The number of absentee ballots returned in the Contested Election represents a greater than 500% increase over the 2016 General Election and a greater than 400% increase over the 2018 General Election. *Id.*

155.

The state received over a million more ballots in the Contested Election than the 2016 and 2018 General Elections. *Id.*

156.

The number of returned absentee ballots that were rejected in the Contested Election was 4,471, yielding a 0.34% rejection rate. *Id.*

157.

The number of returned absentee ballots that were rejected in the 2016 General Election was 6,059, yielding a 2.90% rejection rate. *Id.*

158.

The number of returned absentee ballots that were rejected in the 2018 General Election was 7,889, yielding a 3.46% rejection rate. *Id.*

159.

Stated differently, the percentage of rejected ballots fell to 0.34% in 2020 from 2.9% in 2016 and 3.46% in 2018, despite a nearly sixfold increase in the number of ballots returned to the state for processing.

160.

The explosion in the number of absentee ballots received, counted, and included in the tabulations for the Contested Election, with the simultaneous precipitous drop in the percentage of absentee ballots rejected, demonstrates there was little or no proper review and confirmation of the eligibility and identity of absentee voters during the Contested Election.

161.

Had the statutory procedure for signature matching, voter identity and eligibility verification been followed in the Contested Election, Georgia's historical absentee ballot rejection rate of 2.90-3.46% applied to the 2020 absentee ballot returned and processed, between 38,250 and 45,626 ballots should have been rejected in the Contested Election. *See* **Exhibit 10**.

RESPONDENTS VIOLATED GEORGIANS' FUNDAMENTAL RIGHT TO A TRANSPARENT AND OPEN ELECTION

162.

A fair, honest, and transparent vote count is a cornerstone of democratic elections. INTERNATIONAL INSTITUTE FOR DEMOCRACY AND ELECTORAL ASSISTANCE, INTERNATIONAL ELECTORAL STANDARDS, GUIDELINES FOR REVIEWING THE LEGAL FRAMEWORK OF ELECTIONS (2002).

163.

All citizens, including Georgians, have rights under the United States Constitution to the full, free, and accurate elections built upon transparency and verifiability. *Purcell v. Gonzalez*, 549 U.S. 1, 4, 127 S. Ct. 5, 7 (2006) (per curiam).

164.

Citizens are entitled and deserve to vote in a transparent system that is designed to protect against vote dilution. *Bush v. Gore*, 531 U.S. 98, 104-05, 121 S. Ct. 525, 529-30 (2000); *Anderson v. United States*, 417 U.S. 211, 227 (1974); *see also Baker v. Carr*, 369 U.S. 186, 208, 82 S. Ct. 691, 705 (1962).

165.

This requires that votes be counted, tabulated and consolidated in the presence of the representatives of parties and candidates and election observers, and that the entire process by which a winner is determined is fully and completely open to public scrutiny. INTERNATIONAL ELECTORAL STANDARDS at 77.

166.

The importance of watchers and representatives serving as an important check in elections is recognized internationally. *Id.*

167.

Georgia law recognizes "the fundamental right of citizens to vote ***and to have their votes counted accurately.***" *Martin* at 194 (emphasis added).

168.

The right to have one's vote counted accurately infers a right to a free, accurate, public, and transparent election, which is reflected throughout Georgia election law. *Cf. Ellis v. Johnson*, 263 Ga. 514, 516, 435 S.E.2d 923, 925 (1993) ("Of particular importance is that the General Assembly has provided the public with the right to examine . . . the actual counting of the ballots, . . . and the computation and canvassing of returns . . . .").

169.

Georgia law requires "[s]uperintendents, poll officers, and other officials engaged in the conducting of primaries and elections . . . shall perform their duties in public." O.C.G.A. §21-2-406.

170.

Each political party who has nominated a candidate "shall be entitled to designate ... state-wide poll watchers." O.C.G.A. § 21-2-408 (b)(2).

171.

Poll watchers "may be permitted behind the enclosed space for the purpose of observing the conduct of the election and the counting and recording of votes." O.C.G.A. § 21-2-408 (d).

172.

"All proceedings at the tabulating center and precincts shall be open to the view of the public." O.C.G.A, § 21-2-483(b).

173.

Under O.C.G.A. § 21-2-493, "[t]he superintendent shall, at or before 12:00 noon on the day following the primary or election, at his or her office or at some other convenient **public place** at the county seat or in the municipality, of which **due notice of shall have been given** as provided by Code Section 21-2-492, **publicly commence** the computation and canvassing of returns and continue the same from the day until completed." (Emphasis added.)

174.

During the tabulation of votes cast during an election, vote review panels are to convene to attempt to determine a voter's intent when that intent is unclear from the ballot, consisting of equal Republican and Democratic representation. *See* O.C.G.A. § 21-2-483(g)(2).

175.

The activities of the vote review panel are required to be open to the view of the public. *See* O.C.G.A. § 21-2-483(a).

176.

Moreover, Respondent Raffensperger declared that for the Risk Limiting Audit:

Per the instructions given to counties as they conduct their audit triggered full hand recounts, **designated monitors will be given complete access to observe the process from the beginning.** While the audit triggered recount **must be open to the public and media, designated monitors will be able to observe more closely.** The general public and the press will be restricted to a public viewing area. **Designated monitors will be able to watch the recount while standing close to the elections' workers conducting the recount.**

Political parties are allowed to designate a minimum of two monitors per county at a ratio of one monitor per party for every ten audit boards in a county . . . . **Beyond being able to watch to ensure the recount is conducted fairly and securely,** the two-person audit boards conducting the hand recount call out the votes as they are recounted, **providing monitors and the public an additional way to keep tabs on the process.**[5]

177.

Respondents, jointly and severally, violated Petitioners' fundamental right to a free, accurate, public, and transparent election under the Constitution of the State of Georgia in the Contested Election and the Risk Limiting Audit. *See* composite Affidavit Appendix attached hereto and incorporated by reference as **Exhibit 17**.

178.

Respondents, jointly and severally, violated provisions of the Georgia Election Code mandating meaningful public oversight of the conduct of the election and the counting and recording of votes in the Contested Election and the Risk Limiting Audit. *Id.*

---

[5] Office of Secretary of State Brad Raffensperger, *Monitors Closely Observing Audit Triggered Full Hand Recount: Transparency is Built Into Process* (Nov. 17, 2020),
https://sos.ga.gov/index.php/elections/monitors closely observing audit triggered full hand recount transparency is built into process.

179.

Respondents, jointly and severally, failed to adhere to Respondent Raffensperger's own guidelines promising a free, accurate, public, and transparent process in the Risk Limiting Audit. *Id.*

RESPONDENTS HAVE ADMITTED MISCONDUCT, FRAUD, AND WIDESPREAD IRREGULARITIES COMMITTED BY MULTIPLE COUNTIES

180.

The Secretary of State has admitted that multiple county election boards, supervisors, employees, election officials and their agents failed to follow the Election Code and State Election Board Rules and Regulations.[6]

181.

The Secretary of State has called The Fulton County Registration and Elections Board and its agents' ("Fulton County Elections Officials") job performance prior to and through the Election Contest "dysfunctional."

182.

The Secretary of State and members of his staff have repeatedly criticized the actions, poor judgment, and misconduct of Fulton County Elections Officials.

---

[6] Note: These are samples and not an exhaustive list of the Secretary of State's admissions of Respondents' failures and violations of Georgia law.

183.

Fulton County Elections Officials' performance in the 2020 primary elections was so dysfunctional that it was fined $50,000 and subject to remedial measures.

184.

Describing Respondent Barron's Fulton County Elections in the Election Contest, Secretary Raffensperger stated, "Us and our office, and I think the rest of the state, is getting a little tired of always having to wait on Fulton County and always having to put up with [Fulton County Elections Officials'] dysfunction."

185.

The Secretary of State's agent, Mr. Sterling, said initial findings from an independent monitor allegedly show "generally bad management" with Fulton's absentee ballots.[7]

Fulton County Elections' Deception and Fraud

186.

The Secretary of State's Office claims it is currently investigating an incident where Fulton County election officials fraudulently stated there was a "flood" and "a pipe burst," which was later revealed to be a "leaky" toilet.

---

[7] Ben Brasch, *Georgia Opens 2 Investigations Into Fulton's Elections Operations*, The Atlanta Journal Constitution (Nov. 17, 2020), https://www.ajc.com/news/atlanta news/georgia opens 2 investigations into fultons elections operations/EVCBN4ZJTZELPDHMH63POL3RKQ/.

187.

At approximately 10:00 p.m. on November 3, 2020, Fulton County Election Officials, who were handling and scanning thousands of ballots at the State Farm Arena, instructed Republican poll watchers and the press that they were finished working for the day and that the Republican poll watchers and the press were to leave. The Fulton County Elections Officials further stated that they would restart their work at approximately 8:00 a.m. on November 4, 2020.

188.

The Fulton County Election Officials lied.

189.

Deliberate misinformation was used to instruct Republican poll watchers and members of the press to leave the premises for the night at approximately 10:00 p.m. on November 3, 2020. **Exhibits 12, 13, and 14** attached hereto and incorporated by reference.

190.

After Fulton County Elections Officials **lied and defrauded** the Republican poll watchers and members of the press, whereby in reasonable reliance the Republican poll watchers and members of the press left the State Farm Arena (where they had been observing the ballots being processed), without public transparency Fulton County Elections Officials continued to process, handle, and transfer many thousands of ballots. *See* **Exhibit 14**.

191.

Fulton County Elections Officials' fraudulent statements not only defrauded the Republican poll watchers and the press, but also deprived every single Fulton County voter,

Georgian, American, and Petitioners of the opportunity for a transparent election process and have thereby placed the Election Contest in doubt.

Spalding County Elections & Voter Registration Supervisor and Her Agents' Failures

192.

Respondent Raffensperger has called for the resignation of the Spalding County Elections and Voter Registration Supervisor, who has, as of this filing, resigned.[8]

193.

Respondent Raffensperger cited "serious management issues and poor decision-making" by Election Supervisor Marcia Ridley during the Contested Election.

Floyd County Elections & Voter Registration Supervisor and Her Agents' Failures

194.

Respondent Raffensperger has called for the resignation of the Executive Director of the Floyd County Board of Registrations and Elections for his failure to follow proper election protocols.[9]

---

[8] David Wickert, *Georgia Officials Call for Spalding Election Director to Resign*, The Atlanta Journal Constitution (Nov. 17, 2020), https://www.ajc.com/politics/election/georgia officials call for spalding election director to resign/YYUISCBSV5FTHDZPM3N5RJVV6A/.

[9] Jeffrey Martin, Georgia Secretary of State Calls for Resignation of County Election Director After 2,600 Ballots Discovered (Nov. 16, 2020), https://www.newsweek.com/georgia secretary state calls resignation county election director after 2600 ballots discovered 1547874.

RESPONDENTS CONSPIRED TO DISREGARD THE ELECTION CODE AND TO SUBSTITUTE THEIR OWN UNLAWFUL EDICTS

195.

In violation of O.C.G.A. § 21-2-386 et seq. the State Board of Election promulgated a rule that authorized county election board to begin processing absentee ballots on the third Monday preceding the election, provided they give the Secretary of State and the public notice of such intention to begin processing absentee ballots.

196.

Failure to follow the process directed by the statute is a derogation of the Election Code and denies voters the ability to cancel their absentee ballot up until Election Day.

197.

Respondents, jointly and severally, were complicit in conspiring to violate and violating the Election Code.

198.

As a direct and proximate result of Respondents multiple, continued, and flagrant disregard of the Election Code, the outcome of the Contested Election is not capable of being known with certainty.

199.

Petitioners incorporate by reference and reallege all prior paragraphs of this Petition and the paragraphs in the Counts below as though set forth fully herein.

200.

Despite Respondents receiving substantial funding from the Center for Technology and Civic Life (CTCL), Respondents failed to use such funds to train the election workers regarding signature verification, the proper procedures for matching signatures, and how to comply fully with the Election Code. **Exhibit 11** attached hereto and incorporated by reference.

201.

Due to the lack of uniform guidance and training, the signature verification and voter identity confirmation was performed poorly or not at all in some counties and served as virtually no check against improper voting. *See* **Exhibit 9**.

RESPONDENT SECRETARY OF STATE MUST ALLOW AND CONDUCT AN AUDIT OF THE SIGNATURES ON ABSENTEE BALLOT APPLICATIONS AND ABSENTEE BALLOTS IN ORDER TO DETERMINE WHETHER THE SIGNATURES WERE PROPERLY MATCHED PRIOR TO BEING COUNTED AND INCLUDED IN THE TABULATIONS

202.

The data regarding the statistically tiny rejection rate of absentee ballots cast and counted in the Contested Election gives rise to sufficient concerns that there were irregularities that should be reviewed and investigated.

203.

Petitioners have brought these concerns about the signature matching and voter verification process to the attention of Respondent Raffensperger **on five separate occasions** since the Contested Election, requesting that the Secretary conduct an audit of the signatures on the absentee ballot applications and absentee ballots, via Letter on November 10, 2020; Letter on November

12, 2020; Letter on November 23, 2020; Email on November 23, 2020, and again via Letter on November 30, 2020. **Exhibit 18** attached hereto and incorporated by reference.

204.

The Secretary of State is obligated by law to "to permit the public inspection or copying, in accordance with this chapter, of any return, petition, certificate, paper, account, contract, report, or any other document or record in his or her custody." O.G.C.A. § 21-2-586(a).

205.

Failure to comply with any such request by the Secretary of State or an employee of his or her office shall [constitute] a misdemeanor." O.G.C.A. § 21-2-586(a).

206.

The Secretary of State's refusal on five separate occasions to comply with requests to produce the signatures used to request absentee ballots and to confirm the identities of those individuals requesting such ballots in the contested election is a violation of O.G.C.A. § 21 2 586(a).

207.

In order for the Secretary of State to comply with O.G.C.A. § 21-2-586(a), professional handwriting experts recommend a minimum of Ten Thousand (10,000) absentee ballot signatures be professionally evaluated. **Exhibit 16** attached hereto and incorporated by reference.

208.

Petitioners respectfully request that the Court order the production of the records of the absentee ballot applications and absentee ballots, for purposes of conducting an audit of the signatures on absentee ballot applications and absentee ballots cast in the Contested Election.

THERE ARE MYRIAD REPORTS OF IRREGULARITIES AND VIOLATIONS OF THE ELECTION CODE DURING THE CONTESTED ELECTION

209.

Petitioners have received hundreds of incident reports regarding problems, irregularities, and violations of the Election Code during the Contested Election.

210.

From those reports, Petitioners have attached affidavits from dozens of Citizens of Georgia, sworn under penalty of perjury, attesting to myriad violations of law committed by Respondents during the Contested Election. *See* **Exhibit 17**.

211.

The affidavits are attached to this Petition as an Appendix, with details of the multiple violations of law. *Id.*

212.

Also included in the Appendix are sworn declarations from data experts who have conducted detailed analysis of irregularities in the State's voter records. *See* **Exhibits 2, 3, 4, and 10**.

COUNTS

COUNT I:
ELECTION CONTEST
O.C.G.A §21-2-521 *et seq.*

213.

Petitioners incorporate by reference and re-allege paragraphs 1 through 212 this Petition as set forth herein verbatim.

214.

Respondents, jointly and severally, have violated the Constitution of the State of Georgia.

215.

Respondents, jointly and severally, have violated the laws of the State of Georgia.

216.

Respondents, jointly and severally, have violated the Election Code.

217.

Respondents, jointly and severally, have violated State Election Board Rules and Regulations.

218.

Respondents, jointly and severally, have violated the basic tenants of an open, free, and fair election.

219.

Respondents, jointly and severally, have failed in their duties to their constituents, the people of the State of Georgia, and the entire American democratic process.

220.

The Contested Election has been timely and appropriately contested per O.C.G.A. § 21-2-522 et seq.

221.

As a direct and proximate result of Respondents' actions, the Contested Election is fraught with misconduct, fraud, and irregularities.

222.

Due to the actions and failures of Respondents, many thousands of illegal votes were accepted, cast, and counted in the Contested Election, and legal votes were rejected.

223.

The fraud, misconduct, and irregularities that occurred under the "supervision" of Respondents are sufficient to change the purported results of the Contested Election.

224.

The fraud, misconduct, and irregularities that occurred under the "supervision" of Respondents are sufficient to place the Contested Election in doubt.

225.

Respondents' misconduct is sufficient to change the purported results in the Contested Election in President Trump's favor.

226.

Respondents' misconduct is sufficient to place the purported Contested Election results in doubt.

227.

Respondents, jointly and severally, erred in counting the votes in the Contested Election.

228.

Respondents' error in counting the votes in the Contested Election would change the result in President Trump's favor.

229.

Respondents, jointly and severally, erred in declaring the Contested Election results in favor of Mr. Biden.

230.

Respondents' systemic negligent, intentional, willful, and reckless violations of the Georgia Constitution, Georgia law, as well as the fundamental premise of a free and fair election created such error and irregularities at every stage of the Contested Election from registration through certification and every component in between that the outcome of the Contested Election is in doubt.

231.

As a result, there is substantial doubt as to the outcome of the Contested Election, and the Contested Election and any certification associated therewith shall be enjoined, vacated, and nullified and either a new presidential election be immediately ordered that complies with Georgia law or, in the alternative, that such other just and equitable relief is obtained so as to comport with the Constitution of the State of Georgia.[10] *See* O.C.G.A. § 21-2-522.

COUNT II:

VIOLATIONS OF THE GEORGIA CONSTITUTION'S EQUAL PROTECTION PROVISION

232.

Petitioners incorporate by reference and re-allege paragraphs 1 through 212 f this Petition as set forth herein verbatim.

233.

The Constitution of the State of Georgia provides, "Protection and property is the paramount duty of government and shall be impartial and complete. No person shall be denied the equal protection of the laws." Ga. Const. art. I, § I, para. II.

234.

Under Georgia's Equal Protection Clause, "the government is required to treat similarly situated individuals in a similar manner." *State v. Jackson*, 271 GA 5 (1999), *Favorito v. Handel*, 285 Ga. 795, 798 (2009) (citation and quotations omitted). *See* **Exhibit 15**.

235.

This requires establishing a uniform procedure for all counties to conduct absentee voting, advance voting, and Election Day in-person voting.

---

[10] In the event this Court enjoins, vacates, and nullifies the Contested Election, the Legislature shall direct the manner of choosing presidential electors. U.S. art II, § 1; *see also Bush v. Gore*, 531 U.S. 98.

236.

Respondents, jointly and severally, failed to establish such uniform procedure for the verification of signatures of absentee ballots.

237.

Respondents, jointly and severally, failed to establish a uniform level of scrutiny for signature matching.

238.

Respondents, jointly and severally, failed to train those who would be conducting signature verification on how to do so.

239.

The burdens of applying for and voting an absentee ballot were different in various counties throughout the State of Georgia.

240.

Electors voting via by absentee mail-in ballot were not required to provide identification, other than a matching signature.

241.

Electors voting in person were required to show photo identification and verify the voter's identity.

242.

The burdens of applying for and voting via absentee mail-in ballot were different from those for absentee in person.

243.

Georgia voters were treated differently depending on how they voted (i.e., whether by mail or in person), where they voted, when they voted, and for whom they voted.

244.

An elector in one county casting a ballot would not have his or her ballot treated in a similar manner as a voter in a different county.

245.

Electors in the same county would not have their ballots treated in a similar manner as electors at different precincts.

246.

Electors in the same precinct would not have their ballots treated in a similar manner whose votes were tabulated using different tabulators.

247.

Respondents, jointly and severally, failed to establish uniform procedures for treating similarly situated electors similarly.

248.

Respondents' systemic failure to even attempt uniformity across the state is a flagrant violation of the Constitution of the State of Georgia.

249.

Such a violation of the rights of the Citizens of Georgia constitutes misconduct and irregularity by election officials sufficient to change or place in doubt the result of the Contested Election.

250.

As a result, there is substantial doubt as to the outcome of the Contested Election, and the Contested Election and any certification associated therewith should be enjoined, vacated, and nullified and either a new presidential election be immediately ordered that complies with Georgia law or such other just and equitable relief is obtained so as to comport with the Constitution of the State of Georgia. *See* O.C.G.A. § 21-2-522.

COUNT III:
VIOLATIONS OF THE GEORGIA CONSTITUTION'S DUE PROCESS PROVISIONS

251.

Petitioners incorporate by reference and re-allege paragraphs 1 through 212 of this Petition and Count II as set forth herein verbatim.

252.

Pursuant to the Constitution of the State of Georgia, "No person shall be deprived of life, liberty, or property except by due process of law." Ga. Const. art. I, § I, para. I.

253.

Moreover, "All citizens of the United States, resident in this state, are hereby declared citizens of this state; and it shall be the duty of the General Assembly to enact such laws as will protect them in the full enjoyment of the rights, privileges, and immunities due to such citizenship." Ga. Const. art. I, § 1, para. VII.

254.

The right to vote is a fundamental right.

255.

When a fundamental right is allegedly infringed by government action, substantive due process requires that the infringement be narrowly tailored to serve a compelling state interest. *Old S. Duck Tours v. Mayor & Aldermen of City of Savannah*, 272 Ga. 869, 872, 535 S.E.2d 751, 754 (2000).

256.

By allowing illegal ballots to be cast and counted, Respondents diluted the votes of qualified Georgia electors.

257.

By allowing illegal ballots to be cast and counted, Respondents, by and through their misconduct, allowed the disenfranchisement of qualified Georgia electors.

258.

Respondents, jointly and severally, violated the Due Process protections of qualified Georgia Electors guaranteed by the Georgia State Constitution.

259.

As a result, there is substantial doubt as to the outcome of the Contested Election and any certification associated therewith should be enjoined, vacated, and nullified and either a new presidential election be immediately ordered that complies with Georgia law or such other just and equitable relief is obtained so as to comport with the Constitution of the State of Georgia.

COUNT IV:
DECLARATORY JUDGMENT AND RELIEF

260.

Petitioners incorporate by reference and re-allege paragraphs 1 through 259 of this Petition as set forth herein verbatim.

261.

This claim is an action for a declaratory judgment pursuant to O.C.G.A. §§ 9-4-1 et seq.

262.

An actual controversy is ripe and exists between Petitioners and Respondents with regard to the misconduct, fraud, and irregularities occurring in the Contested Election, specifically including but not limited to:

   a. The illegal and improper inclusion of unqualified voters on Georgia's voter list;
   b. allowing ineligible voters to vote illegally in the Contested Election;
   c. whether the Contested Election results are invalid;

d. whether the Consent Decree is unauthorized under Georgia law such that it is null and void, and unlawfully interfered with the proper administration of the Election Code;

e. whether the results of the Contested Election are null and void.

263.

It is necessary and proper that the rights and status amongst the parties hereto be declared.

264.

This Honorable Court is a Court of Equity and therefore endowed with the authority to hear and the power to grant declaratory relief.

265.

As a result of the systemic misconduct, fraud, irregularities, violations of Georgia law, and errors occurring in the Contested Election and consequently in order to cure and avoid said uncertainty, Petitioners seek the entry of a declaratory judgment providing that:

a. ineligible and unqualified individuals are unlawfully included on Georgia's voter role;

b. unregistered, unqualified, and otherwise ineligible voters cast their votes during the Contested Election;

c. the Consent Decree is unauthorized under Georgia law and is therefore null and void; and

d. the results of the Contested Election are null and void.

COUNT V:

REQUEST FOR TEMPORARY RESTRAINING ORDER AND PRELIMINARY AND PERMANENT INJUNCTIVE RELIEF

266.

Petitioners incorporate by reference and re-allege paragraphs 1 through 265 of this Petition as set forth herein verbatim.

267.

Petitioners seek an emergency temporary restraining order, as well as preliminary and permanent injunctive relief per O.C.G.A. § 9-11-65, to:

a. Order expedited discovery and strict compliance with all open records requests;

b. Order Respondents to respond to this Petition within 3 days;

c. Require Respondents to immediately fulfill their obligations under the Election Code to properly maintain and update Georgia's list of registered voters to remove ineligible voters;

d. Prevent Respondents from allowing unqualified, unregistered, and otherwise ineligible individuals from voting in Georgia elections, including but not limited to the upcoming January 5, 2021 run-off[11];

e. Require an immediate audit of the signatures on absentee ballot applications and ballots as described in Exhibit 16;

f. Enjoin and restrain Respondents from taking any further actions or to further enforce the Consent Decree;

g. Prevent the certification of the results of the Contested Election;

---

[11] To the extent ineligible voters have already voted absentee for the January 5, 2021, runoff, those votes should be put into a provisional status.

h. Enjoin the Secretary of State from appointing the Electors to the Electoral College;

i. **Order a new Presidential Election to occur at the earliest opportune time**; and

j. For such other relief that this Court deems just and proper under the circumstances.

268.

In the absence of an emergency temporary restraining order and preliminary and permanent injunctions, Petitioners (and the Citizens of Georgia and the United States) will suffer irreparable harm for which there is no adequate remedy at law, while injunctive relief will cause no harm to Respondents.

269.

Immediate and irreparable injury, loss, or damage will result to the Petitioners (as well as the Citizens of Georgia and the United States) if the requested emergency injunctive relief is not granted.

270.

There will be immediate and irreparable damage to the Citizens of Georgia by allowing an illegal, improper, fraudulent, error-ridden presidential election to be certified, thereby improperly appointing Georgia's electors for Mr. Biden even though the Contested Election is in doubt.

271.

There will be irreparable damage to the Citizens of Georgia through their loss of confidence in the integrity of the election process by virtue of the illegal votes included in the tabulations of the Contested Election, which outweighs any potential harm to Respondents.

272.

Granting the requested relief will not disserve the public interest.

273.

Petitioners will be irreparably injured in the event the prayed for injunctive relief is not granted.

274.

It is further in the public interest to grant Petitioner's request for emergency injunctive relief so that Georgia voters can have confidence that the January 5, 2021, Senate election is conducted in accordance with the Election Code.

275.

As early as possible, notice to Respondents of Petitioners' motion for emergency injunctive relief will be made via email and / or telephone.

276.

Petitioners are further entitled to the injunctive relief sought herein because there is a substantial likelihood of success on the merits.

277.

The damage to Petitioners is not readily compensable by money.

278.

The balance of equities favors entry of a temporary restraining order and injunctive relief against Respondents and would not be adverse to any legitimate public interest.

WHEREFORE, Petitioners respectfully pray as follows for emergency and permanent relief as follows:

1. That this Court, pursuant to O. C. G. A. § 21-2-523, expeditiously assign a Superior Court or Senior Judge to preside over this matter;

2. That this Court issue a declaratory judgment that systemic, material violations of the Election Code during the Contested Election for President of the United States occurred that has rendered the Contested Election null and void as a matter of law;

3. That this Court issue a declaratory judgment that systemic, material violations of the Election Code during the Contested Election violated the voters' due process rights under the Georgia Constitution have rendered the Contested Election null and void as a matter of law;

4. That this Court issue a declaratory judgment that systemic, material violations of the Election Code violated the voters' equal protection rights under the Constitution of the State of Georgia that have rendered the Contested Election null and void as a matter of law;

5. That the Court issue an injunction requiring all Respondents to decertify the results of the Contested Election;

6. That the Court order a new election to be conducted in the presidential race, in the entirety of the State of Georgia at the earliest date, to be conducted in accordance with the Election Code;

7. *Alternatively*, that the Court issue an injunction prohibiting the Secretary of State from appointing the slate of presidential electors due to the systemic irregularities in the Contested Election sufficient to cast doubt on its outcome;

8. That the Court order expedited discovery and hearing, since time is of the essence, given the legal requirements that the presidential electors from the State of Georgia are to meet on December 14, 2020, and that the electoral votes from the State of Georgia are to be delivered to and counted by the United States Congress on January 6, 2021;

9. That this Court issue a declaratory judgment that the Consent Decree violates the Constitution of the State of Georgia and the laws of the State of Georgia;

10. *Alternatively*, that the Consent Decree be stayed during the pendency of this matter;

11. That the Court order Respondents to make available 10,000 absentee ballot applications and ballot envelopes from Respondents, as per Exhibit 16, and access to the voter registration database sufficient to complete a full audit, including but not limited to a comparison of the signatures affixed to absentee ballot applications and envelopes to those on file with the Respondents;

12. That the Court order the Secretary of State and other Respondents to release to Petitioners for inspection all records regarding the Contested Election pursuant to O.C.G.A. § 21-2-586;

13. That the Court order all Respondents to immediately identify and remove felons with uncompleted sentences, cross-county voters, out-of-state voters, deceased voters, and other ineligible persons from Respondents' voter rolls within the next 30 days;

14. That the Court declare that all rules adopted by the Respondents Secretary of State or the State Election Board in contravention of the Georgia Election Code be invalidated, specifically regarding the authentication and processing of absentee ballots, to wit State Election Board Rule 183-1-14-0.9-.15;

15. That the Court order such other relief as it finds just and proper.

Respectfully submitted this 4th day of December, 2020.

SMITH & LISS, LLC

/s/ Ray S. Smith III

RAY S. SMITH, III
Georgia Bar No. 662555
Attorney for Petitioners Donald J. Trump, in his capacity as a Candidate for President, and Donald J. Trump for President, Inc.

Five Concourse Parkway
Suite 2600
Atlanta, Georgia 30328
Telephone: (404) 760-6000
Facsimile: (404) 760-0225

MARK POST LAW, LLC

/s/ Mark C. Post

MARK C. POST
Georgia Bar No. 585575
Attorney for Petitioner David J. Shafer, in his capacity as a Registered Voter and Presidential Elector Candidate pledged to Donald Trump for President

3 Bradley Park Court
Suite F
Columbus, Georgia 31904
Telephone: (706) 221-9371
Facsimile: (706) 221-9379

Key Document R

Introduction by Thomas Fensch

USAerospace Partners
G7

Illustrious Mr. President:

I confirm my direct knowledge that activities undertaken here in Italy have had a negative impact for the President of the U.S. regarding the manipulation of the electoral vote of November 3rd and 4th, 2020.

I confirm that Leonardo SpA at its Pesara facility, using advanced military encryption capabilities, changed the US election result from President Trump to Joe Biden. The data switch was conducted by the head of the IT department of Leonardo SpA in coordination with senior US intelligence officials (CIA), three of whom work at the US Embassy in Via Venetto in Rome. A senior US Embassy Official held regular meetings with General Claudio Graziano, EU military commander, and Ignazio Moncada, president of FATA SpA, a company owned by Leonardo SpA, the largest aerospace trust company based in Italy with its American counterpart, Leonardo DRS.

On December 3rd, the head of the IT department was arrested in Naples, where he remains. We had direct and continuous contact within the organization with the IT manager who agreed to testify to the US authorities concerning what happened to the electoral data — how they were changed at the Pesscara / Fucino facilities, were loaded with information technology on military satellites, and what data is contained in an electronic key to demonstrate the changing of the data from President Trump who was clearly the winner to Joe Biden on November 4th, 2020.

Our associates in the conservative part of the Italian secret services have been working since the beginning of November, 2020, to ensure that the truth is known and that the American people realize the result voted for: the re-election of President Trump.

Rome, December 27th, 2020.

The Director
Carlo Goria

USAerospace Partners
G7

Illustrious Mr. President:

I confirm my direct knowledge that activities undertaken here in Italy have had a negative impact for the President of the U.S. regarding the manipulation of the electoral vote of November 3rd and 4th, 2020.

I confirm that Leonardo SpA at its Pesara facility, using advanced military encryption capabilities, changed the US election result from President Trump to Joe Biden. The data switch was conducted by the head of the IT department of Leonardo SpA in coordination with senior US intelligence officials (CIA), three of whom work at the US Embassy in Via Venetto in Rome. A senior US Embassy Official held regular meetings with General Claudio Graziano, EU military commander, and Ignazio Moncada, president of FATA SpA, a company owned by Leonardo SpA, the largest aerospace trust company based in Italy with its American counterpart, Leonardo DRS.

On December 3rd, the head of the IT department was arrested in Naples, where he remains. We had direct and continuous contact within the organization with the IT manager who agreed to testify to the US authorities concerning what happened to the electoral data — how they were changed at the Pesscara / Fucino facilities, were loaded with information technology on military satellites, and what data is contained in an electronic key to demonstrate the changing of the data from President Trump who was clearly the winner to Joe Biden on November 4th, 2020.

Our associates in the conservative part of the Italian secret services have been working since the beginning of November, 2020, to ensure that the truth is known and that the American people realize the result voted for: the re-election of President Trump.

Rome, December 27th, 2020.

The Director
Carlo Goria

INTRODUCTION BY THOMAS FENSCH

Key Document S

DAG Call with Ken Kohl   12/30/20

- KK asking if DOJ will file complaint he has drafted & forwarded
    → DAG — Not going to discuss that w/ you, we have
            your draft, we are looking at it,
            we have ?s (e.g. standing) — OSG + Civ Dn.
                                          looking at it.
- "I am acting at the direction of the President"
    — DAG — "Is he your client?"
- "I have made my representations on to you on that"
- "I will be reporting back to the President on this conversation."
- "Historic moment. Election stolen. Need to act to save the republic"

- DAG: Understand your perspective, we will make our own
        decision on this. Not appropriate to relay that
        to you as outside counsel.

INTRODUCTION BY THOMAS FENSCH

Key Document T

Engel, Steven A. (OLC)

From:	Engel, Steven A. (OLC)
Sent:	Thursday, December 31, 2020 9:02 AM
To:	Donoghue, Richard (ODAG)
Subject:	one pager
Attachments:	US v. Penn OJ suit.docx

Introduction by Thomas Fensch

Evaluation of Potential Original-Jurisdiction Suit in the Supreme Court

- There is no legal basis to bring this lawsuit. We cannot ethically file a suit without a legal basis, and we are certain that if we did so, the Justices would promptly dismiss it. Anyone who thinks otherwise simply does not know the law, much less the Supreme Court. If there were a legal mechanism available, we would pursue it. But there is not. And this case is definitely not it.

- This is very much my own view, but I wanted to make that I had the benefit of the views of the best lawyers at the Department. I asked Rich, I asked the Acting Solicitor General, and I asked Steve Engel to review this closely and let me know if there were anything we could do. They were unanimous in their conviction that this suit cannot be brought.

- <u>US can't sue.</u> The United States, as a government, does not have any standing to challenge whether the States complied with their state electoral procedures. The Trump campaign or the candidate plainly does. A would-be presidential elector who wants to vote likely would. But the United States, as a government, does not have a legal stake in the winner of the presidential election or whether individual states comply with their own laws.

- There is no "parens patriae" basis for the lawsuit. The drafters of the complaint could not identify a single case in the history of the Supreme Court where the United States ever brought a case like this. There is no legal doctrine that says that the United States may bring a lawsuit whenever it believes there has been a legal violation by a State.

- <u>The lawsuit does not ask for relief that could make any difference</u>. The lawsuit would be brought against the States, but there is no longer any role left for the States in the presidential election. They have appointed their electors, and the electors have now cast their votes and sent them to Congress. There is nothing that the States could lawfully do now to stop Congress from opening and counting those votes next Wednesday, and therefore, the time to challenge the States has passed.

- <u>The Supreme Court won't hear the case</u>. The Supreme Court rarely hears cases that are exclusively in its original jurisdiction as we saw with *United States v. Texas*. But this case is not even within its original jurisdiction. This case could have been brought in federal district court months ago, and that makes it certain that the Court would not even hear it.

Key Document U

Introduction by Thomas Fensch

Engel, Steven A. (OLC)

From: Engel, Steven A. (OLC)
Sent: Thursday, December 31, 2020 4:20 PM
To: Donoghue, Richard (ODAG)
Subject: any update?

I'm going to have to head out of the office soon, since (b) (6) (b) (6) But I'll be available by cell ((b) (6) and could obviously come back to the office if need be.

Steven A. Engel
Assistant Attorney General
Office of Legal Counsel
U.S. Department of Justice
950 Pennsylvania Ave., N.W.
Washington, D.C. 20530
Office: ((b) (6)
steven.a.engel@usdoj.gov

Key Document V

Introduction by Thomas Fensch

Rosen, Jeffrey A. (ODAG)

From: Rosen, Jeffrey A. (ODAG)
Sent: Thursday, December 31, 2020 6:14 PM
To: Hovakimian, Patrick (ODAG)
Cc: Donoghue, Richard (ODAG)
Subject: Re: Tonight

We are now on way back to DOJ. Might need your help. Could you wait?

Sent from my iPhone

> On Dec 31, 2020, at 6:01 PM, Hovakimian, Patrick (ODAG) <phovakimian4@jmd.usdoj.gov> wrote:
>
> I told Nate he should go ahead and go home if he'd like.
>
> I'm heading out in a minute too, but available by phone if needed.
>
> Patrick Hovakimian
> (b) (6)

Key Document W

INTRODUCTION BY THOMAS FENSCH

Donoghue, Richard (ODAG)

From: Donoghue, Richard (ODAG)
Sent: Friday, January 1, 2021 4:28 PM
To: Rosen, Jeffrey A. (ODAG)
Subject: Re: [EXTERNAL] Fwd:

At least it's better than the last one, but that doesn't say much.

> On Jan 1, 2021, at 4:22 PM, Rosen, Jeffrey A. (ODAG) <jarosen@jmd.usdoj.gov> wrote:
>
> Can you believe this? I am not going to respond to message below.
>
> **From:** Meadows, Mark R. EOP/WHO <(b) (6)>
> **Sent:** Friday, January 1, 2021 4:13 PM
> **To:** Rosen, Jeffrey A. (ODAG) <jarosen@jmd.usdoj.gov>
> **Subject:** Re: [EXTERNAL] Fwd:
>
> There have been allegations of signature match anomalies in Fulton county, Ga. Can you get Jeff Clark to engage on this issue immediately to determine if there is any truth to this allegation
>
> Sent from my iPhone
>
>> On Jan 1, 2021, at 3:22 PM, Rosen, Jeffrey A. (ODAG) <Jeffrey.Rosen38@usdoj.gov> wrote:
>>
>> Got it. Thanks.
>>
>> **From:** Meadows, Mark R. EOP/WHO <(b) (6)>
>> **Sent:** Friday, January 1, 2021 3:09 PM
>> **To:** Rosen, Jeffrey A. (ODAG) <jarosen@jmd.usdoj.gov>
>> **Subject:** Re: [EXTERNAL] Fwd:
>>
>> You should have it now
>>
>> Sent from my iPhone
>>
>>> On Jan 1, 2021, at 2:51 PM, Rosen, Jeffrey A. (ODAG) <Jeffrey.Rosen38@usdoj.gov> wrote:

Did not receive the video link. Can you re-send?

INTRODUCTION BY THOMAS FENSCH

Key Document X

SUBVERTING JUSTICE

Meadows, Mark R. EOP/WHO

From:	Meadows, Mark R. EOP/WHO
Sent:	Friday, January 1, 2021 6:56 PM
To:	Jeff Rosen
Subject:	2020 Ballot Security - New Mexico Complaints.docx
Attachments:	2020 Ballot Security - New Mexico Complaints.docx

Can you forward this list to your team to review the allegations contained herein. Steve Pearce is the chairman of the Republican Party for NM (b) (6)

Sent from my iPhone

Introduction by Thomas Fensch

New Mexico List of Complaints

1. Poll Challengers removed from the Absentee Ballot Certification Process
    a. RPNM notified the Secretary of State in timely fashion and she refused to allow challengers access to the process
    b. RPNM took this complaint to the NM Supreme Court (4 Democrats, 1 Republican) in timely fashion; they refused to hear the case.
    c. Local races were lost by a few votes in several counties where the Party was not present to verify the Absentee Ballots.
2. Poll Challengers were unable to adequately do their job
    a. Some counties forced them away from the ballot counting process, sometimes as much as 50 feet away, making it impossible to verify correct procedures were used.
    b. Republican Poll Challengers were met with outright hostility by some county clerks.
3. Dominion Machines are the only machines used in New Mexico
    a. Many Anomalies were encountered
        i. Vote dumps in the middle of the night when no counting was taking place
        ii. In each instance of vote dump, the Democrat candidate was the beneficiary.
    b. Three automatic recounts took place
        i. Republican challengers were met with hostility and attempts to keep them out of the recount
        ii. Dominion Representatives were allowed into each recount.
        iii. Our data team had noticed a pattern in all the Dominion machines where vote totals below 120 votes had one pattern but when the total votes in the machine exceeded that number, the voting pattern was significantly different.
        iv. In order to test their theory, RPNM instructed our challengers to request that the 100 sample ballots be fed thru the machine a second time.
            1. The Dominion Representatives objected strenuously
            2. The theory was never tested because the County Clerks in each instance gave in to the pressure from the Dominion Representatives.
    c. Our Data Team has reviewed voter files back to 1992
        i. They have identified anomalies that have become increasingly sophisticated through the years
        ii. Recent data patterns suggest between 10-20% vote shifts in recent years, including the 2020 Presidential Election.
4. Absentee ballot requests
    a. We have documented cases of absentee ballots being requested by someone other than the voter, the signature not the same name as the voter and live absentee ballots were mailed.
5. Other Irregularities
    a. Multiple documented cases of dead people voting
    b. Multiple cases of persons who moved out of the state years ago receiving ballots.
6. The Trump Legal team
    a. Has filed a lawsuit against the SOS

- b. Has filed two IPRA requests to the SOS
    - i. The SOS responded that they would provide the information by 30 December, 2020
    - ii. On 31 December, she notified the Trump team she would not provide the information until January 14, 2021.
7. Notarized Affidavits
    - a. RPNM has in hand many signed and notarized affidavits of problems individual voters encountered.
    - b.

Introduction by Thomas Fensch

Key Document Y

SUBVERTING JUSTICE

Rosen, Jeffrey A. (ODAG)

From: Rosen, Jeffrey A. (ODAG)
Sent: Friday, January 1, 2021 7:13 PM
To: Donoghue, Richard (ODAG)
Subject: RE: [EXTERNAL] Brad Johnson: Rome, Satellites, Servers: an Update - YouTube

Yes. After this message, I was asked to have FBI meet with Brad Johnson, and I responded that Johnson could call or walk into FBI's Washington Field Office with any evidence he purports to have. On a follow up call, I learned that Johnson is working with Rudy Giuliani, who regarded my comments as "an insult". Asked if I would reconsider, I flatly refused, said I would not be giving any special treatment to Giuliani or any of his "witnesses", and re-affirmed yet again that I will not talk to Giuliani about any of this.

From: Donoghue, Richard (ODAG) <ricdonoghue@jmd.usdoj.gov>
Sent: Friday, January 1, 2021 3:39 PM
To: Rosen, Jeffrey A. (ODAG) <jarosen@jmd.usdoj.gov>
Subject: Re: [EXTERNAL] Brad Johnson: Rome, Satellites, Servers: an Update - YouTube

Pure insanity.

On Jan 1, 2021, at 3:22 PM, Rosen, Jeffrey A. (ODAG) <jarosen@jmd.usdoj.gov> wrote:

From: Meadows, Mark R. EOP/WHO <(b) (6)>
Sent: Friday, January 1, 2021 3:08 PM
To: Rosen, Jeffrey A. (ODAG) <jarosen@jmd.usdoj.gov>
Subject: Fwd: [EXTERNAL] Brad Johnson: Rome, Satellites, Servers: an Update - YouTube

Sent from my iPhone

Begin forwarded message:

> **From:** Mark Meadows (b) (6)
> **Date:** January 1, 2021 at 3:06:53 PM EST
> **To:** "Meadows, Mark R. EOP/WHO" <(b) (6)>
> **Subject: [EXTERNAL] Brad Johnson: Rome, Satellites, Servers: an Update - YouTube**
>
> https://www.youtube.com/watch?

Introduction by Thomas Fensch

v=YwtbK5XXAMk&feature=youtu.be<

Sent from my iPhone

Key Document Z

INTRODUCTION BY THOMAS FENSCH

Clark, Jeffrey (CIV)

From: Clark, Jeffrey (CIV)
Sent: Saturday, January 2, 2021 9:50 AM
To: Rosen, Jeffrey A. (ODAG)
Subject: Re: atlanta

I spoke to the source and am on with the guy who took the video right now. Working on it. More due diligence to do.

Jeff

Sent from my iPhone

> On Jan 2, 2021, at 8:52 AM, Rosen, Jeffrey A. (ODAG) <jarosen@jmd.usdoj.gov> wrote:
>
> ? Were you able to follow up?
>
> Sent from my iPhone
>
>> On Jan 1, 2021, at 8:24 PM, Clark, Jeffrey (CIV) <jefclark@civ.usdoj.gov> wrote:
>>
>> ? Thanks
>>
>> Sent from my iPhone
>>
>>> On Jan 1, 2021, at 8:24 PM, Rosen, Jeffrey A. (ODAG) <jarosen@jmd.usdoj.gov> wrote:
>>>
>>> ?
>>> BJ Pak's cell (b) (6)

Key Document AA

Introduction by Thomas Fensch

Mtg w/ DAG + Jeff Clark — 6th fl.   1/2/21
— Saturday
— called in by DAG

① DNI Briefing — no evidence of ballot/data tampering in IC
— influence only

— JC has referenced conversation w/ him

② GA — largest Ballot Warehouse in GA + has overflow co
— he called head of GBI — not interested
— then called Bobby Christine — but very new | conducted surveillance on warehouse on Kty St
— thinks he saw trucks move ballots to shredding location

Cobb City — woman who worked at facility testified at GA Sen. Mtg. that she saw shred trucks at election location

Based on the 2 GA allegations of ballot shredding in GA, JC wants, once again, to send letter saying   across state
(1) DOJ believes there is significant fraud, and
(2) GA Legislature should call itself into session and select new electors

This is entirely unacceptable to GA.

DAG and I make it clear that the Department will not send out such a letter as long as we are in charge of it.

JC reiterates that POTUS has offered him Acting AG position + that he has committed to let him know on Monday whether he wants to do that.

Another difficult meeting.

(margin notes:) He acknowledged that he did not tell SDCh he was told federal law requires that ballots be preserved for 22 months

Key Document BB

Introduction by Thomas Fensch

Rosen, Jeffrey A. (ODAG)

From: Rosen, Jeffrey A. (ODAG)
Sent: Saturday, January 2, 2021 7:13 PM
To: Donoghue, Richard (ODAG)
Subject: RE: Two Urgent Action Items

Rich, thanks for responding to this earlier. I confirmed again today that I am not prepared to sign such a letter. Jeff

From: Donoghue, Richard (ODAG) <ricdonoghue@jmd.usdoj.gov>
Sent: Monday, December 28, 2020 5:50 PM
To: Clark, Jeffrey (ENRD) <JClark@ENRD.USDOJ.GOV>
Cc: Rosen, Jeffrey A. (ODAG) <jarosen@jmd.usdoj.gov>
Subject: RE: Two Urgent Action Items

Jeff,

I have only had a few moments to review the draft letter and, obviously, there is a lot raised there that would have to be thoroughly researched and discussed. That said, there is no chance that I would sign this letter or anything remotely like this.

While it may be true that the Department "is investigating various irregularities in the 2020 election for President" (something we typically would not state publicly), the investigations that I am aware of relate to suspicions of misconduct that are of such a small scale that they simply would not impact the outcome of the Presidential Election. AG Barr made that clear to the public only last week, and I am not aware of intervening developments that would change that conclusion. Thus, I know of nothing that would support the statement, "we have identified significant concerns that may have impacted the outcome of the election in multiple states." While we are always prepared to receive complaints and allegations relating to election fraud, and will investigate them as appropriate, we simply do not currently have a basis to make such a statement. Despite dramatic claims to the contrary, we have not seen the type of fraud that calls into question the reported (and certified) results of the election. Also the commitment that "the Department will update you as we are able on investigatory progress" is dubious as we do not typically update non-law enforcement personnel on the progress of any investigations.

More importantly, I do not think the Department's role should include making recommendations to a State legislature about how they should meet their Constitutional obligation to appoint Electors. Pursuant to the Electors Clause, the State of Georgia (and every other state) has prescribed the legal process through which they select their Electors. While those processes include the possibility that election results may "fail[ ] to make a choice", it is for the individual State to figure out how to address that situation should it arise. But as I note above, there is no reason to conclude that any State is currently in a situation in which their election has failed to produce a choice. As AG Barr indicated in his public comments, while I have no doubt that some fraud has occurred in this election, I have not seen evidence that would indicate that the election in any individual state was so defective as to render the results fundamentally unreliable. Given that, I cannot imagine a scenario in which the Department would recommend that a State assemble its legislature to determine whether already-certified election results should somehow be overridden by legislative action. Despite the references to the 1960 Hawaii situation (and other historical anomalies, such as the 1876 Election), I believe this would be utterly without precedent. Even if I am incorrect about that, this would be a grave step for the Department to take and it could have tremendous Constitutional, political and social ramifications for the country. I do not believe that we could even consider such a proposal without the type of research and discussion that such a momentous step warrants. Obviously, OLC would have to be involved in such discussions.

Document ID: 0.7.2774.173057
SJC-Pre-CertificationEvents-03092021-000200

I am available to discuss this when you are available after 6:00 pm but, from where I stand, this is not even within the realm of possibility.

Rich

From: Clark, Jeffrey (ENRD) <JClark@ENRD.USDOJ.GOV>
Sent: Monday, December 28, 2020 4:40 PM
To: Rosen, Jeffrey A. (ODAG) <jarosen@jmd.usdoj.gov>; Donoghue, Richard (ODAG) <ricdonoghue@jmd.usdoj.gov>
Subject: Two Urgent Action Items

Jeff and Rich:

(1) I would like to have your authorization to get a classified briefing tomorrow from ODNI led by DNI Radcliffe on foreign election interference issues. I can then assess how that relates to activating the IEEPA and 2018 EO powers on such matters (now twice renewed by the President). If you had not seen it, white hat hackers have evidence (in the public domain) that a Dominion machine accessed the Internet through a smart thermostat with a net connection trail leading back to China. ODNI may have additional classified evidence.

(2) Attached is a draft letter concerning the broader topic of election irregularities of any kind. The concept is to send it to the Governor, Speaker, and President pro temp of each relevant state to indicate that in light of time urgency and sworn evidence of election irregularities presented to courts and to legislative committees, the legislatures thereof should each assemble and make a decision about elector appointment in light of their deliberations. I set it up for signature by the three of us. I think we should get it out as soon as possible. Personally, I see no valid downsides to sending out the letter. I put it together quickly and would want to do a formal cite check before sending but I don't think we should let unnecessary moss grow on this

(As a small matter, I left open me signing as AAG Civil after an order from Jeff as Acting AG designating me as actual AAG of Civil under the Ted Olson OLC opinion and thus freeing up the Acting AAG spot in ENRD for Jon Brightbill to assume. But that is a comparatively small matter. I wouldn't want to hold up the letter for that. But I continue to think there is no downside with as few as 23 days left in the President's term to give Jon and I that added boost in DOJ titles.)

I have a 5 pm internal call with the SDNY + OASG + ENRD Toyota team, as I am trying to settle that before 1/20. But I am free to talk on either or both of these subjects circa 6 pm+.

Or if you want to reach me after I reset work venue to home, my cell # i (b) (6)

Jeff

INTRODUCTION BY THOMAS FENSCH

Key Document CC

Engel, Steven A. (OLC)

From: Engel, Steven A. (OLC)
Sent: Saturday, January 2, 2021 8:09 PM
To: Donoghue, Richard (ODAG)
Subject: Re: Call

Sure. What's your cell?

Sent from my iPhone

On Jan 2, 2021, at 8:08 PM, Donoghue, Richard (ODAG) <ricdonoghue@jmd.usdoj.gov> wrote:

Steve,

Not urgent, but give me a call when you have 5 minutes free tonight. I want to update you on today's events.

Thanks,

Rich

INTRODUCTION BY THOMAS FENSCH

Key Document DD

Draft — January 3, 2021

Deliberative

Predecisional

E-mail to component heads, Chair/Vice Chair of AGAC, ODAG/OAG staff

Dear all —

Apologies for the impersonal nature of this e-mail.

This evening, after Acting Attorney General Jeff Rosen over the course of the last week repeatedly refused the President's direct instructions to utilize the Department of Justice's law enforcement powers for improper ends, the President removed Jeff from the Department.

PADAG Rich Donoghue and I resign from the Department, effective immediately.

Jeff loves the Department of Justice, as we all do. Preserving and defending the institutional integrity of the Department remains Jeff's paramount concern. The decision of whether and when to resign and whether the ends of justice are best served by resigning is a highly individual question, informed by personal and family circumstances. Jeff asked me to pass on to each of you that whatever your own decision, he knows you will adhere always to the highest standards of justice and act always – and only – in the interests of the United States.

It has been a high honor to serve with each of you.

Best,

Pat

Patrick Hovakimian

Associate Deputy Attorney General

United States Department of Justice

(b) (6)

INTRODUCTION BY THOMAS FENSCH

Key Document EE

jefclark@civ.usdoj.gov

From: jefclark@civ.usdoj.gov
Sent: Sunday, January 3, 2021 4:37 PM
To: Smith, Douglas (CIV)
Subject: Re: DC

Come to DOJ. Legal pad in hand.

We will get dinner

Sent from my iPhone

> On Jan 3, 2021, at 2:57 PM, Smith, Douglas (CIV) <Douglas.Smith@usdoj.gov> wrote:
>
> ? On way to airport. Probably back around 6 something.
>
> Douglas Smith
> Deputy Assistant Attorney General
> Civil Division
> U.S. Department of Justice
> 950 Pennsylvania Avenue, Room 3131
> (b) (6)
>
>> On Jan 3, 2021, at 1:42 PM, Clark, Jeffrey (CIV) <jefclark@civ.usdoj.gov> wrote:
>>
>> ?
>> Try to get back as soon as you can.
>>
>> Jeff
>>
>> **From:** Smith, Douglas (CIV) <Douglas.Smith@usdoj.gov>
>> **Sent:** Sunday, January 3, 2021 2:38 PM
>> **To:** Clark, Jeffrey (CIV) <jefclark@CIV.USDOJ.GOV>
>> **Subject:** Re: DC
>>
>> Sorry just saw this will don have a flight back tonight but will try to get back earlier.
>>
>> Douglas Smith
>> Deputy Assistant Attorney General
>> Civil Division
>> U.S. Department of Justice
>> 950 Pennsylvania Avenue, Room 3131

INTRODUCTION BY THOMAS FENSCH

(b) (6)

> On Jan 3, 2021, at 11:31 AM, Clark, Jeffrey (CIV) <jefclark@civ.usdoj.gov> wrote:
>
> ?Doug, please get back to DC immediately.
>
> We can talk when you are back. Thanks,
>
> Jeff
>
> Sent from my iPhone

Key Document FF

Introduction by Thomas Fensch

Hovakimian, Patrick (ODAG)

From:	Hovakimian, Patrick (ODAG)
Sent:	Sunday, January 3, 2021 9:07 PM
To:	Murray, Claire M. (OASG); Wall, Jeffrey B. (OSG); Delrahim, Makan (ATR); Engel, Steven A. (OLC); Demers, John C. (NSD); Burns, David P. (NSD); Burns, David (CRM); Dreiband, Eric (CRT)
Cc:	Donoghue, Richard (ODAG)
Subject:	RE: Call this afternoon

I have only limited visibility into this, but it sounds like Rosen and the cause of justice won. We will convene a call when Jeff is back in the building (hopefully shortly). Thanks.

From: Hovakimian, Patrick (ODAG)
Sent: Sunday, January 3, 2021 4:28 PM
To: Murray, Claire M. (OASG) <cmmurray@jmd.usdoj.gov>; Wall, Jeffrey B. (OSG) <jbwall@jmd.usdoj.gov>; Delrahim, Makan (ATR) <Makan.Delrahim@ATR.USDOJ.GOV>; Engel, Steven A. (OLC) <saengel@jmd.usdoj.gov>; Demers, John C. (NSD) <John.C.Demers@usdoj.gov>; Burns, David P. (NSD) <dburns@jmd.usdoj.gov>; Burns, David (CRM) <David.Burns@CRM.USDOJ.GOV>
Cc: Donoghue, Richard (ODAG) <ricdonoghue@jmd.usdoj.gov>
Subject: Call this afternoon

Apologies for the Sunday reach-out. Please join Rich and me for a call at 4:45 p.m. Dial-in below.

(b) (6)   , participant passcode   (b) (6)

Patrick Hovakimian
Associate Deputy Attorney General
United States Department of Justice
(b) (6)

Key Document GG

Introduction by Thomas Fensch

Engel, Steven A. (OLC)

From:	Engel, Steven A. (OLC)
Sent:	Sunday, January 3, 2021 9:28 PM
To:	Hovakimian, Patrick (ODAG)
Cc:	Murray, Claire M. (OASG); Wall, Jeffrey B. (OSG); Delrahim, Makan (ATR); Demers, John C. (NSD); Burns, David P. (NSD); Burns, David (CRM); Dreiband, Eric (CRT); Donoghue, Richard (ODAG)
Subject:	Re: Call this afternoon

Still at WH. But that is correct.

Sent from my iPhone

On Jan 3, 2021, at 9:07 PM, Hovakimian, Patrick (ODAG) <phovakimian4@jmd.usdoj.gov> wrote:

I have only limited visibility into this, but it sounds like Rosen and the cause of justice won. We will convene a call when Jeff is back in the building (hopefully shortly). Thanks.

From: Hovakimian, Patrick (ODAG)
Sent: Sunday, January 3, 2021 4:28 PM
To: Murray, Claire M. (OASG) <cmmurray@jmd.usdoj.gov>; Wall, Jeffrey B. (OSG) <jbwall@jmd.usdoj.gov>; Delrahim, Makan (ATR) <Makan.Delrahim@ATR.USDOJ.GOV>; Engel, Steven A. (OLC) <saengel@jmd.usdoj.gov>; Demers, John C. (NSD) <John.C.Demers@usdoj.gov>; Burns, David P. (NSD) <dburns@jmd.usdoj.gov>; Burns, David (CRM) <David.Burns@CRM.USDOJ.GOV>
Cc: Donoghue, Richard (ODAG) <ricdonoghue@jmd.usdoj.gov>
Subject: Call this afternoon

Apologies for the Sunday reach-out. Please join Rich and me for a call at 4:45 p.m. Dial-in below.

(b) (6), participant passcode: (b) (6)

Patrick Hovakimian
Associate Deputy Attorney General
United States Department of Justice
(b) (6)

Key Document HH

Introduction by Thomas Fensch

Donoghue, Richard (ODAG)

From: Donoghue, Richard (ODAG)
Sent: Sunday, January 3, 2021 10:09 PM
To: Pak, BJay (USAGAN)
Subject: Please call ASAP

(b) (6)

Key Document II

Introduction by Thomas Fensch

Pak, BJay (USAGAN)

From:	Pak, BJay (USAGAN)
Sent:	Monday, January 4, 2021 7:41 AM
To:	Winzenburg, Karen (USAEO)
Cc:	Ellis, Corey (USAEO); Donoghue, Richard (ODAG)
Subject:	Resignation Letters
Attachments:	BJP Resignation Letter to the President.pdf; BJP Resignation to the Attorney General.pdf

Karen
Happy New Year. Please find attached my resignation letters addressed to the President and the Acting Attorney General. It has been an honor working with you.
Thank you

BJP

U.S. Department of Justice
United States Attorney
Northern District of Georgia

600 U.S. Courthouse
75 Ted Turner Drive S.W.
Atlanta, Georgia 30303

Telephone: (404) 581 6000
Fax: (404) 581 6181

January 4, 2021

President Donald J. Trump
The White House
Washington, D.C. 20500

Dear Mr. President:

    I am hereby submitting my resignation as United States Attorney for the Northern District of Georgia, effective today, January 4, 2021.

    I deeply appreciate the opportunity to have served as United States Attorney. I wish you and your administration the best of luck and success.

Sincerely,

Byung J. "BJay" Pak
United States Attorney

INTRODUCTION BY THOMAS FENSCH

U.S. Department of Justice
United States Attorney
Northern District of Georgia

600 U.S. Courthouse
75 Ted Turner Drive S.W.
Atlanta, Georgia 30303

Telephone: (404) 581 6000
Fax: (404) 581 6181

January 4, 2021

Hon. Jeffrey A. Rosen
Acting Attorney General of United States
United States Department of Justice
Robert F. Kennedy Building, Room 5111
950 Pennsylvania Avenue, NW
Washington, D.C. 20530

Dear Mr. Attorney General:

    I am hereby submitting my resignation as United States Attorney for the Northern District of Georgia, effective today, January 4, 2021. It has been a great honor and privilege to have served these past three plus years as a United States Attorney by Presidential appointment.

    Serving as a United States Attorney has been the highest honor and most fulfilling duty of my public career. The position has allowed me to serve the nation, positively impact my community, fight for justice for all victims, and restore the citizens' confidence in the government. Thank you for your support and the support of the Department of Justice during my tenure.

    I deeply appreciate the opportunity to have served as the United States Attorney for the Northern District of Georgia. I wish you all the best.

Sincerely,

BJay Pak

Byung J. "BJay" Pak
United States Attorney

cc: Corey Ellis, Acting Director, EOUSA

Key Document JJ

INTRODUCTION BY THOMAS FENSCH

Pak, BJay (USAGAN)

From: Pak, BJay (USAGAN)
Sent: Monday, January 4, 2021 7:46 AM
To: USAEO-USAttorneys
Cc: Donoghue, Richard (ODAG)
Subject: Farewell USAs

Dear Colleagues:

I hope all of you had a nice and safe holiday season. Today, I submitted my resignation to the President and the Acting Attorney General communicating my intention to step down as U.S. Attorney for the Northern District of Georgia.

Like all of you, serving as the U.S. Attorney has been the greatest honor of my professional career. But serving with such a talented and dedicated group of USAs made it even more special. If I look back at my almost a decade serving the Department of Justice (and USAO-NDGA office in particular), the most memorable and fulfilling moments involve working very closely with our law enforcement partners in keeping our communities safe. I take with me fond memories and the utmost respect I have for each and every one of you, and knowing that as a group, we made our country better, and safer, even though we were facing unprecedented challenges. I do wish and hope that at least some of you will consider continuing to serve our country -- our nation needs patriots like you to uphold the rule of law.

This is not a goodbye but a farewell. I will definitely keep in touch and look forward to the next time we are able to gather as a group.

As for me, no matter what position I am in, or what role I may play in the future, I want you to know you have my unwavering respect and support. If I can be of any assistance, please do not hesitate to contact me. I can be reached at:

BJay Pak
(b) (6)
(b) (6)

God bless you, and please stay safe and healthy.

Regards

BJP

BJay Pak
United States Attorney
Northern District of Georgia
75 Ted Turner Dr., SW, Suite 600
Atlanta, GA 30303

Key Document KK

INTRODUCTION BY THOMAS FENSCH

Brooke, Francis J. Jr. EOP/WHO

From: Brooke, Francis J. Jr. EOP/WHO
Sent: Tuesday, January 5, 2021 5:20 PM
To: Moran, John (ODAG)
Subject: FW: Photos of Acting Atty. Gen. Rosen from Oval Office 12/31/2020
Attachments: P20201231JB-0332_2.jpg; P20201231JB-0335_2.jpg; P20201231JB-0385_2.jpg; P20201231JB-0429_2.jpg; P20201231JB-0477_2.jpg

From: Wiggins, Jeremy G. EOP/WHO <(b) (6)>
Sent: Tuesday, January 5, 2021 5:17 PM
To: Brooke, Francis J. Jr. EOP/WHO <(b) (6)>
Subject: FW: Photos of Acting Atty. Gen. Rosen from Oval Office 12/31/2020

From: Hansen, Daniel E. EOP/WHO <(b) (6)>
Sent: Tuesday, January 5, 2021 1:17 PM
To: Wiggins, Jeremy G. EOP/WHO <(b) (6)>
Subject: Re: Photos of Acting Atty. Gen. Rosen from Oval Office 12/31/2020

Re: Photos of Acting Atty. Gen. Rosen from Oval Office 12/31/2020. **For Personal Use Only-not for Publication**

Here is edit from that day with Acting Atty. Gen. Rosen

Regards

Dan H

From: "Hansen, Daniel E. EOP/WHO" <(b) (6)>
Date: Tuesday, January 5, 2021 at 10:37 AM
To: "Wiggins, Jeremy G. EOP/WHO" <(b) (6)>
Subject: Re: Photos from Oval Office

We will take a look for this

Regards

Dan H

From: "Wiggins, Jeremy G. EOP/WHO" <(b) (6)>
Date: Tuesday, January 5, 2021 at 10:23 AM
To: "Hansen, Daniel E. EOP/WHO" <(b) (6)>
Subject: Photos from Oval Office

Hello Dan,

I hope all is well. The Acting Attorney General, Jeff Rosen, reached out to me and was wondering if he could get photos from his meeting with the President last Thursday, December 31st? I think Joyce was the photographer. Is this something you could help with? I know the AG would greatly appreciate any help you could provide. Thank you.

Best,
Jeremy

Jeremy Wiggins
Associate Director and Policy Coordinator
National Economic Council
(b) (6)

Introduction by Thomas Fensch

Introduction by Thomas Fensch

Introduction by Thomas Fensch

www.ingramcontent.com/pod-product-compliance
Lightning Source LLC
Chambersburg PA
CBHW081404080526
44589CB00016B/2477